What people are saying abou

"Deborah is the Deepak Chopra of survival jobs. During my downtime as a sit-com writer Deborah's creative suggestions on how to cushion my financial burdens while still pursuing writing proved invaluable. They should turn this book into a movie starring Harrison Ford—I hear he's good."

Brian Kahn, writer,
Malcolm & Eddie (UPN)

"This book should be the rising actor, artist, or entertainment professional's bible. It offers great ideas and flexible ways to make money and gives you specific information on the materials, the market, and the salary for each job. This is the whole package."

Wes Stevens, voice-over agent,
Talent Group Inc.

"*Survival Jobs* should be on every artist's bookshelf, right next to the compilation of Shakespeare's plays."

Tate Donovan, actor

". . . a fact-filled, meticulously researched book, *Survival Jobs* takes away the angst and presents clear, concise information."

K Callan, author/actress

"A book like this is invaluable and long overdue. Deborah Jacobson provides the reader with substantial, practical information delivered with wit and charm."

Tony Ferrar/Scott Maziroff,
Ferrar Maziroff Associates Talent Agency

"While reading this book I was amazed to see how many jobs I had stumbled upon during slow times and how many jobs I would have liked to try if I had only known about them. This book would have taken away the stress I felt during those 'slow times,' which definitely affected my auditions."

Adam Philipson, Broadway actor/UCLA student

"Filled with ideas. Survival Jobs shows you can survive with a little smarts and a lot of moxie."

M. K. Lewis, author,
Your Film Acting Career

"The worst thing about being a struggling artist is the struggling part. Survival Jobs takes the struggle out of the struggling artist!"

Vance DeGeneres, writer,
Prime Time Emmy Awards and Grammy Awards, Ellen

"When I started out in show biz, I took a job as a nighttime security guard in a dangerous part of town. If only I had had Survival Jobs then . . . come to think of it, because I'm still in show business (last I checked), I think I'll keep a copy of it handy."

Ron Darian, writer,
Mad About You

"Yes! Finally a truly helpful, useful, and practical industry book. Survival Jobs dispels the myth that acting and eating are mutually exclusive. If only the book itself were edible, it would be perfect!"

Dan O'Connor, actor/artistic director of Theater Sports

"Survival Jobs is filled with fabulously fun, insightful, and creative ways to make a buck while waiting for your big break."

Pamala Ellis, owner of Ellis Talent Group

"Finally, here is a book extensive and creative enough so that virtually anyone can find the 'perfect job.' This book is well-organized, clear, and entertaining. Survival Jobs is about more than survival; it's about getting a life. I am recommending it to my classes already."

Joel Asher, acting coach/director

"Deborah has shown me that my 'down time' can not only be profitable but can be fun and rewarding as well."

David Starzyk, actor

Survival Jobs

154 Ways to Make Money While Pursuing Your Dreams

Deborah Jacobson

Broadway Books New York

Broadway Books titles may be purchased for business or promotional use or for special sales. For information, please write to: Special Markets Department, Bantam Doubleday Dell Publishing Group, Inc., 1540 Broadway, New York, NY 10036.

BROADWAY BOOKS and its logo, a letter B bisected on the diagonal, are trademarks of Broadway Books, a division of Bantam Doubleday Dell Publishing Group, Inc.

FIRST EDITION

Designed by Ralph Fowler

Library of Congress Cataloging-in-Publication Data
Jacobson, Deborah.
Survival jobs : 154 ways to make money while pursuing your dreams / by Deborah Jacobson. — 1st ed.
p. cm.
Includes index.
ISBN 0-7679-0150-9 (pbk.)
1. Vocational guidance—United States. I. Title.
HF5382.5.U5J33 1988
331.7'02'0973—dc21 97-40022
CIP

98 99 00 01 02 10 9 8 7 6 5 4 3 2 1

To my husband, **Jordan,**

with whom all things are possible

and to our daughter, **Maya,**

for adding so much love and

laughter to our lives

Acknowledgments

Hundreds of people contributed to the production of this book. I am deeply appreciative to all those who wholeheartedly shared their numerous ways of earning money, their employment or lack thereof, and their Rolodexes for further interviews!

I am filled with gratitude and respect for all of you who have helped advance the idea that there are plenty of part-time, flexible, and even fun ways to make money while pursuing your dreams. As they say at the Academy Awards, "I'm sorry there is not room or time (it would fill a book) to list everyone who helped, and if I left you out, please accept my sincere apology." I thank: Pamela Newkirk-Arkin, Gleason Bauer, Rebecca Brooks, David Bruskin, Dorrit Cowan, Walter and Shelley Dominguez, James Dumont, Steven Frenkel, Cynthia Gale, Ellen and Arthur Giglio, Marcie Gilbert and Adam Philipson, Lisa Givot, Harrison Held, Shari Joffe, Gail Johnston, Stefanie Kane, Brian Kahn, Gary Laramore, Steve Leder, Josh Levin, David Lowe, Marg Mackleon, Scott Maziroff, Shawn Murray, Dan O'Connor, Gene Pack, Chris Paine, Jane Raitt, Gina Ramirez, Maria Rinaldi, Dale Rehfeld, David Starzyk, Vivian Strauss, Brynna Sibilla, Meredith Thomas, Scott Tyler, and Laura Patinkin-Urken.

Special thanks to:

K Callan, the wonderfully talented actress and author of five books for artists, who was my mentor at the beginning and is now also my friend.

Gwen Feldman at Samuel French Bookstore, for her time and support, and for putting my self-published edition at the cash register!

Aaron Silverman at SCB Distributors, for getting my self-published edition in bookstores across the country.

John Feins at Borders Bookstore in Los Angeles, for his generosity in promoting me when I was a first-time author.

Retha Powers at Quality Paperback Book Club, for that wonderful phone call I received when I was three months pregnant and sick in bed. I thought it was a prank call from a friend but it really was you, calling to buy my self-published edition.

Sharone Katz, Kim Starzyk, and Tara Wilson, for their generous assistance with many aspects of this book and, more importantly, for their friendship.

My agent, Simon Green, for his immeasurable talents, energy, tenacity, and humor. Thank you for taking this book to the level of excellence we knew was possible. (Sorry I can't sing your name in print, Simon!)

My editor, Suzanne Oaks, for bringing her ideas, energy, and insight to this book.

Ann Campbell, for her detailed editorial talents and enthusiasm.

My Aunt Marilyn (AKA "soul sister") and my beautiful mother, Barbara Frenkel, for reading and improving my first drafts with loving, uplifting notes.

My Uncle Larry, the owner of Kustom Cards International Inc., for his abounding generosity in creating promotional pictures and bookmarks that helped make my self-published edition such a success.

My mother-in-law, Renee Jacobson, for her amazing resourcefulness in gathering information and her continued support.

My parents, Barbara and Michael Frenkel, for giving me roots so I am grounded and wings so I can fly. I love you and am truly grateful.

To my husband, Jordan, my "Be-Sheret" of life. I thank you for contributing your amazing talents and sense of humor to this book and my life, and for your tremendous support. It is an honor being your partner.

And finally, I thank God for my talents and the angels who surround me with beauty.

Table of Contents

2 Nine to Five . . . Not

Pick a Shift That Works for You

Foreword

Deborah Jacobson saved my life—literally. It never occurred to me that I could do anything else besides waitressing while pursuing an acting career, that anything else would be flexible enough or bring in enough income. But I hated it. And when you hate part of your life, it bleeds into everything else. It was affecting my auditions, my marriage, and my health. I was depressed. I felt like I had no choices.

Then Deborah came into my life with her wonderful list of jobs. Still I scoffed at them (they weren't fully researched yet), because when you are in the middle of impossibility, possibility is almost unrecognizable. Nevertheless, I was one of her first guinea pigs, and for that I will be eternally grateful.

I now have a pet care business that I share with my husband, who is also an actor, and we work on the weekends with developmentally disabled people. For extra money now and then we cater and participate in market research focus groups, and have also done food demos and handed out movie passes. The point is, the choices are endless. Just keep trying different things until you find the job or jobs you like.

I now feel as though I contribute something to the world in a way that fulfills me and lets me have fun. And what's more, that feeling of fulfillment is now spilling over into the rest of my life, and I am starting to make money as an actress.

Now you, too, can pursue your dreams *and* support yourself financially. This book is your first step in the right direction. If you get half as much out of it as I did, your life will greatly improve.

KIM FITZGERALD
mom/actress/pet care business owner/social worker

Survival Jobs completely changed the way I thought about making money part-time. I am an actress who spent many years unhappily waiting tables. Not that there is anything wrong with waiting tables—it can be a lucrative way to earn a living, and it allowed me to take acting and dance classes and attend auditions during the day. However, I began feeling enslaved by it. I felt like I'd bought into the "lie" that artists must suffer and starve. Well, *Survival Jobs* changed all that for me. Aside from the many ideas and job options it presented, there was something Deborah said in her introduction that really opened my eyes. She said, if you don't like the job you're doing full-time, do it part-time, and do something else to earn money on other days. Believe it or not, that thought never occurred to me! I had become obligated to a job that wasn't important, and had lost sight of the options available. Now I have a couple of different jobs that I love, and I arrange my schedule so that I never get burned out on a particular one. *Survival Jobs* encourages you to examine your strengths—the ones you already have and the ones you *want* to have—and to use them creatively to make your living. After all, creativity is what I want to support—so why turn it off in order to survive?

Because I enjoy my survival jobs, I feel less discouraged when my acting career has its ups and downs. I recently made my directing debut with a new play—a big accomplishment, considering that just one short year ago (pre–*Survival Jobs*) I was thinking about giving up on theater altogether! Thanks, Deborah, for helping me enjoy more of my life, more of the time!

PAMELA NEWKIRK-ARKIN
actress/child care/pet care/children's entertainment

Introduction

This book is about sustaining your dreams.

I wrote *Survival Jobs* to reach out to the thousands of people who need a part-time, flexible way to earn money. Whether you are an artist needing financial support till your big break comes along, a student paying your way through school, a mom or dad wanting to work fewer hours and spend more time at home with your family, or one of the millions of Americans who need an extra job simply to pay the bills, save for their children's education, or finance a trip to Europe, this is the book that will help you.

At one time or another, I myself have fallen into all these categories. While attending college, I worked part-time in the evening, on weekends, and during summer months. After graduating, I chose to pursue an acting career in New York and then Los Angeles, and I was constantly in need of "survival jobs." By the time I became a mother, I had used my skills and a few of the jobs I talk about in this book to create part-time work that enabled me to earn full-time income right out of my home (as Dr. Laura Schlessinger says: I am my kid's mom!).

All told, I have held more than 25 survival jobs. I was always in search of a more creative, higher-paying way to make money. Eventually I realized that, to have as much control over my life and time as I wanted, I needed to go into business for myself. The first business I owned combined my love for animals with my entrepreneurial skills. I began a pet care business (see chapter 7), which generated income immediately. I simply took a walk in my neighborhood during peak "dog-walking hours" and went to "doggie parks," introducing myself and distributing fliers. I also placed fliers and business cards in pet hospitals and pet stores around town. Soon I had a thriving business and had to hire out.

The other business I started I call a "factory go-between" (see chapter 1). While living in Los Angeles, I became a rep for an out-of-town factory that offered a high-quality product at an extremely competitive price. I was essentially the middle man; customers came to our home, placed their orders, and paid, and I then sent the order to "my factory." The factory delivered directly to my customers, so I never saw them again except for reorders.

Through speaking at seminars and book events, I have found that often people don't realize that the talents and skills they *already possess* can be used to earn money—sometimes lots of it. Many people dog-sit for neighbors, paint houses, plan parties, build things, play a musical instrument, take excellent photographs, sing, have a flair for design, or are computer savvy. Believe it or not, these are actually skills that can be used to make money now! And with that in mind, here are a few things to consider when setting out to find the survival job that's right for you.

When searching for the appropriate survival job, be aware of your own personality and scheduling needs. Use your most energetic, productive time for yourself and for your creativity (or to be with your kids!). If you are an artist and the best time for you to write or paint is in the morning, work a survival job in the evening. If you're an actor, leave your days free to audition. It may even benefit you to work several survival jobs at once. This way, you can expand your social circles and networking possibilities, and more importantly, you won't feel trapped in one job. That is an awful feeling . . . I know from experience. So instead of working at the same restaurant or office five times a week, work there two or three days (or nights) and try something else of interest in my book.

If you come across a job in this book that grabs your attention but you feel apprehensive about marketing it, remember that you can hire others to market your idea or to do whatever you don't feel comfortable with or don't have time for. People often have a hard time giving up control, thinking, "Only I know how to do it right," or "It will take just as much time to train someone else." But these thoughts can keep you from expanding your business and freeing up *your* time to follow *your* dreams. I have learned that hiring others to handle certain aspects of my business (and my life!) gives me more time to be productive in the areas I excel in. Furthermore, it can be extremely lucrative to hire another person on an hourly basis to distribute fliers, business cards, and brochures that will spread the word about your service over the years.

Bartering is also a wonderful way to raise awareness for your new business venture. A woman recently asked me for a way to get her cake decorating business off the ground. She took my advice, and instead of spending money on gifts for special occasions such as birthday parties, bar and bat mitzvahs, and weddings, she offered to make the cake. Word traveled quickly, and soon she had a thriving business.

If you come across a job that piques your interest but your skills in that particular area are limited, take a few classes at a community college or local community center, or apprentice at a reputable company to get your foot in the door. I can't stress enough the value of apprenticing or assisting a professional in a business you have interest in. Most people and corporations welcome low-cost or free help, and you will benefit by gaining valuable knowledge and contacts without having to spend your own dollars on costly classes. A man interviewed for this book for the freelance illustrator job (see chapter 6) made a very valid point: "When you take a class, you are usually in a room filled with people who know very little. When you apprentice, you are the only one who knows very little and thus will soak up information daily from a team of experts."

I originally self-published a version of this book. I bought a few books on self-publishing (Dan Poynter's *Self-Publishing Manual* is terrific), took a class given by the Learning Annex in Los Angeles, and hooked up with a few people who had successfully self-published. Whenever a person approaches me about self-publishing a book or starting a particular business venture, I always suggest talking to someone who has mastered it.

I believe that how you earn your income, your financial situation, and your ability to feel good about yourself are intrinsically connected to your success in life. As of the final draft of this book, my husband, who is an actor and writer, and I have sold our factory go-between home business (see chapter 1), and are now able to share in the wonder of raising our daughter, Maya. I am writing and giving seminars on survival jobs in my spare time, and I am in school working toward my master's in sacred music, fulfilling my dream of becoming a cantor (the leader of musical liturgy in the Jewish religion). One of my survival jobs, varied musical work (see chapter 3) was actually part of the process I followed to become a cantor. Who knows where *your* survival job will lead *you* when you channel your natural talents into making money?

All aspects of your life—your spouse or significant other, your family, God, your community, and your creative inspirations—deserve to have you at your best. If the situation you are in is not working, change it! Better to do what you love part-time than not at all.

Who knows? Your story may be similar to mine. Your part-time survival jobs may turn into an extremely profitable and rewarding career.

I wish you great success in all your endeavors.

DEBORAH JACOBSON

1

You're the Top

For the CEO in You

Apartment Manager

Trade in your park bench for a roof over your head.

If you never thought it was possible to stay home, eat potato chips, watch TV, and get paid for it, guess again!

Being an apartment manager is perfect for couch potatoes, writers, artists, moms, seniors, or anyone who stays home a lot. Some building owners will even hire people who already have a 9 to 5 job as long as they carry a beeper. I know many couples who worked as apartment managers for a number of years to save for a down payment on a home—what a great idea!

Basically, an apartment manager is responsible for collecting rent, keeping the building and surrounding area clean, and knowing whom to call in an emergency. Some positions may even require light maintenance. The actual labor involved in this job will depend on your tenants and the size and quality of the complex. Most large complexes (over 50–75 units) have special maintenance crews. Typically a small, 10- to 20-unit building is easiest to handle. Some building owners prefer couples, but this is not a requirement. The main attributes that apartment owners generally look for are honesty, common sense, good credit, stability, and an ability to fill vacancies.

Most large cities have apartment associations that offer certified resident manager training courses. For example, the Apartment Association of Greater Los Angeles offers a training course approximately 12 times a year. It costs between $350 and $400, and the placement rate is around 80 percent. After completing the course, you can place an ad in the Apartment Association's employment bulletin—an excellent way to get a job. Most courses are extremely informative and well-respected among apartment building owners. Another option is exploring a course in your city that is subsidized by the government. For example, at Los Angeles City College Community Services, an apartment management course is offered for $85. You can also try calling the local chamber of commerce regarding an apartment managing course.

Whether you receive free rent and utilities plus salary will depend on the building you are managing. Smaller units often offer only a rent reduction or free rent, while larger buildings will pay a weekly salary as well. This is often negotiable depending on your experience. Some management companies even offer health benefits and profit sharing.

To find an apartment manager position, check the classified section of your newspaper, contact building owners and management firms directly, and network with other apartment managers. You will need to submit a current résumé and a list of references. Also helpful is *The Encyclopedia of Associations,* which can be found at your local library: one for national associations and several volumes for different regions. The National Apartment Owners and Managers Association is in Watertown, Connecticut, and the National Apartment Association is in Washington, D.C.

Good Luck

BENEFITS: salary plus free rent and utilities or rent reduction, sometimes profit sharing and health benefits.

PITFALLS: overbearing owners and tenants, calls at all hours.

SOURCES: classified section of newspaper; Apartment Association of Greater Los Angeles, (213) 384–4131; Los Angeles City College Community Services, (213) 669–1031; National Apartment Owners and Managers Association; National Apartment Association, (202) 842–4050; building owners and management firms.

NEEDS: prior experience, good credit, some basic maintenance ability.

> *"I took the apartment management course in California and recently had to move to Dallas 'cause of an illness in the family. I contacted other managers for recommendations of people to call and had no problem getting a job. In fact I had a number of offers. I now manage a 90-unit building with salary plus an apartment, utilities, and free cable."*
>
> JIM PLATTER, apartment manager/builds computers/retired, Dallas

Designing Greeting Cards and Postcards

**Roses are red, they don't grow in a ball park—
write pretty verses and work for Hallmark!**

The gift card industry is a thriving business. The average person receives about 30 cards a year. A neighborhood post office recently estimated that a third of all first-class mail consists of greeting cards. If you possess photographic, writing, or artistic abilities, you can become part of this booming industry.

Designing cards allows you to be creative and work at home on your own time. It also provides the excitement of seeing your work displayed. To be successful, marketing abilities are a must. If marketing is not your forte, consider hiring someone else to help out.

You can turn anything into a postcard or gift card. I have seen beautiful cards with dried flower designs, twigs, and original artwork. To get started, go to an art store, library, or bookstore and read a few books on card making. These can be found in the art technique section. The creative process comes next. If you are drawing or painting your cards, draw a rough sketch first and then finalize it in pen and ink. To save some money, go to a paper supply company that sells different kinds of paper wholesale. Such companies often can be found in industrial areas.

Next, you can silk-screen your design or go to a copy center and laser print the sketches. You can then paint the prints with dry pigments, pastel sticks, or other media. After coloring your cards, spray them with an acrylic paint for protection. Explore your designs, reproduce them, and test them out.

Marketing your prototypes is the next step, and there are many ways to go about doing this. Visit a variety of stores and gift shops with your portfolio and meet with the card buyer. You may need to make an appointment, but oftentimes if you have a professional and courteous manner, you can just walk in and be seen. Many small stores and specialty shops buy their cards from independent artists. If a store is interested, it will typically order a small amount first and pay you upon delivery. Another good way to sell your work is at craft bazaars and flea markets (see "Swap Meets and Flea Markets" in this chapter). You can find out about these through friends and newspapers, and by networking with crafts people.

You can also sell your designs through card distributors. They will buy the rights and produce the cards. To locate a distributor that is right for you, go to a store and see which cards are similar to yours. Look on the back of the card to see what company produces it, and write directly to the distributor or manufacturer, requesting its market list, catalog, and submission guidelines. Remember to enclose an SASE (self-addressed, stamped envelope) and *be certain to copyright your material first.* For more information call the Library of Congress in Washington, D.C., (202) 707–3000. Always put your name and phone number (preferably a service number) on your cards. You never know who may see your work and want to contact you.

Submission procedures vary among greeting card publishers. Some prefer individual card ideas on 3-by-5 cards, others prefer receiving a number of complete ideas on 8.5-by-11 bond paper. The typical submission includes five to 15 card ideas with a cover letter.

Income will vary depending on how much of your work actually sells.

Craft shows and flea markets usually charge a booth fee, and you keep all profits. Stores typically pay you half of what each card is sold for. If your work is put into the store on consignment, about 75 percent of the card price is a fair return for you. Greeting card companies and distributors offer individual payment plans, per-card payments, and royalties.

You can consult a number of sources for information on the greeting card industry. The book *Writer's Market: Where and How to Sell What You Write* contains a listing of greeting card companies and their requirements. *The Greeting Card Industry Directory* lists names, addresses, and product lines of all exhibitors at the National Stationery Show. Trade magazines such as *Greetings* and *Paper Retailer* may be helpful.

Good Luck

BENEFITS: work at home, creative, exciting to see your work produced.

PITFALLS: income varies.

SOURCES: network with crafts people; go to card stores, specialty stores, and craft stores; contact companies listed in *Writer's Market: Where and How to Sell What You Write;* read trade magazines such as *Greetings,* 309 Fifth Avenue, New York, NY 10016; and *Paper Retailer.* For more information write to Greeting Card Creative Network at 1200 G Street N.W., Suite 760, Washington, DC 20005, and the Greeting Card Association, 1350 New York Avenue N.W., Suite 615, Washington, DC 20005, (202) 393–1778.

NEEDS: artistic or photographic talent and vision, marketing ability.

IDEA: Writing prose for greeting cards is another possibility. If you have the talent, contact card companies with writing samples, using the information above. Check out the book, *How to Write and Sell Greeting Cards, Bumper Stickers, T-Shirts and Other Fun Stuff* by Molly Wigand.

"About two years ago my partner and I started our own greeting card line called Greetings from Little Jimmy—hip, humorous cards. I write them and my friend Jeff designs them. When we first started we silk-screened them and sold them at small shops in Chicago. Just recently we went national. I enjoy doing it and it comes easily to me—I write about five cards a day. Jeff and I have been friends since fifth grade so we work well together. Seeing people crack up when they read the cards is very satisfying."

JOHN MCCRAY, writer/director/greeting card company co-owner, Chicago

Designing or Refinishing Furniture

Was woodshop your favorite high school class?

Last year I bought a beautiful, distressed wooden coffee table from a soap opera star who had started to make and sell furniture after he was killed off on his show. What had started as a hobby and a way to bring in some extra cash eventually became a lucrative side business. Distressed finishes and colorful, creatively painted furniture are extremely popular right now, and plenty of people and stores alike love to buy custom-made furniture at wholesale prices.

Making or refinishing furniture is fun and creative, and challenges your artistic abilities. As a self-employed artist you can create as many or as few pieces as you like, or as many as needed to supplement your income. You can sell your own designs or take custom orders, and most importantly, your schedule is your own.

You need basically two things: a place to work and furniture. The place could be your own backyard, a garage, or a studio. Pieces of furniture are easy to come by, and can be gathered from garage sales, flea markets, thrift stores, or even the city dump. I have seen old door frames turned into desk tops and coffee table tops, old school desks stripped and shellacked over with colorful stamps or comic strips, and discarded bathroom furniture pieces painted with vibrant colors and brought back to life. It is exciting to see what one can do with a little imagination and some paint.

The next step, of course, will be marketing the items. Remember, if marketing is not your strength, think about hiring someone else to do it for a percentage of the profit. There are a number of ways to sell your furniture: set up shop right in front of your home on the weekends; advertise with neighborhood fliers and by word-of-mouth; or sell your work at flea markets and furniture or craft stores. After you complete a few attractive pieces, have some quality photographs taken and create a portfolio of your work to show to independent stores. I have seen furniture sellers bring a few of their pieces to flea markets (see "Swap Meets and Flea Markets," this chapter) along with their portfolios and take custom-made orders on the spot. Have business cards handy to pass out to potential customers at these markets.

Another way to sell your work independently (and probably at a higher profit than a store can offer) is by spreading the news among friends. This is exactly how I got my coffee table. The actor who made it traded his work for headshots. I noticed his work at my friend's house, and asked for his number. Trade furniture pieces for services or classes, sell discounted pieces to well-connected friends, advertise in local papers, and place fliers on cars. Get your work noticed and receive a fair price for it.

Your income will depend on how many pieces you sell and your profit margin (including time and material costs). Price similar items at stores, figure out your minimum hourly wage, and negotiate from there.

Good Luck

BENEFITS: creative, challenging, self-employed.

PITFALLS: unsteady salary, time spent gathering wood or furniture.

SOURCES: flea markets listed in the yellow pages or classifieds under "Swap Meets" or "Flea Markets" or local newspaper weekend calendar sections, thrift stores, garage sales, garbage receptacles.

NEEDS: artistic talent, patience, tools and paint, woodworking skills.

Factory Go-Between

Be the president of a company.

Most people are unaware of many untapped business opportunities. Being a factory go-between is one of them. A factory go-between is a rep for an established factory or company who sells merchandise for the factory and makes a profit on each item. For example, two law students in New York connected with a factory in the Midwest that manufactures in-line skates and accessories. They negotiated a deal with the factory owners to get merchandise at or below wholesale cost (irregulars and last season's merchandise). They then papered the town and schools with fliers that advertised the names and prices of popular skates and provided a phone number for orders. This concept can be applied to most items (clothing, electronics, and flatware, to name a few) as long as a factory is willing to supply the product.

Working as a factory go-between takes little effort once you get set up and organized. You have no overhead, you spend little time taking orders, and once the factory receives the order, you are out of the picture. The customer pays you, you pay the factory, and the factory sends the merchandise with your logo or label directly to the customer. Make sure you have a clear understanding with the factory that all products *must* be quality or size guaranteed.

Wages are totally dependent on your profit margin (how much more you charge per item than the factory) and your advertising efforts.

To hook up with a wholesale distributor or manufacturer, you may need to do some research. Look through various magazines, mail order ads, newspapers, and the yellow pages for companies selling a product of interest, and then contact the owners, expressing your interest in being a rep.

Good Luck

BENEFITS: your own business, little overhead.

PITFALLS: income varies depending on product and marketing.

SOURCES: contacting manufacturers or businesses listed in various magazines, mail order ads, newspapers, and the yellow pages.

NEEDS: marketing ability, product to sell.

"My wife (the author of this book!) and I had a very successful business out of our home as a factory go-between. While living in Los Angeles, a city where actors and models need many copies of publicity prints (headshots) we became the middleman with a factory in the Midwest that my wife had found out about through a local photographer. We basically acted as 'reps' for this factory. They did incredible work at a much lower price than stores in L.A. could compete with, and we were able to negotiate even lower prices to make a nice profit on our end. Actors would come to our home, place their orders, and write us a check (we accepted credit cards, too), and we would express our orders to the factory twice a week. The prints were sent directly to our cus-

tomers, so we never saw them again except for reorders! We basically collected the money and guaranteed our quality. Our customers only stayed for about 15 minutes so we were easily earning $100+ an hour. Not bad for never leaving your home, huh? My wife, who set up the whole business, is an entrepreneurial genius . . . but I guess from reading this book you already know that."

JORDAN JACOBSON, dad/writer/actor, Los Angeles and New York

Headshot Photographer

Your home photo album is so professional that it would put Annie Leibovitz to shame.

There are over 100,000 union actors and probably double that number who are non-union, and they *all* need headshots! Not to mention models, musicians, authors, and many others who need publicity prints. The headshot is an actor's calling card. Casting directors need to see a photograph of an actor before he or she is even called in for the audition. In cities such as New York, Los Angeles, Chicago, and Orlando, an inexhaustible supply of actors constantly need to update their headshots, and busloads of talented transplants migrate each year to entertainment havens, seeking the gold rush of TV and film!

A good headshot photographer must love taking pictures and must have a knack for capturing a person's essence in a photograph (eyes are the key). Being a photographer while pursuing another area in the arts allows you to continue to be creative while earning a living. The job itself includes taking the photographs, developing and reviewing the contact sheets, and selecting the ones you think are best. It's a flexible job in that you are always able to coordinate the time of the shoot with your personal schedule.

If you don't have a background in photography, introductory six- to ten-week photography courses are offered at most community colleges and adult-ed schools. The startup costs for becoming a headshot photographer are reasonable. You will need a decent 35-millimeter camera and lens, which starts at about $275, and, of course, film. Create a portfolio to show prospective clients by shooting volunteer actors and models for free or at cost. Try contacting local agencies for referrals. Shooting a few high-profile clients for free in exchange for a reference will be invaluable in the long run. To promote your business, advertise in the trades and theatrical publications found at performing arts bookstores or newsstands (*Backstage, Dramalogue, Theater Week, The Working Actors Guide* by Mani Flattery), and post your business cards at theaters and casting offices.

Income varies widely: $150–$2,500 a week depending on your fee and your bookings. A good photographer charges, on average, $150–$300 for a two-roll session. This price often includes one or two developed 8-by-10s.

Another way to generate income as a photographer is to take pictures of children at Little League games, karate studios, and any other sports and recreational classes. Parents love pictures of their children performing. Or try photographing people at special events. When my husband and I finished the Los Angeles Marathon (have to boast about that!) there was a guy who took our picture and then put it in a plastic circular magnet for a fee—what a great idea! I still have it displayed on my refrigerator. You can also take portraits of people with their pets or their children, or even expand to photograph weddings, parties, and other social gatherings. There are endless possibilities to secure employment as a photographer.

Good Luck

BENEFITS: great profit margin, creative, networking, self-employed, barter for other services, work at home.

PITFALLS: unsteady income.

SOURCES: advertise in theatrical publications found at performing arts bookstores or newsstands: *Backstage,* (310) 474–6161 or (212) 764–7300; *Dramalogue,* (213) 464–5079; *Theater Week; The Working Actors Guide* by Mani Flattery; also, place your brochure or cards on bulletins where actors congregate, referrals through freebies or agents.

NEEDS: a good 35-millimeter camera and lens, experience, a photography course, work well with actors.

IDEA: *Careers for Shutterbugs and Other Candid Types* by Cheryl Mclean offers dozens of career opportunities for anyone who loves working with a camera. Another excellent book is *Photographer's Market: Where and How to Sell Your Photographs* by Michael Willins.

Home Clothing Sales

Ralph Lauren would call you for fashion tips if he had your phone number.

Everyone likes a bargain, and home clothing sales provide just that. Home clothing sales involves contacting clothing manufacturers and gathering discounted goods on consignment to sell privately in your home. You will usually receive overcuts, samples, damages, or last season's merchandise. The manufacturers will tell you what the garments cost, and you can mark them up accordingly to earn a profit.

To run a successful home clothing sale, you will need some specific skills. First, you must be an organized person. It is imperative to keep accurate records of garments sold and how much money each manufacturer is owed. Many manufacturers are only willing to give out their clothing at the end of each season—on consignment, with a promise that you will pick up and return the goods within three days (pick up Friday and return Monday). Another avenue, if you have the cash, is to buy overruns that didn't sell for a variety of reasons or close-out merchandise (irregulars, which are slightly damaged, and discontinued items) below wholesale. This will enable you to sell it all year and then, if need be, take it to a swap meet or flea market (see "Swap Meets and Flea Markets," this chapter). You need space to store garments on racks and a database of customers. Presentation is likewise important. All garments must be steamed, price-tagged and easily accessible. A mirrored dressing room area, even if it is only a bathroom or bedroom, is essential.

People you know in the clothing industry are great for leads, and often knowing someone in the business is the key to getting merchandise "on loan." Most companies won't trust just anyone with their goods, and you are responsible for all garments taken. If you are looking to buy, check the yellow pages under "Clothing—Wholesale and Manufacturers" and call directly. I suggest asking for a meeting with the production manager, manufacturer, or owner and presenting your idea with authority, conviction, sales ability, and most importantly, references!

To let people know about your sale, place fliers where people congregate—yoga centers, salons, supermarkets, health clubs, dance and aerobic studios, and popular audition spots. You may also want to advertise in your community newsletter. Be sure to keep a record of all customers so that you can inform them of the next sale.

Income varies. Some people earn up to $3,000 in a weekend selling clothes. Your success will greatly depend on your merchandise, promotional techniques, and customer base.

Good Luck

BENEFITS: easy cash, fun, do it when you want to.

PITFALLS: unsteady money, need room to store and organize the goods.

SOURCES: contacts in wholesale manufacturing, yellow pages under "Clothing—Wholesale and Manufacturers."

NEEDS: organized, responsible, good sales technique, database of customers.

Mail Order Business

Two words: home shopping.

There is a reason that hundreds of companies such as Victoria's Secret send you a "free" catalog every week: It works. Millions of people love the idea of ordering products from the privacy and security of their home.

This particular moneymaking opportunity is perfect for those with an entrepreneurial spirit. To get started you need an idea, a P.O. box to receive orders and payment, and some money for advertising. A few popular ideas are kitschy sexual stuff, gag gifts, information on how to make money fast or get something for free that normally costs money, lists of places to write for free samples, information on how to solve credit problems, recipes, and, of course, the old standbys: diet and beauty products.

Money spent on advertising can range from $20 to hundreds of dollars depending on the papers or magazines you choose.

One woman I interviewed ordered by mail a list of foundations that give grants to people looking to consolidate their debt. Upon receiving the information, she was inspired to start her own mail order business with additional resources she had gathered. She wrote her own flier, took out an ad in a magazine called *Jackpot Junkies* (figuring readers would be desperate for her information), and for months after earned substantial money.

To gather ideas, look in magazines and newspapers to see what others are selling. There are a number of books on the subject at your local bookstore or library. A few popular ones are *101 Great Mail-Order Businesses* by Tyler Hicks, *Home-Based Mail Order* by William J. Bond, and *How I Made $1,000,000 in Mail Order* by E. Joseph Cossman.

NOTE: to protect a printed product, copyright it. Write to the Registrar of Copyrights, Library of Congress, Washington, D.C. 20559, (202) 707–3000.

Good Luck

BENEFITS: can make a lot of money easily, work from home; initial investment is low if you're selling information.

PITFALLS: other people see your ad and copy the idea.

SOURCES: books on the subject to get the business up and running, magazines and newspapers for ideas.

NEEDS: a good idea, sought-after information or product, money to advertise, ability to write appealing advertisements, perseverance.

> *"I made $2,000 a month repackaging an old idea and selling it through the mail. I didn't need to make copies of my information packet until the orders came in, so my overhead was minimal. It was exciting finding checks in my mailbox. Unfortunately, soon after people copied my idea, so I stopped."*
>
> LYNN HAYWORTH, actress/mail order business/furniture painter, Milwaukee

Massage Therapist

You are proud of your overdeveloped hand muscles.

Massage may be the second oldest known profession (the oldest known profession is not a job this author recommends). It has been practiced for approximately 5,000 years.

Getting a massage is definitely on my top five list of pleasures—next to playing with my daughter, making love with my husband, traveling, and eating. I find it relaxing and luxurious. My whole being feels better after a massage. And there are many proven health benefits. Being a massage therapist has a number of advantages: You are participating in the healing of another person and learning about the human body, which is fascinating. You make a good income with a flexible, part-time schedule once you have established your clientele. You can barter for services like haircuts and privately run classes. Trading massages with other massage therapists is another big plus, not to mention paying off your tuition by giving discounted sessions while attending massage school. Working for a chiropractor, hotel, spa, or gym will pay less than your own service, but it will guarantee you a steady income while you build your client base.

Check the yellow pages to find massage therapy schools. State requirements differ, so call the local board of education or licensing department for information on certification. Often, massage is regulated through your city government, so call your city or town hall and ask for the department of business licensing. Most cities have a number of schools that offer eight- to 12-week part-time courses. For example, the California Healing Arts College offers an eight-week part-time course for $1,450. Conversely, the state requirements in New York are rather stringent. You need over 605 hours of schooling to sit for the New York state licensing exam. The Swedish Institute on West 26th Street in New York City offers a one-year program for $6,500. The class meets for about three hours a day, five days a week.

If your finances are tight, there are other options. Many healing arts centers (check your yellow pages or directory assistance) offer massage courses at less costly prices. They don't offer certification to practice massage, but they do teach technique and provide information that should enable you to pass the licensing exam in many cities. You can then take other body-related courses at your own pace.

You will also need to buy a massage table, which costs approximately $500 new. For a used table, check your local classifieds or independent papers (*The Recycler* in Los Angeles and the *Village Voice* in New York are excellent) and bulletin boards at massage schools.

Most massage schools have bulletin boards with lists of job openings. Check the help wanted section of the paper for spa and health club job opportunities (see "Working in a Health Club," chapter 4) or contact health clubs directly using your yellow pages. I know a few people who have bought massage chairs and set up shop in local health markets and office buildings, offering "quickie" massages.

Speak to the manager or owner of a store near you; a short massage in a neighborhood store, or, for that matter, any business, could increase sales. Many film producers hire part-time or full-time massage therapists to work on the set, giving relief to the actors.

For a 60- to 90-minute massage, the average rate is $65 (it ranges from $40 to $125). Higher rates are common for home visits. For a 15-minute neck and shoulder massage, $10–$15 is the going rate.

Good Luck

BENEFITS: good wages, meet different people, contribute to people's health, barter for services.

PITFALLS: tuition, building clientele.

SOURCES: American Massage Therapy Association, (847) 864–0123; California Healing Arts College, (310) 826–7622; Swedish Institute, (212) 924–5900; classifieds; yellow pages; spas; gyms; chiropractors.

NEEDS: education, certification, and massage license.

"I actually became a massage therapist because of Deborah and her list of survival jobs. I had been managing a restaurant in New York and they moved me out to Los Angeles. I soon realized a change in careers was necessary. I have always been fascinated by the human body. Massage has changed my life. It is tremendously rewarding being able to work with athletes, pregnant women, and regular folks in need of deep tissue work. I recently got employee of the

month at the Pacific Athletic Club and have decided to go for a master's degree in physical therapy. Thanks, Deborah."

CARLO BRUNO, massage therapist, Beverly Hills

"When I was 16, I was dropped from a ballet lift, and the only relief from pain was my weekly massage. That led to my initial interest in the field. I continued to work in musical theater but soon tired of the theater politics and all the negative energy I was experiencing. I decided to pursue a massage license to see what it would be like. Well, it became so fulfilling that I left showbiz for good (although I still taught dance until I had my daughter two years ago). I now have a steady clientele out of my home, am able to be home with my daughter, Lina, and am working with cancer patients and people with immune diseases, which is incredibly rewarding. Becoming a massage therapist was one of the best things I ever did."

ELLEN GIGLIO, mom/massage therapist/dancer, New York

Mobile Auto Detailing

Does the word buffing excite you?

Mobile auto detailing is a popular service, especially in cities with frequent inclement weather or air pollution. People are always willing to pay good money to keep their cars in top shape. Mobile auto detailing involves driving to your client's car and giving it a thorough cleaning inside and out, shampooing the seats and carpeting, and polishing and buffing all interior and exterior surfaces.

Going into business for yourself, or with a partner, as an auto detailer can be quite lucrative. Owning your own business guarantees flexibility. And, like many of the jobs in this book, auto detailing can also be used to barter for other services. An actor I know who does mobile auto detailing trades his services for headshots and classes. Keep in mind that you must be in decent physical condition, as this job involves physical labor.

To gain the necessary knowledge and experience, work for an auto detailing shop first (check the yellow pages), or get your own car detailed by a mobile unit and ask specific business questions. To start up your own auto detailing business you will need to invest approximately $1,500–$2,500, which will cover the cost of all the equipment you will need. To make things easier, you may want to have a trailer built that hooks up to the back of your car and enables you to carry the necessities, like a gasoline power pump, generator, steamer, and polisher. Most importantly, you will need to obtain a license. For information on obtaining a license or certificate, call your city's tax and permit division or the county clerk's office. It is also a good idea to check with your car insurance agent for quotes on minor insurance since you will be dealing with other people's personal property.

Naturally, to build a good customer base you will need to advertise your services. Word-of-mouth is always the best way to generate interest, but fliers are also quite effective. Public garages and professional office complexes are a great place to target steady customers—they can afford regular service and you can polish their cars during their business hours. Ideally, you should find steady clients who will employ your services on a monthly basis. Another idea is to hire yourself out to auto dealers, who often like to "prep" cars for sale.

The process of mobile auto detailing a car typically takes two to three hours. The going rate is $85–$150 for the job.

Like most jobs, the harder you work, the more money you will make.

Good Luck

BENEFITS: lucrative, flexible.

PITFALLS: hard physical labor, startup costs, securing customers.

SOURCES: yellow pages, work at an auto shop for experience, advertise in local papers, distribute fliers at professional office complexes.

NEEDS: a car, insurance, money for equipment, experience, sales technique.

Mobile Disc Jockey

Dick Clark and Wolfman Jack are your idols.

These days most people are on a budget, and the cost of a band or full orchestra for an event can really put a dent in the wallet. A DJ is more cost-effective than hiring a full band, and many people actually prefer a DJ, so they get to hear their favorite songs sung by the original artists. There is nothing worse than a guy in a cheap tuxedo doing his version of a Bruce Springsteen classic. A DJ's duties include MC-ing, spinning records, and getting people on the dance floor. Playing appropriate music during the event is essential, for example, classical during mealtime, and swing and top 40 for dancing.

This is a great job for musicians or anyone who loves music, people, and parties. The ideal DJ possesses an extensive knowledge of current music as well as popular oldies. Above all, he or she must have the ability to feel out the crowd and know intuitively what music they want to hear. I was warned by a number of DJs that some parties, especially children's parties, can be high-maintenance, since parents tend to transfer a lot of their anxiety onto you. According to my sources, corporate and college parties are less stressful.

If you are just starting out, I suggest that you intern with another DJ to learn the ropes. You can earn $100 a night changing CDs or records while the DJ uses the microphone and plays games. To work for an established entertainment company, check the yellow pages under "Disc Jockeys" or "Entertainers."

When the time comes to start your own business, you will need to buy or rent equipment: a few good speakers, an amp, a mixer, and a turntable (the old-fashioned way) or a special two-CD player with pitch control. This equipment can be purchased at most specialty music stores and will cost approximately $1,000. You will also need about 100 CDs. Join a few of the music clubs advertised in newspapers and magazines, such as Columbia House and BMG—you can get a lot of free and discounted music. Putting together a demo tape for review by prospective parties is essential to your success. To generate business you can work some free or discounted gigs—church, temple, college, or theater company parties would be good places to start—and pass out your business cards. Advertise in your local paper or on bulletin boards. As always, word-of-mouth is the best advertisement.

The standard rate for a DJ is typically $125–$200 an hour. If you are a novice, I suggest a rate of about $100 an hour until you develop a reputation. There is usually a four-hour minimum. You can always charge time and a half if the host wants you to play beyond the previously scheduled hours.

Most of the DJs I spoke to emphasized the importance of being on time, presentable (a suit for most parties), and accommodating. One DJ said he is always set up and ready to go 30–60 minutes before the event begins. Remember, the host is counting on you for the success of the party.

Good Luck

BENEFITS: fun, meet people, learn music, good pay.

PITFALLS: unsteady cash flow if it's your own business.

SOURCES: yellow pages under "Disc Jockey" or "Entertainers."

NEEDS: professional, knowledgeable in current music and oldies, equipment and CDs if it's your own business, advertising.

Multilevel Marketing

The salesperson inside you must be let loose!

Multilevel marketing (MLM) has been hailed by many as the job of the nineties. Almost anyone can be successful at it with a little work, planning, and believing in the product or service being sold. The whole idea of multilevel or network marketing is to sell a product or service directly to others, who then become users and potential new sellers (your "downline"). You (the original seller) get a commission on both your individual sales and your downline sales. The more people who sell for you in your downline, the more money you make. For example, selling to five customers who each sell to five others creates 25 customers from whom you receive commissions. Depending on the number of people in your downline, untold numbers of customers are possible.

A major plus of this job is working from your home. You create your own work schedule. On the downside though, since this is a commission-only job, income fluctuates. Additionally, you may need to spend money to familiarize yourself with the products you will be selling. A few popular MLM companies you may have heard of include Herbalife, NuSkin, and Melaleuca.

MLM typically involves signing an agreement with the provider of a product or service to become a personal user and to market to others. With some companies there is a sign-up fee. Also, a minimum commitment to stock inventory is often required or advisable so you have samples or demonstrators for prospective customers. *Be careful* not to become involved with an MLM company that requires you to buy and stock more products than can be easily used or sold. The marketing plans of MLM companies vary considerably, as do the terms and conditions of the contracts. The most lucrative usually involve consumable products that customers use and reorder, like cosmetics, cleaners, vitamins, or long distance phone carriers. Consumable products produce "residual income," a monthly profit generated after the initial sale, based on reorders.

Income varies considerably depending on the product and your marketing abilities. Some people make as much as $40,000 a month and others make $100–$200 a month.

There are thousands of MLM companies to choose from. Pick up a copy of *USA Today* and look at the classifieds in the back under "Independent Agents." Any reputable MLM company will provide frequent informational seminars.

Good Luck

BENEFITS: self-employed, opportunity for high income, residuals, flexible hours, work out of home.

PITFALLS: commission only, spending money to familiarize yourself with the product, sometimes stocking high-volume inventory.

SOURCES: *USA Today* classifieds under "Independent Agents."

NEEDS: belief in product/service, entrepreneurial spirit.

"What I like best about the company I work for is there is no paperwork, billing, or collecting product in my home. Residual income provides me with a monthly $1,000 check from customers I enrolled a year ago! I work from home, it's flexible, and I love the products."

ANN CLARKE, real estate broker/MLM, Hanover, New Hampshire

Party Promoter

Celebrate good times, come on!

Were you the kid who invited 200 friends over to your house as soon as your parents went out of town? Have you ever been at a party, specifically a singles event, and thought, "I could plan a much more interesting party than this!" Well, here is a job for you.

College students, young professionals, people in their 40s on up, Christian and Jewish singles, and vegetarians are attracted to great parties as a way to meet other like-minded individuals. A party promoter puts these parties together. Judging from the city and climate you live in, you'll need to find an interesting venue to hold a party in and an eye-catching way to promote it. Depending on the age you're catering to, sports parties, ballroom or swing dancing parties, or virtual reality parties can be much more interesting and successful than the typical affair with a rented room and a DJ.

One party promoter told me he always keeps track of new places by reading various publications and local magazines that review "hot spots." Recently he read an article on a new café that opened as part of a boathouse. He rented it for a night and had a successful party called Party on the Dock of the Bay.

Successful parties require promotion, direct mailing, and advertising. Word-of-mouth is always best. Send out simple postcards to keep costs minimal or create elaborate invitations in hopes of attracting a larger, more exclusive crowd. When your parties are a hit, your mailing list will grow and people will keep on returning to the events you organize.

When going into business, contact your local county clerk's office to set up a corporation, self-proprietorship, or partnership. Liability insurance is important as well. When booking a space, you can go in person or handle arrangements by phone. You may need to give a deposit and show a portfolio with past invitations and write-ups.

Salary will vary depending on how successful your party is compared to costs involved. When you book a place, you typically guarantee a certain number of people or bar revenue. Earnings can vary from a few hundred bucks a party up to $10,000.

Good Luck

BENEFITS: flexible hours, social connections, potential to earn a lot of money.

PITFALLS: promotion costs, stressful at time of parties, feeling responsible for people having a good time.

SOURCES: when starting a business perhaps team up with organizations such as temples, churches, or dating services; finding venues to hold parties.

NEEDS: business acumen, liability insurance, promotional talents.

"I was a lawyer and wanted more control over my own life on a daily basis. This gives me the ability to allocate my free time and my business time. I no longer practice law (much to the dismay of my parents) and have time to write between putting parties together. And there is satisfaction in seeing an event go extremely well."

JEFF STRANK, ex-lawyer/writer/party promoter, New York

Personal Shopper

"I'd rather be shopping."

Are you always on the best-dressed list? If you have an eye for color, ability to make wise fashion decisions, and enjoy shopping, consider becoming a personal shopper.

Personal shoppers give personal assistance to customers depending on their needs and tastes. By hiring you, clients will actually save money by making specific purchases that satisfy their needs. You help clients weed out unworn, unflattering, or outdated items in their wardrobes.

Department stores hire personal shoppers, or you can choose to work independently. Department stores often look for personal shoppers who have retail experience and a design background or flair for fashion. Working for a department store will enable you to know when all the sales are to assist your customer and give you a steady paycheck—department stores usually give commission plus salary. On the downside, you are limited to choosing clothes from that particular store, and because you are working on commission, you may feel pressure to "sell" the client, which may not be in his or her best interest. Working independently allows for greater freedom, albeit an unsteady paycheck. Your job often consists of going through your client's closet and deciding what works and what doesn't—spring cleaning! If you work independently, it is valuable to have an "in" with wholesale houses.

Pay varies. Department stores generally pay $7–$9 an hour plus a small commission—maybe 3 percent. As an independent personal shopper, expect to earn $25–$50 an hour and $100 to go through a client's closet. Some personal shoppers gather a percentage fee of what is actually purchased. At showrooms, the client saves money on the items purchased, and the shopper can often receive up to 20 percent of the actual sale.

For employment in a department store, contact human resources or look in the classifieds. Independent work is often obtained by word-of-mouth. Advertise in local papers and in community, church, or temple newsletters. Place ads at salons and health clubs. Offer to barter your services when starting out to spread the word.

Good Luck

BENEFITS: flexible, fun to shop, assisting a client.

PITFALLS: in department stores, you're limited to their clothing; when self-employed, work can be unsteady and it may take time to gather a clientele.

SOURCES: department stores, advertising, word-of-mouth.

NEEDS: fashion and color sense, people skills, knowledge of various manufacturers.

IDEA: Being an image consultant is a rewarding and lucrative field as well.

"For a number of years, I worked as a personal shopper for department stores and now have a private clientele built through word-of-mouth. One of my current customers heard about me from her decorator. I enjoy using my talents in fashion and sharpening a person's wardrobe."

ESTHER RUTMAN, mom/personal shopper, Cleveland

Plant Leasing and Maintenance

You have several green thumbs.

Given the concrete jungles we live in today, having greenery around us has become both a necessity and a trend. A restaurant may have as many as 40 to 50 plants, banks with the typical high ceilings may have 12 to 15 very large plants, and hotel lobbies are filled with greenery. A plant leasing and maintenance business involves leasing and caring for these plants and assuring customers of weekly visits to keep their plants healthy and attractive.

You will need to have a general knowledge of familiar plants, since each type has different light, water, and food requirements. Some of the specifics you will need to learn are: Which plants can thrive behind tinted windows? What is the impact of direct and indirect sunlight? Which plants are low in pollen? Which plants are the heartiest? Reading books and working in a plant store or greenhouse are good ways to learn about these basic characteristics.

Many existing services supply rental/maintenance agreements. To work for an existing business (a great way to learn the ropes), look in the yellow pages under "Plants, Interior Design and Maintenance" or "Plants, Living—Renting and Leasing." To start your own business, try to work out an agreement with a neighborhood nursery for discounts on supplies and plants. A large vehicle is necessary for transportation of plants; use your own or rent a truck as needed.

Some nurseries may even be willing to transport and care for the plants if you act as the leasing agent.

You will need to advertise your services in local papers and by word-of-mouth. Or you can create a flier and distribute it to your target markets.

Your income will vary depending on the number of steady clients you have. To find out competitive pricing call a few companies listed in the yellow pages. The average monthly rent is 15–20 percent of the wholesale price. Leasing a few plants to an office will probably cost them a minimum of $100 per month. Leasing a plant such as a ficus for an empty home up for sale (so it looks more attractive to potential buyers) costs about $20 per week.

Good Luck

BENEFITS: self-employed, great for plant lovers.

PITFALLS: unsteady income until regular clientele is established.

SOURCES: Yellow pages under "Plants, Interior Design and Maintenance" or "Plants, Living—Renting and Leasing," visiting local nurseries and working out a deal.

NEEDS: plant knowledge, a green thumb, marketing abilities.

IDEA: A similar approach can be applied to aquarium maintenance for all you fish lovers out there!

Product Manufacturer "Artisan"

Santa wanted to hire you, but you didn't meet the height requirement.

Was arts and crafts always one of your favorite classes as a kid? Who would have guessed that your artistic talents might actually have a practical use and allow you to generate a more than substantial income? There are a wealth of success stories in this field, from the young women who invented "hard candy" nail polishes to your neighbor designing and selling jewelry. I have interviewed many creative people who use their skills on a small scale by selling to specialty stores, as well as those who have eventually expanded to hire reps all over the world and become the owners of million-dollar corporations.

A few ideas that have worked in the past are dipped plaster pieces (the angel craze), custom-made pillows and tapestries, gift baskets, hats, candles, uniquely designed lampshades, mirrors and frames, dress designing, bath oils, and flavored cooking oils in decorative bottles. Craft magazines sold at newsstands will also fuel you with ideas.

There are many ways to market your product. You can do it personally by bartering your crafts or giving them as gifts, which will spread the word and create other inquiries and sales. A woman recently thanked me for a simple suggestion that I gave her at a seminar of mine. She wanted to get her cake decorating business off the ground, so I told her to get business cards made up and to start volunteering to bake the cake for celebratory functions and private parties as her gift. Word traveled quickly, and soon she was the owner of a successful cake decorating business.

You can sell your products and network at flea markets and fairs (see "Swap Meets and Flea Markets," this chapter). Find out where art shows are taking place, and where the main mart in your city is located. Marts often have reps to meet with. Reps require a commission—10 percent for clothing lines and 15–20 percent for accessories is standard—but they can really broaden the market for your product. If you have good marketing skills, you may also want to approach local dealers and shop owners.

Earning potential varies greatly, from a few thousand dollars a year to millions, depending on how much energy you invest in your business. On the plus side, this type of work can often be started with minimal initial investment. And as orders come in, so will deposits to offset costs.

Good Luck

BENEFITS: creative, work at home, flexible schedule, your own boss, adding beauty to the world.

PITFALLS: often slow process of making, selling, and marketing the products.

NEEDS: creativity, imagination, ability to put colors and textures together, artistic skills.

> *"When I moved to the U.S. from Italy where I had worked consistently as an actress, I found I needed another source of income. I thought, 'What can I do that will allow me to be home, raising my son?' I used to be an artist so I decided to utilize those skills, making beautiful things I enjoy. I hired a rep and now my products are in boutiques around the country."*
>
> VIRGINIA CASE, mom/actress/owner of Flora (floral-related products such as aromatherapy pillows, lamp shades, and mirrors), Los Angeles

Résumé Service

People are more impressed with your résumé than they are with you.

In today's ultracompetitive market, everyone needs a professional résumé. It's a person's calling card, it makes a statement, and it sets the candidate apart from hundreds of others. Not everyone has the time, the inclination, or the know-how to create a top-notch résumé, and that's where a résumé service comes in.

A résumé service can provide any of the following: advice on résumé content and style, the format design, computer storage of the résumé for future updates, and laser copies of the résumé. Some services also do bios, cover letters, logos, labels, and personalized mailers. You can set up your résumé service to deal with a specific group or profession or broaden it to deal with the general public's needs—whatever most suits you. A friend of mine started the very popular résumé service for actors called Imagestarter, based in Los Angeles. His theatrical photo-résumés combine an actor's headshot on the same page as his or her credits.

Flexibility is a major advantage here, as you can set your own hours and work out of your home. To run a résumé service, you will need a computer, disks, a word processing program, and a laser printer. Computer proficiency and a thorough understanding of résumé writing, formats, and content are building blocks of your success. It is also important to be able to offer different aesthetically pleasing designs. Libraries usually have several different résumé books, or you can purchase one from a bookstore. And if you have a high-quality laser printer and a few paper-quality choices, you can charge money to make copies, too.

To get started, advertise in local publications and trade papers. If you are marketing to a specific profession such as acting, advertise at theaters, acting schools, and casting places, and in the trade papers found at performing arts bookstores and newsstands. *The Working Actors Guide* by Mani Flattery is a well-received industry book that has a section on résumé services. And of course word-of-mouth is best.

Find out the going rate for designing a résumé by calling competitors in your area. Designing a work résumé for the general public usually costs $50–$60. The going rate for designing an actor's résumé is $25–$35. Updates typically start at $5–$15. It takes approximately an hour to design a résumé. Certain cases may require a consulting fee.

Good Luck

BENEFITS: work out of your home, be your own boss.

PITFALLS: unsteady income.

SOURCES: advertise in local publications or in populated places, word-of-mouth.

NEEDS: a computer, printer, programs.

"I started doing résumés as a side business because so many friends had asked me to help put together their résumés. It was a good way to make some grocery money, and now I've expanded to doing a newsletter for my agent's office for clients (she takes it off what I owe her each month), personalized greeting cards, invitations, etc. I enjoy working on my computer and I'm teaching myself new things every day."

ANNIE CHRISTIANSON, actress/résumé service/trade show presenter/apartment manager, Seattle

Secretarial/Word Processing Service

You can actually tell the difference between copy and parchment paper.

There's an important reason for National Secretaries Day: no office or business can run efficiently without a top-quality secretary or assistant. These days, freelance secretaries are in high demand because many companies are scaling back and sizing down, preferring to contract out for individual projects. Large corporations and hospitals have enormous monthly dictation and transcription needs, not to mention the small business owners or individuals who need occasional assistance.

Secretarial and administrative services can involve organizing offices and files, answering phones, setting appointments, typing manuscripts, sending out mass mailings, doing personal and business correspondence, and performing special job-specific tasks. Some services also include desktop publishing, graphic design services, and personalized mailers.

For employment with an established company, you can work through a temp agency (see "Temp Work," chapter 6) listed in the yellow pages or look through the classified section of your paper under "Secretary" or "Administrative Assistant." Working through a temp agency allows you to get your feet wet and learn the ropes before starting your own business.

To start your own service, you will need business supplies such as a computer, printer, fax machine, business cards, stationery supplies, and a word processing program. I recommend reading a few books on starting a home business as well as on freelance secretarial services. It is also helpful to keep books on proper grammar, punctuation, and business-style writing handy. It may take more time and energy to start your own business, but in the end, the monetary rewards will be greater. Additionally, you are eligible for tax deductions when working out of your home, and your hours can be as flexible as you desire.

Advertising your services in the yellow pages or trade publications such as *Backstage* and *Publishers Weekly* are good ways to get the word out. Go to a newsstand and flip through some papers and magazines and decide which ones would be lucrative to advertise in. *The Working Actors Guide* by Mani Flattery, which can be purchased at most theatrical bookstores, has an extensive list of secretarial services, and you can add yours to this publication.

The pay will vary from project to project. You will need to set a fair hourly wage for your time and expertise, and price services accordingly. An easy way to do this is by calling other secretarial services to determine the fair market value. Profits will depend on location, efficiency, and hustle. You can even include a pickup and delivery charge for your services.

Good Luck

BENEFITS: flexible hours, work out of your home.

PITFALLS: up-front costs to purchase supplies and equipment.

SOURCES: temp agencies, advertising in local publications and at populated places.

NEEDS: excellent knowledge of computers and secretarial skills.

"I recently answered an ad in the paper for a secretarial position, working out of my home for a home inspector. He installed a phone line with voice mail in my home. He covers the bill, pays me a base salary plus commission. I set up his appointments and answer his phone calls. It works out well, as I can be home with my little girl."

DEBBIE SKAJA, mom/at-home secretarial work/baby-sitting, Chicago

Sketch Artist

Turn your doodles into oodles of cash.

This is a fun, creative job for someone who has sketch portrait skills or a fashion illustrator/designer background. You can find work as a sketch artist in a variety of industries. Storyboards (sketches of each scene in a script) are used to help directors visualize different scenes for TV and film projects. Sketching portraits or caricatures at parties (especially popular at bar and bat mitzvahs) and social functions is also a possibility. Another interesting job for someone who draws well is working at the sheriff's office as a police identification artist, although this is more appropriate for someone who is experienced at sketching from a verbal description.

If you are just starting out, you may want to offer your services for free so you can put together a portfolio and make contacts. Student films and non-union commercials can be a great place to start. Check the trades for advertisements. When you have accumulated enough sketches, create a portfolio of your best work that demonstrates the breadth of your skills.

Ascertain the proper contact persons at a variety of studios and set up appointments to show your portfolio. If you can't get an appointment, you may be able to drop off your work. Then they can review it on their own time. As always, use any contacts you have.

The Pacific Coast Studio Directory (the yellow pages of studios in Los Angeles), *The New York Production Guide (N.Y.P.G.), The Illinois Production Guide, LA 411,* and *The Hollywood Creative Directory* are a few books that can assist you in finding studios and production companies. These books as well as others are available at performing arts bookstores or may be ordered by mail from Samuel French Theater & Film Bookstore in Los Angeles at (800) 8ACT–NOW.

To advertise your service for parties, contact party planners by looking in the yellow pages under "Party Planning Services" and "Entertainers."

You can also advertise in the classified section of local papers and magazines. A parents' magazine can be a terrific resource.

For storyboard artists, pay will vary depending on union versus non-union work. Salary is negotiable for independent jobs depending on how much work is actually needed. When negotiating, decide what is equitable for your time and talent on a daily or hourly basis. Call some competitors in your area to find out the going rate.

Good Luck

BENEFITS: creative, fun, networking.

PITFALLS: irregular work, variable wage, tough to get started.

SOURCES: *The Pacific Coast Studio Directory, The New York Production Guide (N.Y.P.G.), The Hollywood Creative Directory, The Illinois Production Guide,* and *LA 411,* industry contacts.

NEEDS: sketching and portraiture skills.

Start Your Own 900 Number

You've already spent so much money on 900 numbers, why not start your own?

The 900 number industry started in 1984. MCI, Sprint, and AT&T entered the field in 1987, and by 1989, certain financial and administrative changes allowed entrepreneurs and small businesses to get involved. In 1991 the 900 number industry made $1 billion in revenue. Revenues have increased every year since, translating into vast and varied opportunities for budding entrepreneurs.

Because of new FCC regulations, the 900 number image is more acceptable now (it used to be associated strictly with phone sex lines). It has been reshaped by the interest of Fortune 500 companies. *Consumer Reports,* the *Wall Street Journal,* the Better Business Bureau, Procter & Gamble, and the Pope have all used 900 numbers. Examples of 900 services include opinion polls, stock information, jokes, customer or product support, and horoscopes. Hundreds of professionals and celebrities are providing information while making money.

Not surprisingly, a 900 number can be extremely profitable for you as well. Basically, a 900 service is a caller-paid service that provides access to a variety of information and entertainment. You simply get an idea, put it on a 900 number, and then the long distance carrier does the billing and collecting. Costs vary greatly, depending on what you set up with the service bureau and your advertising budget. Expect to spend a few hundred dollars on the low end to a few thousand dollars and up on the high end. If you work through a service bureau your initial costs can be on the low end, as the service bureau buys the hardware and software, hires the programmer, sets up the line, gets it approved by the long distance carrier, and provides necessary support. If you want to be really "hands off" about it, you can get the bureau to answer prerecorded calls for you. In return, the service bureau gets a percentage of your business. The 900 service bureau subscribes directly to a common carrier, such as MCI, by leasing multiple 900 numbers directly. Call your long distance company for further information. For $4, MCI will send you a 14-page brochure introducing the 900 service, including guidelines, and a list of service bureaus.

Do your research and choose the service bureau that meets your needs from the many available. In addition, many independent adult learning schools such as the Learning Annex (found in a number of major cities) have offered courses on starting a 900 number company. Another idea is to visit a library in your area and locate books and articles on the subject, and research your options. A few popular books are *900 Know-How* by Robert Mastin; *The Directory of 900 Service Bureaus: How to Select One* by Audiotex News; and *Money-Making 900 Numbers: How Entrepreneurs Use the Telephone to Sell Information* by Carol Morse Ginsburg and Robert Mastin.

Initially, you will need cash flow to market your line, but since a lot of money can be made with these numbers, you may recoup quickly. A number of years ago, a physician in Los Angeles started a 900 number line called Be Abused While Being Amused, offering a different insulting joke each day. At one point, he was making thousands of dollars a day! Cleverness and timing can pay off. But be forewarned, this kind of income is the exception not the rule.

A neighbor of mine, experienced in the 900 number industry, and not as lucky as the physician mentioned above, advises anyone serious about making money in today's marketplace to devise a service line that provides hard, fact-based information that is difficult or impossible to obtain elsewhere. He suggested hooking up with a professional—such as a doctor, lawyer, or real estate broker—and giving prerecorded, factual information for which there is a preestablished need.

When it comes to marketing, consider hiring an ad agency to help develop a campaign—it is money well spent, as the ad is all you have to make the initial connection with your audience. Another idea is to get a media partner so you don't have to pay for ads. I think a surefire success strategy would be to hook up with a tabloid television program, using the 900 number as a poll to interact with the show's audience.

Good Luck

BENEFITS: chance to make a huge profit, hands-off business if prerecorded.

PITFALLS: up-front costs, advertising expenses, irregular income.

SOURCES: MCI, (900) 733–6249. The Learning Annex for a course: San Francisco, (415) 788–5500; San Diego, (619) 544–9700; Los Angeles, (310) 478–6677; New York, (212) 371–0280; and Toronto, (416) 964–0011. The library for books and magazine articles. *The Directory of 900 Service Bureaus: How to Select One* by Audiotex News, (800) 735–3398; *900 Know-How* by Robert Mastin, and *Money-Making 900 Numbers: How Entrepreneurs Use the Telephone to Sell Information* by Carol Morse Ginsburg and Robert Mastin, (401) 849–4200. Service bureaus include: Accelerated Voice, (415) 281–3173; Creative Call Management, (213) 462–2255; ICN, (561) 272–5667; Network Telephone Services, (800) 727–6874; MM1/America's Best 900#, (800) 664–9007; and Scherers Communications, (800) 356–6161.

NEEDS: an idea, a 900 number.

Swap Meets and Flea Markets

Prevent yourself from spending money on the weekends—work!

Anyone can make money at flea markets (or swap meets, as they are sometimes affectionately called), providing they have the right items at the right prices.

The concept of swap meets took off in California in the early sixties, and today thousands of them are held regularly across the nation. One of the largest flea markets in the country is the monthly Rose Bowl Swap Meet in Pasadena, held on the grounds of the famous Rose Bowl. On the second Sunday of each month, thousands of people attend this meet, where every item you can imagine is on sale. You name it, someone is selling it! You know the old saying: "One person's junk is another's treasure." Items commonly sold are antiques, collectibles, clothing, furniture, plants, paintings, jewelry, toys, and food. But believe me, you can sell *anything*.

Startup costs can be low depending on what you are selling and how you gather items. Space at a swap meet typically costs $20–$80 per day, and you can either sell on consignment or sell things that you and your friends make. I suggest frequenting swap meets and flea markets to get a sense of what merchandise sells well. I know a woman who buys discontinued or irregular in-line skates very cheaply from a manufacturer and sells them at swap meets for a hefty profit. And then there are those who buy antiques and other goods discounted from estate sales (advertised in the paper), and resell at flea markets.

Swap meets and flea markets are generally open from 7 A.M. to 3 P.M., and the vendors usually arrive between 6 A.M. and 8 A.M. You will need to call the flea markets and swap meets you are interested in for specific information and policies. In certain cities, you will need a location-specific permit for each swap meet you work at. You can get one for free from the state board of equalization. Call the one nearest you for more information.

Income from working at swap meets varies. Earning a few hundred dollars a day profit is not uncommon, and the chance to make a lot of money over a short period of time is a huge incentive for this type of work.

Many swap meets and flea markets are available across the country. Check your yellow pages under "Swap Meets" or "Flea Markets." Word-of-mouth is a great way to learn about hot locations for your items, so when you frequent swap meets ask vendors which other meets are the best.

Good Luck

BENEFITS: weekend work, self-employed, meeting people, making a lot of money.

PITFALLS: earnings vary, early day, long day.

SOURCES: calling swap meets and flea markets for specific information, state board of equalization, yellow pages under "Swap Meets" or "Flea Markets," the Rose Bowl Flea Market and Swap Meet at (213) 588–4411, and the Pasadena City College Flea Market at (818) 585–7906. In New York try The Garage at (212) 647–0707.

NEEDS: product to sell, a permit.

Teaching What You Know

Your talents are too abundant and awe-inspiring to keep to yourself.

Every person has a talent or ability that can be shared with others—for a fee of course! The possibilities of what you can teach are endless: accents/dialects, martial arts, yoga, improvisation, writing, computer skills, dance, musical instruments, stand-up routines, on-camera commercial techniques, voice-over workshops, song interpretation, children's theater, magic, photography . . . the list goes on. Think about your talents and hobbies, make a list, ask your friends, browse through catalogs and bookstores for ideas.

Teaching isn't just for teachers. There are countless untold stories of regular people who apply their natural skills and abilities to make a good living teaching others. A professional writer I know recently rented a space at Highways, a cultural arts center in Santa Monica, and taught a successful playwriting workshop. Another friend coaches actors on audition material in his home and has been teaching a cold-reading workshop using an empty studio apartment in his building. My neighbor, a professional singer, rents a piano and gives private voice lessons in her home. A comedian I know converted her garage into a studio and uses the space to teach comedy and acting technique. If you prefer a bit more structure, you can find teaching positions at established schools and learning institutions by submitting a résumé or class proposal.

You will probably need to advertise for students when forming your own classes. Distributing fliers in your community and at theaters (if you're teaching any sort of acting or writing technique), and advertising in specific trade papers, free local publications (*Pennysavers*), and featured sections of local papers are great ways to spread the word. And of course, referrals generally work best.

Pay will vary. Independent learning institutions, universities, community schools, dance schools, music schools, churches and synagogues, senior centers, and private schools (no state certification needed) will have their own pay scales. If you form your own class or teach privately, check around to keep your rates competitive.

Good Luck

BENEFITS: substantial income, learn as you teach, contacts.

PITFALLS: gathering students, teaching what you would rather be doing.

SOURCES: call institutions about teaching requirements, advertising.

NEEDS: patience, good communication skills, more patience.

"After I had my baby, I was too tired to audition for musical theater or do any bus and truck tours. This left me with the 'now what do I do for money' song. At the same time, many of my friends were coming to L.A. to audition for musicals. Since none of us knew good vocal teachers at that time, they asked if I could vocalize them. In a short time I found myself busy with not only my friends but friends of friends. I now have a very lucrative business as a singing teacher and musical coach to adults and children, while also finding time to win two Dramalogue awards as an actress and be a full-time mom."

GAIL JOHNSTON, actress/singer/voice teacher, Los Angeles

Video Production Service

Is America's Funniest Home Videos your favorite TV show?

If capturing people's most personal, prized, intimate moments and exercising your artistry with a video camera is appealing, then a video production service may be the right job for you.

Videographers are hired to videotape a wide range of affairs: weddings, birthdays, anniversaries, bar and bat mitzvahs, reunions, seminars, and theatrical or musical events. The job enables you to attend a variety of functions, meet people, and, if it's your own business, make an excellent hourly wage. Being a videographer is a particularly excellent job for a film student who has access to video equipment. If you're not enrolled in a film school, post a sign at one and hook up with a student. This job is definitely easier and more flexible with two people, especially if the hosts ask you to interview the attendees—one person works the camera while the other walks around with the microphone.

If it's your own business you'll need to market yourself by advertising in community newsletters, local newspapers and magazines, and trade publications; posting fliers; and advertising at expos (events that focus on specific industries). My husband and I found our wedding videographer at a wedding expo. Alternatively, you may want to work for an existing company where you can start as an assistant to learn the ropes. Check the yellow pages under "Video Production Services."

You can buy or rent equipment, either new or used. Check the yellow pages under "Video Recorders and Players." For certain functions, a final edited video is required. Consider hooking up with a video editor or film school student; such people have access to all the equipment for free and know how to use it. A new basic video camera starts at about $500–$700. A rental costs about $50 a day. To buy a used one, look in a *Pennysaver* paper, trade magazine, or classified section of your local paper. Some rental companies also sell used cameras.

The going rate for a videographer is $75–$150 per hour. A typical event such as a wedding will range from $495 to $1,200, depending on hours, experience, and the location of the affair. The going rate for video copies is $25–$35 a tape.

Good Luck

BENEFITS: high hourly wage, creative.

PITFALLS: rental fee or initial investment of equipment.

SOURCES: yellow pages under "Video Production Services," local magazines and newspapers.

NEEDS: camera experience, creative ability, friendly, professional, reliable.

IDEA: A friend in Cleveland told me about a popular video service that records a day in the life. A videographer comes to your home and videotapes your routine with your family, and so on. What a terrific idea!

Wedding Coordinator/Event Planner

At last, you can plan a wedding without your parents' input.

One of the most significant and pressure-filled events in a family's life is the much-anticipated wedding day. Hiring a wedding coordinator to handle all the details (like making sure Aunt Rose doesn't sit next to Aunt Matilda) can help ensure a smooth event. If you enjoy planning parties, have a knack for design, are resourceful, and can remain calm in stressful situations, consider becoming a wedding coordinator.

It is important to be able to personalize each function. Many wedding coordinators meet at their clients' home to get a feel for their taste and style. A wedding coordinator must be familiar with the many aspects of a wedding: local hotels and wedding sites, catering services, florists, bands, where to rent equipment and order invitations. Wedding coordinators often get special prices, thus enabling their clients to save money in many of these areas.

Planning a wedding involves many details, and people hire coordinators for different tasks depending on their budget. You may be contracted as a full-service coordinator, handling everything and hiring everyone for the affair, or you may be hired to handle last-minute details, including presiding over everything on the day of the event.

If you don't have much experience in party planning, it may be a good idea to work in a hotel or catering business for a spell, assisting the director or another upper-level staff member. This is how to make contacts. It is crucial to know the most reliable vendors so that you can give your clients the best prices and services available.

Pay will vary. Call competitors in your area to see what the going rate is. Most wedding coordinators charge a flat fee for the affair, which can range from $500 to a few thousand dollars, or charge 10 percent of the entire cost of the affair. Others work on a consultation basis and are paid an hourly wage, typically $50–$150 an hour.

To find employment, you will need to network. Contacts can be made through organizations, women's groups, bridal shops, churches, and temples. Advertise in local papers or bulletins. Consider getting a booth at a wedding expo, which can be found by contacting editors of bridal magazines or manufacturers of bridal gowns. Build a reputation, and word-of-mouth will build your business.

Good Luck

BENEFITS: creative, fun, organizing a joyous occasion, flexible.

PITFALLS: working under stress, pressure, dealing with nervous parents, being on your feet throughout the affair.

SOURCES: networking, advertising, wedding expos, bridal shops and magazines.

NEEDS: artistic background, knowing reliable vendors, even temperament, resourceful, well organized.

IDEA: Wedding invitations are a lucrative business. You can design and market them yourself or sell them from established catalogs (listed in the backs of bridal magazines). Note that I titled this job "event planner" as well, because there are many business opportunities in planning functions for corporations, bar and bat mitzvahs, sweet-16 parties, private parties, and so on.

"I was a teacher and wanted to be home when I had my daughter. Utilizing creative talents, I began to design centerpieces, cater, and flower arrange on a part-time basis. People kept asking me to do more and more so slowly I gave

up control of each part of an event and became the conductor, hiring others to be the players!"

CAROL SINGER, mom/owner of Celebration Party Planning, Boston

Yard Sales

**Don't throw out your garbage . . .
someone will buy it.**

All over the country, you can find bountiful weekend yard sales. My husband and I have had a few such sales with our old clothes and knickknacks. We've profited a few hundred dollars each time. It's not surprising—selling used articles inexpensively is a great way to make fast cash! It seems like every Saturday and Sunday, there are front yards filled with everything from furniture to clothing.

There are two ways to profit from yard sales: Sell your own stuff, or buy and resell someone else's. Local papers advertise plenty of estate sales, where quality antiques can be bought and then sold to stores for a hefty profit. People who buy out yard and estate sales often do it as a side job. They go early in the morning and buy all the good merchandise for inexpensive prices. Then they go to a higher-income, more crowded area and resell everything at a higher price. On the downside, the income is unsteady and you'll need to work constantly to gather items from people, and to store the goods between sales.

Good places to sell are high-traffic areas or neighborhoods where people are walking around. If you don't live in a busy neighborhood, maybe a friend does. Advertise in community papers (some are free) and post signs in the neighborhood. In some cities, depending on how often you want to participate, a permit may be required.

In this business, you'll never want for merchandise—many people will be happy to give you their "junk" if you come over and haul it away. Consider setting up a business with a friend. If storage is a problem, you can rent a garage for about $50–$80 a month.

Income will vary depending on what you are selling and where. Higher-income neighborhoods yield higher profits.

Good Luck

BENEFITS: immediate cash, flexible hours, weekend work.

PITFALLS: unsteady income, need to gather and store the goods.

SOURCES: local papers, driving or walking around neighborhoods, advertising your services, posting signs.

NEEDS: items to sell, place to sell them, storage area, truck or large car.

"I love the whole garage sale circuit. It's all about buying and selling so I get the benefit of shopping inexpensively, then turning around and selling the next month. It's great fun to get friends together and piggyback the sales, which makes for a really fun afternoon. Garage sales provide me with quick extra money on the weekends, allowing me the freedom to audition and network during the week."

LISA GIVOT, mom/actress/garage sales, Des Moines

2

Nine to Five...Not

Pick a Shift That Works for You

Advertising Sales Representative

Madison Avenue, here I come.

Bet you never guessed that you could turn your enthusiasm for a weekly publication or magazine into a part-time job. Are you a mom or dad who enjoys reading parent magazines? Or a vegetarian who reads *Vegetarian Times* and other health-conscious publications? However passionate you may be about the subject or articles, the heart of every magazine is in the advertisements. Ads are what keep the magazine afloat, and publishers often hire outside people to scout for new ones.

Energetic, creative, and naturally organized people are well suited for this job. Basically, you scout businesses that have placed ads in other publications and try to convince them to advertise in your magazine, and you approach new businesses. You meet the person interested in placing the ad, help create the size and style, knowing what works best in your particular magazine, and send it to the office of the company you work for, which handles the rest. Most of the work is typically done from your home, where you can have separate phone lines installed or two lines on the same phone. For many local magazines and papers, knowing your neighborhood and potential clients who will place ads is helpful.

Salary is typically commission based; normally 15–20 percent of sales. Advertising sales reps in major cities earn an average of $15 an hour. The potential for earnings is usually based on the time invested.

To attain a sales rep position, simply contact weekly publications, newspapers, or magazines that you are interested in working for. Radio and TV stations also hire advertising sales reps. A background in sales is beneficial.

Good Luck

BENEFITS: flexible, create your own hours, work from home.

PITFALLS: fluctuating salary.

SOURCES: contact human resources at newspapers, magazines, TV and radio stations.

NEEDS: energetic, creative, enthusiastic, enjoy working in sales.

> *"This is a perfect job for me. I have two daughters and am an advertising sales rep for* Parent Guide. *This paper is geared toward children so my kids often join me on appointments. I was an avid reader and fan of* Parent Guide *before I became employed by them so it's an easy sell for me."*
>
> SUSAN PACK, mom/advertising sales representative, Long Island, New York

---

Airline Employment

The sound of a 747 sends chills down your spine.

Many positions within the airline industry can accommodate all types of scheduling needs. The jobs I've chosen to discuss here are flight attendant, customer service agent, and reservation sales agent. Flexible shifts, steady pay, and free travel are all excellent benefits of airline employment.

Each airline has its own employment department and hiring procedures. Salary and benefits also vary from airline to airline, so you will have to do your homework before you decide which one best suits your needs. The consensus among the airline employees I spoke with was that Southwest Airlines is a reputable company to work for. Since it is fairly typical of industry standards, I use its policies and procedures as examples.

Flight Attendant

Flight attendants are responsible for ensuring that the flight is a comfortable experience for the plane's passengers and that safety rules are followed at all times. Flight duties include serving beverages and meals to passengers and tending to other needs that may arise. You must enjoy flying, be willing to travel on a constant basis, and be open to working rotating shifts. Eventually, seniority will give you preferential treatment when it comes to shifts and flexibility. Furthermore, it is important to be able to work well with others, as you are part of a team.

The requirements for employment vary from airline to airline, but a few points are standard. You must be at least 20 years of age, with a high school diploma or equivalency. You need excellent verbal and communication skills, as well as the ability to work under tight time constraints. A well-groomed appearance is a must. The job involves few physical demands, but you must be capable of lifting 50-pound items from the floor to above shoulder height. You are required to work between 60 and 85 hours a month. More work is available during holiday season. Keep in mind that once you are hired, there is a mandatory training period.

Salary varies based on experience and the company you work for. Expect to start at $10–$12 an hour. Depending on seniority, it is possible to make up to $24 per hour.

For information check the yellow pages under "Airlines" and ask for the employment number. Or go to specific airline terminals at the airport and request an application.

Good Luck

BENEFITS: free travel, see the world, meet people.

PITFALLS: long hours, being a "waitress in the sky," jet lag.

SOURCES: yellow pages under "Airlines." Southwest Airlines job hotline, (214) 904–4803; TWA job hotline, (314) 895–6699; Northwest job hotline, (612) 726–3600; US Air job hotline, (703) 872–7499; Delta main office, (404) 715–2600; Continental job line, (201) 902–7182 or (713) 834–5300.

NEEDS: at least 20 years of age, high school diploma or equivalency, well-groomed, ability to travel a lot, friendly (although we've all seen otherwise!).

Customer Service Agent

An airline customer service agent greets and tickets passengers. Airports are open 24 hours a day and flights depart and arrive at all hours, so employee scheduling is generally flexible. Part-time work typically involves four hours a day, five days a week. Airlines mainly look for highly motivated, friendly individuals who work well in team situations. You must be at least 19 years of age with a high school diploma or equivalency. College education is preferred. Also required is the ability to type 30 words per minute on a computer keyboard. At most airlines you will need to be able to move 40–50 pounds onto a weighing device called a "rate service."

Salary usually starts at $7 an hour. You may receive up to three raises within the first year, but after this initial period, salary increases occur only on an annual basis and are usually capped at $20 an hour. Traveling for free on standby is one of the great advantages, as are medical benefits and profit sharing.

For more information, check your yellow pages under "Airlines" and ask for the employment number or go to any ticket counter and pick up an application.

Good Luck

BENEFITS: free travel, medical benefits, flexible shifts, steady salary.

PITFALLS: on your feet, work under tight constraints, demanding passengers.

SOURCES: yellow pages under "Airlines." Southwest Airlines job hotline, (214) 904–4803; TWA job hotline, (314) 895–6699; Northwest job hotline, (612) 726–3600; US Air job hotline, (703) 872–7499; Delta main office, (404) 715–2600; Continental job line, (201) 902–7182 or (713) 834–5300.

NEEDS: at least 19 years of age, friendly, ability to type on a computer keyboard.

Reservation Sales Agent

A reservation sales agent is the person you speak to when making travel arrangements. Airlines look for individuals who are at least 18 years of age, with a high school diploma or equivalency. College or course credits are preferred. You must be able to type on a computer keyboard, learn ticketing procedures, articulate airline regulations, and keep on top of all flight specials. A courteous phone manner and good verbal skills are mandatory.

A variety of shifts are available between the hours of 6 A.M. and 1:30 A.M. Busy hours, when more employees are needed, are from 9 A.M. to 1 P.M. and 6 P.M. to 10 P.M. Part-time employees generally work four hours a day, five days a week.

Salary usually starts at $6.50 an hour. Benefits include flying for free on standby, medical coverage, and profit sharing.

For more information, check the yellow pages under "Airlines" and ask for the employment number or go to any ticket counter and pick up an application.

Good Luck

BENEFITS: free travel, medical coverage, flexible shifts, steady salary.

PITFALLS: on the phone all the time, calls are monitored.

SOURCES: yellow pages under "Airlines." Southwest Airlines job hotline, (214) 904–4803; TWA job hotline, (314) 895–6699; Northwest job hotline, (612) 726–3600; US Air job hotline, (703) 872–7499; Delta main office, (404) 715–2600; Continental job line, (201) 902–7182 or (713) 834–5300.

NEEDS: at least 18 years of age, excellent verbal skills and telephone manner, ability to type on a computer keyboard.

Airport Shuttle Service

Traveling without jet lag.

Necessity is the mother of invention. For years, people wanted a quick, easy way to get to the airport without paying the high costs of a taxi or limousine. Enter the airport shuttle service, or, as the industry calls it, the "share ride business."

You may work for a number of companies that offer this service. Most, like the furiously franchising Super Shuttle, require a minimum three-day work week. Shifts are usually ten hours, with a number of shifts available since service is offered 24 hours a day in major cities. Basically, once you check out your van from the company you work for, you're on your own—meaning there is no boss looking over your shoulder and your earnings will depend on how many passengers you pick up.

You must be at least 21 years of age and have a clean driving record. When hired, you will receive one week of training at minimum-wage salary. The standard uniform consists of black pants, white shirt, and black tie.

Pay is commission based. Expect to earn 23–27 percent of gross revenue of the van. Cash tips are your own. The people I interviewed generally earned $7–$12 an hour. To apply for a job, look in the yellow pages under "Airport Transportation Service."

NOTE: Rental car companies need drivers to take people to and from the rental car agency and the airport. For employment opportunities, look in the yellow pages under "Automobile Renting."

Good Luck

BENEFITS: different shifts available, unsupervised.

PITFALLS: within your assigned schedule there is not much flexibility, driving can be exhausting.

SOURCES: any shuttle service at airport. For Super Shuttle, call (800) BLUE-VAN. A few well-known rental companies are Enterprise, (800) 325–8007; Alamo, (800) GO–ALAMO; Avis, (800) 831–2847; Hertz, (800) 654–3131.

NEEDS: love of driving.

> *"After eight years as an abused child of Hollywood as a screenwriter, I needed a survival job that would monetarily support me, where no one would recognize me, and that would take zero brain power."*
>
> JOEL ANDOVER (fictitious name), screenwriter/airport shuttle driver, Los Angeles

Casino Jobs

Double your salary!

The thrill, the rush, the tumult, the "flush." If these words pique your interest, working in a casino may be the perfect job for you.

From the shores of New Jersey, to the Rocky Mountains, to the glitzy desert oasis of Las Vegas, casino establishments now exist in more than 22 states. These gambling paradises frequented by high rollers hoping to make some quick cash are usually open 24 hours a day, seven days a week, which means that you can select from a number of round-the-clock shifts. Casinos provide part-time employment opportunities, such as slot cashiers, cocktail servers, dealers, and casino surveillance personnel.

Slot Cashier

Slot cashiers, often called cage cashiers, assist customers in making change, exchanging cash, and running credit card transactions for chips. You need to be at least 18 years of age, preferably with cashier experience. Expect to earn about $9 an hour.

Cocktail Server

Cocktail servers are often required to have a minimum of two years of cocktail or waiter experience. At the time of your interview, you may be quizzed on the content of different alcoholic drinks. If you want to boost your bartending marketability, there are a number of books to read on mixed drinks—two popular one are *Mr. Boston's Official Bartending and Party Guide,* published by Warner Books, and *Seagrams Bartending Guide,* published by Viking. Cocktail servers usually make minimum wage plus tips.

Dealer

Dealers are generally required to have been to some type of gaming school. In Atlantic City, the Casino Career Institute has trained over 37,000 students since 1978. Most houses require you to be proficient at a minimum of two games, usually blackjack and a choice of craps, poker, baccarat, roulette, minibaccarat, pai gow poker, or pai gow tiles. Many locations ask that you have a casino license. In New Jersey, a casino license costs $350 and is good for three years. Call the New Jersey Casino Control Commission for more information. Dealers are generally paid minimum wage plus tips. Expect to earn $25,000–$35,000 a year part-time.

Surveillance Worker

A surveillance job involves monitoring the games, players, and employees. You are basically an "eye in the sky." In other words, you are hired to protect the casino's assets. You sit in a room with several television monitors and scan the bars, restaurants, and gambling floors. VCRs record the game and bar areas at all times, and you must make certain that the tapes are working and set up for the next shift. If an unusual situation or discrepancy comes up, you are required to review the video and write a report on what happened. There are three shifts available at most casinos: 6 A.M. to 2 P.M., 2 P.M. to 10 P.M., and 10 P.M. to 6 A.M. You are typically scheduled for five shifts a week. You may feel isolated from the hubbub of the casino, but you can listen to music and read in between scanning. The salary usually ranges from $11.25 to $17 an hour.

For employment opportunities check the yellow pages under "Casinos" or use your Web browser, for example, Netscape or Internet Explorer, and choose one of the many search engines available, such as Yahoo, Infoseek, or Excite, and type in Casino.

NOTE: A few books to assist in finding casinos in your area are *Casinos—The International Casino Guide,* published by BDIT; *Where to Play in the USA: The Gaming Guide* by Michael Sankey; and *American Casino Guide* by Steve Bourie.

Good Luck

BENEFITS: steady salary, flexible shifts.

PITFALLS: gambling away your salary; noisy, smoke-filled, crowded environment (granted, that might be a benefit for some).

SOURCES: yellow pages under "Casinos." *Casinos—The International Casino Guide,* published by BDIT, (800) 257–5344; *Where to Play in the USA: The Gaming Guide* by Michael Sankey, (800) 929–3811; *American Casino Guide* by Steve Bourie. Casino Career Institute at (609) 343–4848; New Jersey Casino Control Commission at (609) 441–3749. Also, see Internet information listed above. In California, three popular casinos are the Bicycle Club Casino, (562) 806–4646; the Hollywood Park, (310) 330–2800; and the Commerce Casino, (213) 721–2100. The Foxwoods Casino, in Connecticut, (860) 885–4170, is very popular for the Boston/Providence and New England area. In the New Jersey area, try any of the casinos in Atlantic City. The *Atlantic City Sunday Press* will have many job listings. Tropicana Casino & Resort, (800) 843–8767, is a good one. For a list of hotels/casinos in Las Vegas, contact the Commission on Economic Development at (702) 687–4325.

NEEDS: knowledge of casino games, some casinos require a gaming school certificate.

"I have worked as a croupier [dealer] at charity events and on cruise ships. Gambling is illegal in Florida, so the cruise ships cruise off shore where casino gambling is legal. I average about $50 for three hours. There are about

six to seven companies to register with, so work can be pretty consistent when needed."

CHRIS GEORGE, actress/croupier/pet care/works with children, Hollywood, Florida

---

Catering

Do you want to attend a party every Saturday night?

My friend Allison attended the Oscars this past year, and she wasn't even nominated! How'd she do it? She worked for the Ambrosia Company, an upscale catering and event-planning business in Los Angeles.

Caterers are hired for a wide range of affairs: intimate dinner parties, weddings, bar and bat mitzvahs, film and TV wrap parties (for the cast and crew), as well as gala social and political events. The endless Hollywood parties in Los Angeles keep catering companies busy all year round.

If you work for a caterer, your responsibilities may include unloading trucks, setting up tables and chairs, setting tables and cocktail areas, prepping and serving food, bussing tables, bartending, cleaning up, and then reloading the entire shebang to return to the office. It is important to have a professional attitude and show up on time with a neat, clean appearance. A black tuxedo uniform is essential. I suggest going to a vintage store to look for a used tuxedo: black single-breasted jacket, wing-tipped tux shirt, and a black bow tie and cummerbund. On the job, French service know-how is helpful and sometimes necessary. The basics of French service include holding the platter of food in your left hand while serving individual food items from utensils in your right hand, and always serving from the left and clearing from the right (except for beverages, which are always served from the right). Most caterers will want you to have experience in the food industry.

Catering hours are flexible, usually at night and on the weekend. Around the holiday season the business flourishes, so it is a great time to work hard and save extra dollars for the slower months. The best part of catering—and the reason so many people prefer it over restaurant work—is the variety. Catered events are often held in places like museums and theaters for receptions, giant halls for functions, and private homes for big and small parties alike. And as we've seen, it can be a great way to attend the Oscars or Grammys!

Catering companies typically pay $8–$18 per hour, depending on your experience and the city you live in, with a four- or five-hour guarantee. This means that if the party goes for only an hour and a half, you still get paid for the guaranteed time. Many times, at the end of the night, you will be tipped by the host of the party, but don't expect it *every* time.

There are hundreds of catering companies, and once you begin catering, you'll be able to network and find out which are the better companies to work for. Many companies contract out people to help in the kitchen, serve food, or bartend. One company in Los Angeles called Host Helper will hire you as an independent contractor. This means that the host pays you directly and you then pay Host Helper a placement fee. They consider themselves a marketing arm for people on their registry. For other similar employment opportunities in your city, look in the yellow pages under "Caterers," "Party Service," or "Employment Agencies."

Good Luck

BENEFITS: good salary, varied and interesting locations.

PITFALLS: standing on your feet, physically demanding, unsteady work.

SOURCES: yellow pages under "Caterers," "Party Service," and "Employment Agencies." In Los Angeles, call Host Helpers, (310) 478–7799, and Party Staff, (213) 933–3900. In New York, call For Your Occasion, Inc., (212) 682–6281.

NEEDS: restaurant or food experience, a black tuxedo uniform.

"When I was in graduate school getting my master's in social work, I catered in Portland to help pay the bills. I loved the flexibility (and the food!). At one party I actually served the Funeral Directors of America. It was at a beautiful mansion and I heard an evening of funeral stories—too bad I'm not a writer."

BRYNNA SIBILLA, student/potter/catering, Portland, Oregon

Club Work

Shake your booty while you work . . .

The days of Studio 54 and the Limelight are over, but nightclubs are alive and well, still beckoning the hip, the trendy, and the retro-funky to their doors. And for you nocturnal neophytes, working in a club may be the right gig.

On one hand, club work enables you to meet a lot of people, listen to good music, and be part of the scene. People are out having fun and spending money freely. On the other hand, you will be dealing with smoke-filled rooms, late hours, and *loud* music. If this is not for you, then working in a restaurant or a low-key lounge may be a better idea.

To get a job in a club, check the yellow pages under "Clubs and Cocktail Lounges." Ask your friends or people in music stores to recommend some hot spots, and check the local community paper or the entertainment section of your newspaper for listings of popular hangouts. The main jobs available are bartender, waiter, cocktail waiter, and bouncer/doorman.

Bartender

Sex on the Beach, Kamikaze, and Fuzzy Navel. No, this is not a list of activities you engaged in when you graduated college. These are just three of the mixed drinks you'll need to know as a bartender. A bartender's duties include setting up the bar, stocking beverages, maintaining an inventory of items, cutting fruit for the condiment tray, cleaning glassware, and mixing drinks for bar customers and the wait staff. The hours tend to be later in a club than in a restaurant, often until dawn. Many clubs don't even open until nighttime. Still, bartenders at popular clubs can make $200 a night or more. If you presently lack bartending experience and knowledge of mixed drinks, sign up for a reputable bartending course. Schools usually charge between $300 and $500 for the course, with scholarships and creative financing available. Many schools will help place you in jobs upon completion. A few reputable ones are the National Bartenders School, American Bartenders School, and Professional Bartenders School of New England. Two reputable books on mixed drinks are *Mr. Boston's Official Bartending Guide,* published by Warner Books and *Seagrams Bartending Guide,* published by Viking.

Waiter/Waitress

Where can you still get great tips, always be well fed, listen to hip music while you work, and develop your leg muscles? The old standby, serving food, is still one of the most popular part-time, flexible ways to earn a great wage. And waiting tables in a nightclub offers an added element of excitement. Once again, the hours are a lot later and the dress code may differ. The wages tend to be higher if the shift is longer . . . and the skirt is shorter.

A waiter's job is to take food and drink orders, serve the requested items, and tend to customer needs. Side work involves setting up tables, refilling condiments, polishing glasses and silver, and cleaning counters and work areas. It is important to be efficient and personable. Having a good memory is definitely an asset since you will need to know and recite the daily specials. Sometimes a more extensive knowledge of wine and food is required.

The positive aspects of being a waiter are fast cash, a flexible schedule, and free meals. The hours vary depending on the club and your shift assignment. On the downside, you'll have to work at a frantic pace during peak hours and put up with sometimes erratic income—poor tips can alter your mood pretty darn fast.

Salary consists of minimum wage plus tips. Tips will vary depending on the location and size of the club. An average dinner shift in a midsized club in a major city pays $100 a night.

Before accepting a job at a club, or even applying for one, try to gauge the volume of customers as well as the prices on the menu; tips are commensurate with these factors. To get started, look in the help wanted section of the newspaper, ask friends, or apply at clubs during slow evenings, Sunday–Tuesday at off-peak times (between 3 P.M. and 5 P.M.).

Cocktail Waiter/Waitress

Cocktail waitering is similar to regular waitering, except you are primarily serving drinks instead of food. Unlike the waiter at a restaurant, the cocktail waiter at a club rarely deals with the kitchen.

You start the evening with a bank (a belt pack with money broken down into change for the evening), and you do all your money transactions directly with the customer. You pay the bar directly out of your personal bank, and the customer reimburses you. If a customer pays by credit card, you must run a copy of the card before delivering drinks to ensure payment just in case the customer gets the sudden urge to walk out. Although it's a change of pace from regular restaurant work, the whole system is simple once you learn it.

Unlike other restaurant or club jobs, the waiter does not need to come in as soon as the establishment opens, but rather can arrive just before the busy period, and leave when the crowd dies down. A good cocktail position in a busy club can be quite lucrative, with relatively short hours. Even today, with all the hype about sexual discrimination, most clubs prefer to hire attractive, sexy women as cocktail waitresses (shocking, isn't it?).

To find a job, look in the yellow pages under "Clubs and Cocktail Lounges," ask around, and check out the music and entertainment section of local papers for names of popular clubs. You might try asking people who work in music stores, since they often know the hot spots.

Salary varies greatly, usually from $80 to $200 a night depending on the shift, tipping system ("pooling" or keeping your own), location, and popularity of club.

Bouncer/Doorman

A bouncer's job is primarily to check IDs so that minors don't slip in and to protect club workers and patrons. A bouncer helps establish a pleasant and safe environment so that people can come and have a good time.

Hours are flexible. Bouncing is a nighttime gig starting anywhere between 6 P.M. and 11 P.M. and lasting until about 2 A.M. You can work just a few nights a week or more if you prefer. Typically, one or two bouncers will come in early for happy hour, and then another will arrive every hour or so. By 11 P.M. the club should be fully staffed with about 10–11 bouncers working each night. Benefits include decent pay, meeting a lot of people, making connections, and being "tipped" with phone numbers (whoo-haa). On the negative side, it can become dangerous if people get angry when refused entrance or become drunk and out of control.

To be a bouncer, you need to speak English and communicate effectively. It helps to look intimidating, be in great physical shape, and know a form of martial arts. Usually, male bouncers are preferred.

To get a job as a bouncer or doorman, go through anyone you know who works at a club. Word-of-mouth and personal referrals are the best means to secure a job of this kind. Check out your paper's entertainment section for names of popular night spots or look in the yellow pages under "Clubs."

The pay is $9–$15 an hour depending on experience and duration of employment at a particular club.

Good Luck

BENEFITS: meeting people, making connections, having days free, good money, listening to music.

PITFALLS: Smoke-filled rooms, loud music, late hours, on your feet.

SOURCES: word-of-mouth, yellow pages under "Clubs." National Bartenders School, (800) 556–MIXX (6499); American Bartenders School, (800) 532–9222; Professional Bartenders School of New England, (800) 262–5824 (outside New England: (617) 646–2459). Two reputable books on mixed drinks are *Mr. Boston's Official Bartending Guide,* published by Warner Books, and *Seagrams Bartending Guide,* published by Viking.

NEEDS: restaurant or club experience preferred; for bouncer position, look intimidating, know martial arts (or at least how to break up a fight!).

Coffee Houses

Is caffeine flowing through your bloodstream?

The sentence "Let's go get a cup of coffee" has taken on a whole new meaning in the nineties. Today coffee houses are vibrant, sometimes kitschy places where young Kafka readers and caffeine junkies go to schmooze. These eclectic places offer survival job hunters a social atmosphere and flexible hours, with both full- and part-time shifts available. To become a behind-the-counter worker, a "Barista," you must have an interest in coffee, be willing to stand 90 percent of the time, and be quick on your feet.

You can work at the trendy little coffee house around the corner or at one of the ever-growing national chains, such as Starbucks. Store hours for Starbucks vary depending on location, although many are open from 7 A.M. to 11 P.M. Starbucks provides five days of training, approximately 24 hours total. You will learn all you need to know about coffee, tea, equipment, and general procedures.

The best way to get a job at a coffee house is to apply when a manager is in the store, since personal meetings are always best. Ask around for names of popular coffee houses or check the yellow pages under "Coffee Dealers—Retail." To work at Starbucks or another franchise, call information for locations in your area.

The salary starts between $6.25 and $7 an hour. In many coffee houses where you serve people, you'll also make tips. At Starbucks, a minimum of 20 hours a week entitles you to full health and dental benefits. In addition, a 20-hour work week allows you the option of a 401K retirement plan. Employees are even entitled to buy discounted stock in the company.

Good Luck

BENEFITS: social atmosphere, flexible shifts, comprehensive benefits.

PITFALLS: on your feet, very physical.

SOURCES: call information for Starbucks in your area, yellow pages under "Coffee Dealers—Retail."

NEEDS: quick on your feet, interest in coffee.

Delivering Food for Restaurants

Would you rather deal with your car than with people?

From Joe's Diner to your local five-star restaurant, food establishments everywhere are now jumping on the delivery food bandwagon. Delivering food for restaurants and pizza joints is a terrific way to make quick cash. As a delivery person, you work as an independent contractor; there is no boss hovering over you and you can listen to music or books on tape while making money. Your car will experience wear and tear, and being called the pizza boy or pizza girl might cause you to cringe, but the benefits far outweigh the disadvantages.

Shifts are typically four to six hours, with both nighttime shifts and day shifts available. This job is flexible in that you arrange your own schedule, and in many cases, you can switch a shift if need be.

To qualify to work this job, you need a car and insurance (in New York, the subway or your feet will do the job). Knowledge of the area where you will be working is preferred—which can easily be acquired with a good map. Your time is spent in your automobile, so air conditioning is helpful.

The pay is typically minimum wage plus tips, or $3 per delivery plus tips. The average income from working a five-hour shift at a mid-sized restaurant is about $75.

For specific jobs, check the classified section under "Drivers" or "Restaurants," or the yellow pages under "Restaurants," or inquire at any restaurant or pizza place that provides delivery. Services that deliver from a catalog of local restaurants are popping up in most major cities. If you have the entrepreneurial spirit, consider starting your own.

Good Luck

BENEFITS: flexible, no boss around, can listen to music or books on tape in your car.

PITFALLS: wear and tear on your car.

SOURCES: restaurants that deliver (check yellow pages), classifieds.

NEEDS: working knowledge of the area, a car and insurance in most cities.

"Writing in L.A. disenchanted me and I moved into another interest of mine, working with children. I always wanted to live in Colorado, and since I didn't like the L.A. writers' lifestyle, I moved. I needed to work a number of part-time jobs until I got a permanent position working with kids. One of them was delivering food for a neighborhood restaurant. It was a good flexible job."

WHITNEY MCKAY, writer/working with children/delivering food, Boulder, Colorado

Directory Assistance Operator

The phone is permanently attached to your ear anyway.

Directory assistance operators find phone listings and addresses for callers. This job is actually more of a full-time position, as employees are expected to work 37.5 hours a week. I included it here because split shifts are available, meaning that you can come in for four hours in the morning and then back for four hours in the evening if you like. Some "stations" are open 24 hours a day and others from 7 A.M. to 11 P.M. A phone bar (area with usable phones) is accessible to workers during their breaks, allowing free calls within surrounding counties. There are 15-minute breaks every two hours and a 30-minute lunch or dinner break after four hours.

Directory assistance operators must be on time for their shifts, have good customer service skills, be courteous to callers, and be available to work a variety of hours. When you are hired, you will be required to take a week-long crash course that teaches you everything you'll need to know for the job. Keep in mind, this is a sedentary position and is not a wise choice for anyone who likes to move around. You have to be on the phone for at least two hours at a time. Of course, many of you phone junkies won't have a problem with this idea!

For more information, call your local phone company.

Pay typically starts at $7–$8 an hour, with raises, if appropriate, every six months. The hourly wage usually caps at $16 an hour. Excellent health benefits are provided, including dental and eye insurance.

Good Luck

BENEFITS: steady income, excellent health benefits, varied shifts and split shifts.

PITFALLS: 37.5 hours a week, rude customers.

SOURCES: call your local phone company. In Los Angeles, call Pacific Bell Jobs Hotline, (800) 924–5627. In New York, call Bell Atlantic, (212) 395–2800. For Bell South, call (800) 407–0281.

NEEDS: customer service experience, ability to work various hours and split shifts.

Hotel Jobs

A lifetime supply of mini shampoos and soaps.

Hotels offer a number of flexible, part-time employment opportunities, including bellhop, concierge, doorman, front desk clerk, and room service waiter. Keep in mind when applying for hotel positions that there are advantages to working at larger, more expensive hotels. Above all, you will make more money, and trading shifts is easier since there are more employees.

Bellhop

The bellhop's duties include greeting guests, carrying their bags, escorting people to their rooms, showing the facilities in the room, handling storage of bags, and tending to customers who may have special requests. In hotels that do not have a room service department, the bellhop is responsible for ice, making trips to the store if necessary, and bringing requested items up to the rooms. One perk is that you get to meet people from all over the world.

The bellhop must have a courteous demeanor and a neat appearance. Also, a good working knowledge of spots around town is helpful since guests unfamiliar with the area will often ask questions. The hours vary. Shifts are usually 7 A.M. to 3 P.M., 3 P.M. to 11 P.M., and 11 P.M. to 7 A.M. Note that during the graveyard shift, people do not travel as much, and that therefore tips tend to be scarce.

Most hotels pay $7 an hour plus tips from guests. In an upscale hotel the bellhop can make as much as $800 per week. Group tours have a preset price paid per person for bellhop services. Most hotels offer comprehensive health benefits.

For a complete listing of hotels in your area, check your yellow pages. A few national upscale hotel chains are Nikko, Four Seasons, Biltmore, and Marriott.

Good Luck

BENEFITS: steady salary plus tips, meet people from around the world.

PITFALLS: physical labor, polyester uniform can be hot during the summer.

SOURCES: yellow pages under "Hotels." Nikko, (212) 765–4890; Marriott, 1-888–4MARRIOTT. For the Four Seasons, the Biltmore, or other chains, contact the hotel nearest you directly.

NEEDS: working knowledge of spots around town, neat and courteous.

Concierge

The job of the concierge is a pivotal position in a hotel. Guests will look to the concierge not only for hospitality, but for problem solving. The concierge informs guests about the city, suggesting restaurants, attractions, and places of interest, cautioning people about areas to avoid, and making restaurant and ticket reservations. At some hotels the concierge also handles currency exchange. As a result, the concierge must have strong communication skills to deal with hotel guests and make arrangements with vendors outside the hotel. Extensive knowledge of the city is also important. Many hotels with an international clientele prefer to hire a person who is fluent in one or more foreign languages.

Typical shifts are 7 A.M. to 3 P.M., 3 P.M. to 11 P.M., and 11 P.M. to 7 A.M. The flexibility factor can be a bit tougher with this particular position. Many hotels do have other personnel who can double as concierge, but your ability to switch shifts often depends on the willingness of your coworkers and the rules of the hotel. A terrific benefit of this job is the opportunity to make contacts all over town. On the downside, dealing with the public can be frustrating, and the concierge can often be the brunt of complaints on all levels.

A concierge can make up to $15 an hour plus tips. Rest assured that the ability to get a reservation or secure a spot at a sold-out event does not go unrewarded. Most hotels offer comprehensive health benefits.

For a complete listing of hotels in your area, check the local yellow pages. A few national upscale hotel chains are Nikko, Four Seasons, Biltmore, and Marriott.

Good Luck

BENEFITS: steady salary plus tips, make contacts all over town.

PITFALLS: deal with complaints.

SOURCES: yellow pages under "Hotels." Nikko, (212) 765–4890; Marriott, 1-888–4MARRIOTT. For the Four Seasons, the Biltmore, or other chains, contact the hotel nearest you directly.

NEEDS: friendly, neat in appearance, a schmoozer, working knowledge of the city, fluency in foreign languages is helpful.

Doorman

The doorman of a hotel greets hotel patrons when they arrive, helps them out of their cabs or assists in handling valet parking, directs them to the check-in area, and opens the door for patrons entering and leaving. A hotel doorman must be friendly, neat in appearance, and knowledgeable about the city.

This job offers the opportunity to work outside so you are not under the constant scrutiny of others. There is no "head doorman," so there is a certain freedom attached to this position. Unfortunately, working outside also means exposure to inclement weather. Unless *Singing in the Rain* is your favorite musical, this can be unpleasant. The hours are usually standard hotel shifts: 7 A.M. to 3 P.M., 3 P.M. to 11 P.M., and 11 P.M. to 7 A.M. The shifts can be switched depending on coworkers' availability. During the 11 P.M. to 7 A.M. shift you won't have to work as hard, but you will also receive few or no tips.

The salary is about $7–$10 an hour, and most hotels offer comprehensive health benefits. With tips this job can be extremely lucrative. The doorman will often get tipped both when the customer arrives at and departs from the hotel. A doorman at a busy hotel can earn in excess of $450 per week in tips.

For hotel listings, check the yellow pages under "Hotels." A few national upscale hotel chains are Nikko, Four Seasons, Biltmore, and Marriott.

Good Luck

BENEFITS: steady salary plus tips, working outside.

PITFALLS: standing, exposure to inclement weather, opening and closing the door again and again and again . . .

SOURCES: yellow pages under "Hotels." Nikko, (212) 765–4890; Marriott, 1-888–4MARRIOTT. For the Four Seasons, the Biltmore, or other chains, contact the hotel nearest you directly.

NEEDS: friendly, neat in appearance, knowledge of the city.

Front Desk Clerk

The front desk clerk is responsible for booking hotel reservations and making sure they are accurate upon the guests' arrival. The front desk clerk's main objective is to ensure that the guest's stay is as pleasant as possible. He or she confirms that the room is ready at check-in, deals with any questions or problems the guest may have, and handles checkout. The front desk clerk is also responsible for being aware of vacancies at the hotel at any given time, as well as monitoring the duration of a guest's stay and the charges incurred while at the hotel. The front desk clerk also polices in-hotel activities, checking on room availability from housekeeping, making certain guests check out at the appropriate time, and silencing noisy visitors.

This is a job where courtesy is of the utmost importance. As a front desk clerk, you are usually the first person with whom a guest makes contact inside the hotel. It is important to have a neat appearance and useful to have an extensive knowledge of the city. Foreign language skills are helpful and sometimes required.

Standard hotel shifts are 7 A.M. to 3 P.M., 3 P.M. to 11 P.M., and 11 P.M. to 7 A.M. Hotels often hire people with accounting or night audit skills to work the graveyard shift and balance the day receipts. Flexibility of shifts varies and usually depends on your peers' willingness to cover. On the downside, you will spend your shift standing; you are dealing with the public (pretty scary sometimes!); and you can be besieged by the guest for any reason whatsoever, even a spider in a room.

Most major chains offer a consistent salary and benefits. If you work for a national or international hotel chain, you will usually receive a sizable discount or a complimentary stay at the hotel you work for and its affiliates.

Salary typically ranges from $7 to $12 per hour. If night audit is incorporated, the salary will be higher. The front desk clerk usually does not receive tips.

For hotel listings, check the yellow pages under "Hotels." A few national upscale hotel chains are Nikko, Four Seasons, Biltmore, and Marriott.

Good Luck

BENEFITS: steady salary, hotel discounts.

PITFALLS: no tips, on your feet, dealing with demanding guests.

SOURCES: check the yellow pages under "Hotels." Nikko, (212) 765–4890; Marriott, 1-888–4MARRIOTT. For the Four Seasons, the Biltmore, or other chains, contact the hotel nearest you directly.

NEEDS: neat and courteous, responsible, working knowledge of the city, foreign language skills are helpful.

Room Service Waiter

A hotel room service waiter is the person who delivers meals to a guest's room. When the hotel is full, the room service waiter may deliver hundreds of meals a day. It is important to be neat, clean, and in good physical condition, as this job entails extensive walking.

The hours are standard hotel shifts, 7 A.M. to 3 P.M., 3 P.M. to 11 P.M., and 11 P.M. to 7 A.M., with the exception of the breakfast shift, when the waiter may be required to come in earlier. This is a fairly flexible job as long as your coworkers are willing to trade shifts with you.

This job pays between $5 and $10 an hour plus tips. In a large hotel, a room service waiter can make a good deal of money for the hours worked. Unfortunately, there is no guarantee of a tip each time you deliver.

For hotel listings in your area, check the yellow pages under "Hotels." A few national upscale hotel chains are Nikko, Four Seasons, Biltmore, and Marriott.

Good Luck

BENEFITS: steady salary plus tips, flexible shifts.

PITFALLS: a lot of walking with deliveries, no guarantee of tips.

SOURCES: yellow pages under "Hotels." Nikko, (212) 765–4890; Marriott, 1-888–4MARRIOTT. For the Four Seasons, the Biltmore, or other chains, contact the hotel nearest you directly.

NEEDS: neat, clean, efficient, friendly, good physical condition.

Limousine Driver/Chauffeur

Is Driving Miss Daisy your favorite movie?

A limo driver transports passengers to and from their destination in a luxurious vehicle. I have decided to write about limousine rather than taxi driving, as the consensus is that this is a safer, more pleasant job. The people I interviewed tended to be limo drivers or chauffeurs to specific celebrities, but there are plenty who cater to the public at large.

To qualify to be a limo driver, you need to be 25 years of age or older, have a clean driving record, a driver's license from the state where you plan to drive, and an extensive knowledge of the area. Job flexibility will depend on which company you work for and the schedule you are given. As long as you are responsible and a good driver, most companies are willing to work with your scheduling needs. To get in with a solid, small company that has a select clientele, you will first need to pay your dues by working for one of the larger companies. When you begin, be prepared to work long, odd hours.

Starting salary is customarily minimum wage plus tips. Once you begin work, you will be able to schmooze with other drivers to find out which companies are the best to work for. After learning the ropes, you can even start your own business.

The yellow pages lists many companies under "Limousine Services" and "Employment Agencies—Domestic Help." Check the classifieds under "Chauffeur." A few nationwide services are Carey Limousine, Limo USA, and Thomas Transportation. One large limousine company in Los Angeles is Music Express. In Chicago, try Limousine Network and Limos R Us, and in Boston, try Cooper's Limosine.

Good Luck

BENEFITS: can work off-hours, steady pay.

PITFALLS: odd hours, long hours, proms, dealing with drunks.

SOURCES: yellow pages under "Limousine Services" and "Employment Agencies—Domestic Help," classifieds under "Chauffeur." Carey Limousine, (800) 336–4646 or (800) 585–9333; Limo USA, (800) 659–7053; Thomas Transportation, (800) 526–8143; Music Express, (213) 849–2244; Limousine Network, (708) 430–0023; Limos R Us, (312) 226–5363; Cooper's Limousine, (617) 482–1000.

NEEDS: 25 or older, driver's license from the state you'll be driving in, clean driving record, extensive knowledge of the area, good sense of direction.

Market Research

Do you feel that your opinion is so valuable that you should be paid for it?

Market research solicits and compiles consumer opinions on products as varied as a new television program to choice of coffees, detergents, toilet papers, cars, and even financial investments. There are basically three flexible jobs available: focus groups, outside recruiters, and phone room recruiters.

Focus Groups

Focus groups typically involve six to ten men or women who get together in a group setting and give their opinion on products and television shows. There are even "mock jury" focus groups. Being part of a focus group can be a fun and interesting way to make extra money. Since you are only allowed to participate in a focus group once every three to six months per company, the money is not steady. But not to worry—there are plenty of companies to register with and recruiters to contact. At the very least, it is a nice supplemental income.

To participate in a focus group, you will first need to qualify. Ethnicity, demographics, age, occupation, and product use will determine participation in a particular group. Manufacturers prefer a balanced sampling of opinions for their criteria. When you call to register, you will be required to answer a list of prescreening questions.

When you are contacted to participate in an actual focus group, you will be rescreened with specific product questions. Upon qualifying, you'll be given a time and place to show up for the group session. The jobs last from one to a few hours. Occasionally you will be asked to pick up the new product beforehand, try it at home, and answer questions about it. When you have completed and delivered the questionnaire, you will be paid.

Pay varies from $30–$100 per job. The good news is that it is considered a cash gift, so it doesn't go on your taxes.

For employment opportunities, look in the yellow pages under "Market Research." You will need to call and request to be part of an upcoming research group. Plaza Research, a well-respected market research company, has offices in New York, New Jersey, Los Angeles, Chicago, Denver, Dallas, Atlanta, Philadelphia, Houston, Fort Lauderdale, and San Francisco. The Focus Network has offices in Dallas, Chicago, and New York. There are many local research centers as well. For example, in Los Angeles you will find Creative Data and L.A. Focus. When you begin participating in focus groups, you'll meet people who know recruiters, which will lead to more work.

Good Luck

BENEFITS: easy and fun, quick cash, you become the voice of the masses.

PITFALLS: unsteady work, may have to drive far.

SOURCES: "Market Research" in yellow pages; Plaza Research, (800) 654–8002; Focus Network, in Dallas (800) 336–1417; Chicago, (312) 951–1616, Los Angeles, (818) 501–4794; and New York (212) 867–6700; Creative Data, (818) 988–5411.

NEEDS: transportation to site.

"I've done a number of focus groups where I've given my opinion on new TV shows—usually I love doing them since it's easy cash. The last one I did was kind of rough on me since I was up for the lead! A few other favorites were when I tested out a new Porsche and gave my opinion for $100, and when I gave my opinion on a remodeled hotel room—this 'job' is my kind of work!"

DAVID STARZYK, dad/actor/market research/pet care/social services, Los Angeles

Outside Recruiter

Many market research firms employ recruiters to bring in participants for their focus groups. Once an assignment is completed, you bill the firm based on how many of your recruits show up. This is a terrific job for an assertive individual with good coordinating skills. A sizable database of contacts is invaluable. Flexibility is a big plus with this job; you work out of your home, at your own pace. Be aware that there are deadlines, though. Each individual company will provide you with the structure and guidelines you need to follow.

Pay varies depending on the company you work with. The typical range is $15–$30 a head. The average is ten people for each group.

For more information, contact market research groups listed in the business-to-business yellow pages and those listed above under "Focus Groups." A few companies who hire outside recruiters in Los Angeles are Adept Consumer Testing and ASI.

Good Luck

BENEFITS: flexible, work at home, good wages.

PITFALLS: challenge to break into, always at home with your work.

SOURCES: yellow pages under "Market Research," Adept Consumer Testing, (818) 905–1525; ASI, (818) 637–5600.

NEEDS: database of names, coordinating ability.

"I've been an outside recruiter as my part-time job for over eight years, on and off. It's flexible, as I work from home on my own time, and since I'm an independent contractor, I can take time off when I need to. It's easy to recruit people for focus groups, since I'm providing them with a way to earn money. It's always great when I can get my friends in on a group."

SUSAN MORRIS, writer/outside recruiter, New York and Los Angeles

Phone Room Recruiter

Many market research groups hire employees to work in what is called a phone room. There you recruit individuals from specific lists to participate in focus groups. Unlike telemarketing, you are not selling anything. You are simply inviting people to participate in a group discussion so that *they* can make money. This is an appropriate job for anyone who is outgoing, friendly, and enjoys phone work. Flexible shifts are available. The late-in-the-day 5 P.M. to 9 P.M. shift is a popular one. The salary is approximately $8–$10 an hour.

To find out more information, call "Marketing Research" groups listed in the yellow pages or call the phone numbers listed above under "Focus Groups."

Good Luck

BENEFITS: steady income, flexible shifts.

PITFALLS: cold calling.

SOURCES: yellow pages under "Market Research."

NEEDS: good phone manner.

Messenger

Faster than a speeding bullet, able to grab large packages with a single swipe.

A messenger picks up letters, documents, contracts, checks, or packages, and delivers them from one business or individual to another. Most messenger services require you to have a car, driver's license, registration, liability insurance, and working knowledge of the city (or a good map). In New York City, a car is not required; in fact, most deliveries are made by foot or by bike. A positive attitude, physical fitness, and a presentable appearance are what most companies look for when hiring.

Many messenger services are open 24 hours a day, seven days a week, so a variety of shifts are available. You have the freedom of working alone while making your delivery, and when driving you can pack your car with plenty of music or books on tape. Foot and bike messengers get plenty of exercise. On the negative side, this job can be stressful if you are facing a deadline and find yourself stuck in traffic (*very* common in large cities).

Most messengers work on commission. Typically, services pay 50 percent of the particular job or $6–$7 an hour, plus commission. Overall, you can expect to earn $8–$10 an hour. Since messengers are usually paid by the delivery, the faster you are, the more money you make. But remember to drive carefully!

Messenger services are always looking for reliable workers. Check the yellow pages under "Messenger Service" for a complete listing, or the classifieds under "Messengers" or "Drivers." In New York, a popular and respected company, RDS Delivery, loves hiring actors. In Los Angeles, contact Dynamics, West Express Messenger Service, or Action Messenger Service.

Good Luck

BENEFITS: varied shifts, sense of freedom in car or on bike, decent salary.

PITFALLS: traffic, irregular income when working on commission, dangerous, especially for New York bike messengers.

SOURCES: yellow pages under "Messenger Service," classifieds under "Messengers" or "Drivers." RDS Delivery, (212) 260–5800. In Los Angeles contact Dynamics, (310) 838–7676; West Express Messenger Service, (213) 466–1271; Action Messenger Service, (213) 654–2333.

NEEDS: car or bike, knowledge of your city, driver's license, registration, insurance.

Real Estate Agent

Three words:
location, location, location.

Interacting well with people, enjoying the art of selling, patience, and tenacity are some of the qualities needed for success in the world of real estate. Selling real estate on a part-time basis allows you to juggle your hours to suit your needs. There are different facets to being a real estate agent: A buyer's agent represents the buyer solely, a seller's agent (also called a listing agent) represents the seller. A transaction broker has no fiduciary ("loyalty") to either party involved. He or she simply facilitates the transaction. A dual agent represents the buyer and seller simultaneously, in showing a broker's (employer's) listing. Note that each state has its own governing rules regarding agency.

To become a real estate agent, a college degree is not necessary, but you will need to pass the state exam, and in most cities own a car.

Typically, a real estate principal course has to be taken. You can contact real estate brokerage firms and local colleges for desirable class information, or contact specific real estate schools listed in the yellow pages. Expect to pay several hundred dollars for a real estate license and the course, depending on the state you live in. In many states, once you pass your state exam, brokerage firms solicit for employment. Another way to procure employment is to call firms directly that advertise in the Sunday paper's real estate section. Hanging your license with a broker will provide you with advertising, a desk, phone, fax, copier, information, and voice mail.

Once you are a certified real estate agent, your broker will provide you with MLS (Multiple Listing Service) listings, which is a computer printout of houses for sale in specified areas. Another way to find houses to represent is to look for "fisbos" (for sale by owner) in the real estate classified sections. And yet another method is calling listings that have expired in the MLS to renew with you!

Most successful part-time real estate agents partner with an established agent in their broker's office when getting started, working at a lesser commission. You will often need to do most of the grunt work, which entails detailed paperwork, phone solicitation, and taking out new buyers. On the upside, you will gain experience and have access to higher-quality listings while building your own reputation.

A few common ways to sell properties include advertising on the Internet, through newspapers, on local cable stations, and in specialized real estate magazines often found at supermarkets and gas stations.

Earnings vary tremendously. It helps if you don't have to worry about your income for the first three to six months, since it takes a while to get the ball rolling (closings generally occur after 60–90 days), and being desperate when selling is a serious faux pas. Some part-timers make as much as $30,000–$60,000 a year. Expect to earn 3–6 percent of each sale when listing and selling the property. You'll earn at least 1.5 percent when the commission is split between two brokers (listing and selling sides).

Good Luck

BENEFITS: constantly changing pace and environment, meeting new people, flexible hours, weekend work.

PITFALLS: ask my mother-in-law! fluctuating income, up-front costs, advertising expenses.

SOURCES: Board or Association of Realtors in your city or state. Contact brokerage firms in your area for information. Check the yellow pages under "Real Estate" or "Schools."

NEEDS: real estate license, reliable car, sales ability, personality, and perseverance.

"I can't sit in a chair at a desk for any length of time. This job allows me a lot of freedom, as I can juggle my appointments if need be. I lived in a million-dollar home while it was for sale. My only expense was my time to show it and making sure it looked well kept. Potential to make big money is certainly there."

CHASE DAKOTA, writer/actress/part-time real estate agent, Los Angeles

---

Real Estate Appraiser

You can differentiate between English Tudor and French Provincial.

Appraisers are hired by mortgage brokers, lenders, and banks to appraise a piece of property for current market value. Appraisal is the unscientific art of evaluating a property based on knowledge and information obtained from comparable properties, typically within a mile or two radius or subdivision.

Banks and mortgage lenders want appraisals on anything that they are lending money for. The appraisal plays an important role in whether the lender will lend money to the buyer.

Real estate agents often do appraisals on the side to make extra money. Work is flexible since you often have two to three days to get any given job done. Typically, half the work is done in the field and half is done in research. It takes approximately one hour to complete the computer work and visit the property. Using a camera and an MLS (Multiple Listing Service) program, you can give a quick appraisal by knowing location prices, square footage, and number of rooms.

To become a real estate appraiser, you must go to appraisal school and pass a state exam. To get started, contact local real estate offices, the Board Association of Realtors, and adult-ed schools for class information.

After you meet your state requirements, contact major banks, lenders, brokers, and appraisal companies for employment opportunities.

Wages vary. Expect to earn between $50 and $100 per appraisal in major cities.

NOTE: Another option pertaining to real estate is to work as a photographer for the MLS. Shooting pictures of properties does not require an appraiser license and usually pays $8–$15 an hour.

Good Luck

BENEFITS: flexibility, can do a number of appraisals in a day.

PITFALLS: tedious research

SOURCES: appraisal school, local real estate offices, the Board Association of Realtors, adult-ed schools, hooking up with real estate agents or appraisal companies.

NEEDS: a car, camera, and real estate appraiser license.

Restaurant Work

You will not be a starving (or thirsty) artist!

Although "waitressing on the side" has become something of a cliché, restaurant work continues to be a popular survival job because it provides fast cash and free or discounted meals. Hours vary, it's a social atmosphere, and there are usually plenty of people on staff with whom you can trade shifts.

When looking for a restaurant job, be in tune with your own particular needs and criteria. If you are not a night owl, look for a family-style restaurant or at least one that closes by midnight. Also, pay attention to the surrounding environment. I am a nonsmoking, nondrinking morning person who prefers quiet environments (sounds like a personal ad), but at times I worked in smoke-filled pubs and smoke-filled cafés. These were by far my shortest restaurant experiences. Get the point?

Bartender

A bartender's duties include setting up the bar, stocking beverages, maintaining an inventory of items, cutting fruit for the condiment tray, cleaning glassware, and mixing drinks for bar customers and the wait staff.

Unfortunately, good bartending jobs are not easy to come by, as they are often filled from within or through recommendations. Gaining your employer's trust is a key factor in securing a bartending position, as you are responsible for the cash register. Generally, you deal directly with the owners, not managers. Bartenders tend to be treated with more respect than waiters because customers want that extra shot of alcohol in their drink. As with most restaurant jobs, the hours are flexible. You can work day or evening shifts and switch with other bartenders as needed. Day shifts are usually slower and more peaceful, but you earn less money than at night. However, day shifts can be very profitable in business districts such as New York's Wall Street.

Salary varies widely depending on the restaurant, hours, location, and customers. Shift pay is generally $25–$50 plus tips. Tips are often high, as they include gratuities from bar customers as well as a percentage of the wait staff's take. You can expect to earn an average of $60 a day and $100 a night.

If you are presently lacking in bartending experience and knowledge of mixed drinks, plenty of reputable bartending courses are available. Schools usually charge between $300 and $500 for the course, with scholarships and creative financing often available. Many schools will help place you in jobs upon completion. A few reputable ones are the National Bartenders School, American Bartenders School, and Professional Bartenders School of New England. Two popular books on mixology are *Mr. Boston's Official Bartending Guide,* published by Warner Books, and *Seagrams Bartending Guide,* published by Viking.

Good Luck

BENEFITS: quick cash, free meals.

PITFALLS: competitive position, on your feet for an entire shift, deal with rowdy drunks.

SOURCES: classifieds, word-of-mouth, *Mr. Boston's Official Bartending Guide,* published by Warner Books, *Seagrams Bartending Guide,* published by Viking. Placement service of bartending schools, National Bartenders School, (800) 556–MIXX (6499); American Bartenders School, (800) 532–9222; Professional Bartenders School of New England, (800) 262–4657 (outside New England: (617) 646–2459).

NEEDS: wide knowledge of mixology, experience.

> *"I earn enough money in four nights of bartending to support my acting habit."*
>
> DAVID STRONG, actor/bartender, New York

Hostess/Maître d'

Hostessing involves taking reservations, answering the phone, and greeting and seating people who enter the restaurant. Owners prefer hiring a person who is attractive, neat in appearance, and personable. Your choice of wardrobe will depend on the style of restaurant in which you work. Unfortunately, this job requires that you be on your feet for your entire shift, and when business is slow the job can be dull. On a positive note, you meet a lot of people, and the job provides flexibility. Different shifts are available, and it's usually possible to switch with another host or maître d'.

Hours vary. Some restaurants prefer you to be there before they open to take reservations. Other locations may require you to work only during the busier hours. Choose a place that you are interested in and present yourself during off-hours (3 P.M. to 5 P.M. and 9 A.M. to 11 A.M.). The best way to get a host or hostess position is through a friend's recommendation.

Pay ranges from $6 to $15 an hour, and often you are "tipped out" a small percentage by the wait staff. You may also be tipped by guests who want a good table.

Good Luck

BENEFITS: easy work, meet people, discounted or free meals.

PITFALLS: always on your feet, boring at times.

SOURCES: choose restaurants you are interested in and present yourself during off-hours (3 P.M. to 5 P.M. and 9 A.M. to 11 A.M.)

NEEDS: neat and presentable appearance, courteous manner.

Manager

A manager's duties vary according to restaurant size. They typically include scheduling and monitoring staff efficiency, hiring, firing, bookkeeping, and ordering. The manager serves as a liaison between the floor staff, kitchen staff, and owners, and works to ensure customer satisfaction, which often requires table visits. At the end of the day, a manager closes out by balancing the cash and charges with the computer or register receipts. Computer knowledge is often necessary.

Managing a restaurant offers a steady salary and is a high-profile, respected job. Management tends to be the least flexible restaurant position, since exchanging shifts is limited to the number of managers working in the specific establishment. Prior food service management or headwaitering experience is required, but you can always work yourself up the ranks from within.

Salary varies depending on restaurant size and type. You can expect to make anywhere from $500 to a $1,000 a week and up. To find a management position, check the classifieds or contact employment agencies through the yellow pages. Word-of-mouth and a recommendation are best.

Good Luck

BENEFITS: steady salary, respected position, free meals.

PITFALLS: a lot of responsibility, limited flexibility, long hours, few days off.

SOURCES: classifieds, word-of-mouth, employment agencies.

NEEDS: restaurant experience, computer proficiency.

Waiter/Waitress

A waiter's job is to take food and drink orders, serve the requested items, and tend to customer needs. Side work involves setting up tables, refilling condiments, polishing glasses and silver, and cleaning counters and work areas. It is important to be efficient and personable. Having a good memory is definitely an asset since you will need to know and recite the daily specials. Sometimes a more extensive knowledge of wine and food is required.

The positive aspects of being a waiter are fast cash, a flexible schedule, and free meals. The hours vary depending on the restaurant and your shift assignment. On the downside, you'll have to work at a frantic pace during peak hours, and put up with sometimes erratic income—poor tips can alter your mood pretty darn fast.

Salary consists of minimum wage plus tips. Tips will vary depending on the location and size of the restaurant. An average dinner shift in a mid-sized restaurant in a major city pays $75-$100 a night, and an average lunch shift pays $30–$75.

When looking for a job, be aware that not all restaurants do well. Before accepting, or even applying, try to gauge the volume of customers as well as the prices on the menu; tips are commensurate with these factors. To get started, look in the help wanted section of the newspaper, ask friends, or apply at restaurants during off-hours (3 P.M. to 5 P.M. and 9 A.M. to 11 A.M.).

Good Luck

BENEFITS: fast cash, flexible hours, free or discounted meals.

PITFALLS: unsteady income, on your feet, rude customers.

SOURCES: classifieds, friends, visiting restaurants during off-peak hours (3 P.M. to 5 P.M. and 9 A.M. to 11 A.M.).

NEEDS: prior experience and contacts are beneficial, but not necessary.

> *"Waitressing provides us with extra money, and I enjoy the adult time spent away from my baby two nights a week. It's a neighborhood kind of restaurant, so I have special contact with regular customers of all ages."*
>
> LORI CIAUDELLI, mom/waitress, Doylestown, Pennsylvania

Secret Shopper

You always wanted to be in the FBI but you're afraid of guns.

Would you believe that someone will actually pay you to shop? For years, retailers have hired secret shoppers—also called mystery shoppers—to check up on the service and attitude of employees and evaluate store operations by posing as customers. This helps store, restaurant, and shopping center owners keep an eye on their staff and consequently improves customer service. It allows *you* to actually earn money while unleashing your wildest consumer fantasies.

Companies that hire secret shoppers look for people who blend in with the crowd. Retail or management experience is often preferred. It is often tiring work—you may have to shop at ten different stores within a three-hour period, and you are required to fill out detailed evaluation forms. On the upside, the wages are good, there is no dress code, and you can shop for yourself while on the job. The hours are flexible—usually 15–20 hours per week—but the amount of available work may vary depending on where you live.

The pay is about $10–$15 for evaluation of a store, which can take anywhere from ten minutes to an hour. If you are evaluating a restaurant, a free meal is included.

A few national companies to contact for information are Profitivity, Feedback Plus, and Courtesy Counts. Many of these companies run ads in college newspapers, so check those for employment opportunities. Another idea is to contact large department stores, hotels, or major apartment management firms and ask them which companies they use for this purpose. Some market research companies also hire secret shoppers, so check the yellow pages under "Market Research."

Good Luck

BENEFITS: flexible schedule, no dress code, paid to shop.

PITFALLS: detailed work, tiring—shopping at ten stores in one day can be exhausting (unless you're Ivana Trump).

SOURCES: college newspapers, contacting major stores or hotels, national companies, yellow pages under "Market Research," the "Market Research" section of this chapter. Profitivity, (310) 477–8333; Feedback Plus, (972) 661–8989 ext. 214; Courtesy Counts, (301) 299–5400.

NEEDS: retail experience preferred.

Sitting Open Houses

Sit on your butt and make money.

Real estate agencies often hire people to sit at a table during an open house and hand out material on the house for sale so that the agent can spend more time hustling sales or commissions. When I was in college, my roommate sat open houses on the weekends. It was an excellent part-time job, as she was able to study and write in between handing out information. Some apartment managers and owners also hire people to hand out lease applications.

In certain states, such as Florida, you need to be licensed as a real estate agent to hand out information and show people listings, unless you're working for a developer. But in most cases—like that of my roommate—all you need is a professional and responsible manner. It is important to be reliable, punctual, and above all friendly, since you will be meeting quite a lot of people and will be acting as a representative of the agency you work for.

Weekend work is plentiful, and even in states where a license is needed, you can always work during the week on "brokers' day," when brokers check out new listings. You don't need to be licensed to work a brokers' day.

Wages vary, but you can expect to earn $8–$10 an hour in major cities. You are usually required to work for a minimum of three hours. Shifts can be available all day depending on when the property is being shown. If you are a licensed real estate agent, you can often choose to forgo an hourly wage in exchange for a percentage of the sale.

To get this type of job, all you really need to do is let real estate agents know you're available. One idea might be to design a flier and drop it off with real estate agencies in your area. Read the real estate section of your newspaper and pick out the heavy hitters to contact—they all have many houses to show, and can probably use your help.

Good Luck

BENEFITS: flexible, can catch up on reading or correspondence while sitting.

PITFALLS: tedious if you don't enjoy being alone.

SOURCES: real estate agents or companies.

NEEDS: professional appearance and attitude, reliable and punctual, enjoy working with people.

"When I'm sitting open houses on the weekends, I can bring my daughter along to help—she enjoys playing real estate agent. No sitter is needed and it's a great opportunity to pick up Avon customers."

LORRAINE LECHAMINANT, mom/Avon rep/part-time real estate agent, Boca Raton, Florida

Supermarket Cashier

Have you been able to make change since the first grade?

A supermarket cashier, also known as a checker (market lingo), rings up the customer's groceries and is responsible for collecting the correct amount of money. It's a great part-time job, and the hours and shifts are flexible since many of today's supermarkets are open 24 hours. Some even prefer you to work weekends, which is ideal for anyone who has another job during the week.

One advantage of this job is knowing when all the sales are, which can enable you to save hundreds of dollars on your grocery bill. You also receive full union benefits at major supermarket chains after three months of employment. On the downside, it can be difficult to get a job as a checker if you are just starting out. You may have to invest a few months of low-paying work ($5–$7 an hour) as a grocery bagger (wrapper) in order to be promoted from within.

Cashier pay range is $9–$15 an hour at most union supermarkets. To get a job, simply visit the stores of your choice and ask to fill out an application.

Good Luck

BENEFITS: union support, medical coverage, flexible hours.

PITFALLS: dealing with a major corporation, may need to be promoted from within.

SOURCES: go to supermarkets at desired location and apply.

NEEDS: friendly, some cashier experience or an investment of time doing low-paying work.

Telemarketing

Reach out and touch someone.

Telemarketing involves phone solicitation for a particular product or service. A corporation or an individual will hire you either to "cold call" (call a list of people who have not yet expressed an interest in your product), or to contact individuals who may have expressed an interest, but have not yet purchased the product or service. Most companies provide you with lists of specific people who are in a particular market, sect, or niche that may be interested in what you are selling. The product you market can vary tremendously, from office and computer supplies, to season theater tickets, to dating services. This is a great job for someone who is articulate, has a positive attitude, enjoys the art of selling (it is best to think of it as introducing an important and beneficial service)—*and* can handle rejection.

Telemarketing offers flexibility at a decent and sometimes excellent wage. Shifts vary, but they usually last four to six hours. A morning shift typically ends by 1 P.M., and afternoon and evening shifts are available for late risers. On the downside, you may have to deal with people being rude to you (but at least you can hang up, unless they beat you to it!) and hearing a lot of "not interested," which can be frustrating. If you are working on commission, "not interested" can mean "no rent money" this month.

There are many telemarketing opportunities out there. It is important to trust the product or service you are selling so that you can put your own enthusiasm into your marketing pitch. It often helps when the company you work for offers potential customers a trial or gift certificate over the phone—everyone likes a freebie.

For specific telemarketing jobs, check the classifieds under "Telemarketing," "Sales," or "Part-time Work." Trade papers and college newspapers often list telemarketing jobs as well. Find the one that best suits your needs in terms of service, geographic location, salary, and commission.

Income varies widely among telemarketing jobs, usually ranging from $7 to $20 an hour. Salary plus commission is the norm; others are commission only. The latter can pay extremely well if it's a high-end product or service—some employees earn over $50,000 a year for a 30-hour work week.

Good Luck

BENEFITS: flexible shifts, good salary, often includes health benefits.

PITFALLS: deal with rejection, feel isolated if you're working in a cubicle.

SOURCES: classified section under "Telemarketing," "Sales," and "Part-time," trade papers, and college newspapers.

NEEDS: positive attitude, upbeat personality, knowledge of your product or service, persistence, good communication skills.

"I've worked at over ten telemarketing jobs, and the one I'm doing now is by far the best. I receive salary with commission, plus benefits. I've been here about two years and feel confident about the products we sell: surgical instruments and health care products. It's a high-quality product with a noble purpose, and it's a soft sell since we send samples to technicians. They usually fall in love with our products and buy. The main advantage for me is living a

block away from work—I'm able to go home during lunch and practice my music!"

VINCENT PRESTIANNI, musician/telemarketing, Long Island, New York

---

Valet Parking

Be seen at parties with Steven Spielberg, Janet Jackson, and other glitterati.

You can work at the finest establishments, meet famous people, and stand face to face with the heads of studios. Valet parking is a job that offers glamour and earns a substantial wage. Flexible shifts are available around the clock. The qualifications include having a driver's license, a clean driving record, a social security card, and, as one company put it, the ability to "smile and say hello."

Pay varies. Typically it is minimum wage plus tips, but it may be as high as $7.50 an hour plus tips. When it's all added up, you can expect to make $8–$20 an hour. You can usually earn more money at a busy upscale restaurant or hotel than at private parties.

For employment, check local newspapers and magazines or the yellow pages under "Parking Attendant Service" or "Valet Service." Call hotels or restaurants in your area to find out what valet companies they use. Leon Smith Parking is *the* valet service at the Beverly Hills Hotel. Chuck's Parking in Los Angeles has been in business for over 35 years; it valets 75–100 parties a month. In Boston, try Valet Park of New England; in Washington, D.C., try Valet Parking Systems; and in Richmond, Canada, try Valet Parking Services.

Good Luck

BENEFITS: possibly meet famous people, drive cool cars (albeit for short distances), flexible shifts, steady work.

PITFALLS: you have to give the keys back.

SOURCES: local newspapers and magazines, yellow pages under "Parking Attendant Service" or "Valet Service." Leon Smith Parking, (310) 281–2987; Chuck's Parking,

(818) 788–4300; Valet Park of New England, (617) 451–1393; Valet Parking Systems, (800) 696–7170; Valet Parking Services, (800) 278–8250.

NEEDS: energetic and friendly personality, driver's license, clean driving record, social security card.

> *"Valet parking was an easy, laid-back kind of job. I had very little responsibility, shifts were relatively short, and while we were working we'd go into the restaurant. I got to hang out, make money, and get a free meal."*
>
> ANTHONY GONZALEZ, singer/valet parking/taxicab driver/waiter, San Francisco

---

Video Store Clerk

The alternative to sneaking into movie theaters.

"Play it again, Sam," or in this case, rent it again. It seems like a new video store is opening its doors every few blocks. Everybody loves the convenience, the price, the selection, and the chance to pop popcorn and curl up in front of an old favorite. Each video store needs a number of helpful clerks, and that's where you come in—you look up movies for customers and check out rentals.

Working in a video store is a great part-time job for anyone interested in the film industry. Since you are constantly doing research, you will learn a lot about genres of film and who the different producers, directors, and lead actors are. In large cities, many video stores are open until midnight, which allows for flexibility when scheduling shifts. Knowledge of a wide variety of films is preferred, but not necessary.

Starting salary is normally $5.25–$7 an hour, and most stores offer the added bonus of free rentals and discounts on merchandise. There are many video stores to choose from. Look in your yellow pages under "Video Tapes" and "Discs—Renting and Leasing," and frequent the stores you are interested in. Find out when the manager is in and set up an interview. Many artists have told me that Tower Records and Video is a particularly good place to work, because Tower hires mostly musicians and actors, and is flexible and open-minded when it comes to auditions and interviews. Tower also provides health coverage.

Good Luck

BENEFITS: flexible scheduling, learn about films, free rentals and discounts.

PITFALLS: low starting salary.

SOURCES: neighborhood stores, yellow pages under "Video Tapes" and "Discs—Renting and Leasing." The number for Tower Video in Los Angeles is (310) 657–3344. In New York, call (212) 505–1166 for the downtown location and (212) 496–2500 for the uptown location.

NEEDS: good attitude, social skills, film knowledge preferred.

3

That's Entertainment

There's No Business Like Show Business

Box Office Salesperson

Be "in the theater" without the backstage jitters.

These days it seems like you have to take out a second mortgage on your house to afford a night out at the theater. Theater tickets are expensive, but there *is* a way to see all the latest shows without going into debt: work part-time as a box office salesperson. Working the box office for a theater company or performing arts center will allow you to indulge your taste for the dramatic arts *without* spending enormous amounts of money.

Basically three jobs are involved in this line of work. One is to work directly in the box office assisting customers who step up to the window to purchase tickets. A second way is to work for a company in your area that handles ticket sales for many theaters and performing arts centers, such as Ticketmaster. These companies will hire people to work the box office over the phone. A third way is to work in a theater or performing arts center answering phones and providing details on the show, show times, and other information. Some theaters will employ you simply to answer phones, while others will have you answer questions as well as sell tickets.

There are many shifts to choose from when working box office. Shows are usually "dark" (off for the night in theater lingo) on Mondays. Some performing arts centers however, are open 365 days a year. Holidays in particular are big business—there is even work to be had on Christmas (remember *The Nutcracker*). To find employment, contact theaters and performing arts centers listed in your paper's entertainment section. Also look in the yellow pages under "Theaters."

Pay varies depending on experience and the venue you work. Working box office at a theater while you personally meet people usually pays more. Pay is typically $6–$12 an hour.

NOTE: It doesn't usually pay (sometimes $10), but being a volunteer usher for a performance allows you to see theater for free. When I was an actress in New York, I saw almost every off-Broadway show this way.

Good Luck

BENEFITS: seeing shows (usually from orchestra seats) for free or at a discount, steady hourly wage.

PITFALLS: dealing with people who are upset with policies or cancellation of shows in their subscription.

SOURCES: contacting theaters and performing arts centers.

NEEDS: professionalism, ability to cope with people and their requests or problems.

> *"Being a box office salesperson has given me the opportunity to experience theater, opera, symphonies, and the ballet. I always loved watching opera but could never afford $80 tickets. Now I am able to enjoy a level of culture that would otherwise be inaccessible to me."*
>
> RYAN LEE, actor/box office salesperson, Los Angeles

Casting Session Camera Operator

Lights, camera . . . bucks!

A casting session camera operator tapes actors during auditions as they read commercial copy from cue cards or improvise specific scenarios. Taping is a vital part of the process, as it allows the client (the actual company of the product or service being advertised) to see each audition without being there. Commercial casting directors, busy with upcoming audition breakdowns (defining types needed for commercials), usually hire assistants to run the camera for them during commercial auditions and callbacks. That's where your job comes in.

In an entry-level position, you will simply run the camera. If you have more experience or a casting director trusts you, you might be hired to run the entire day's session. This includes taping and directing. Basically it requires on-the-job training. Knowledge of video equipment is a plus.

This is an excellent job for actors or anyone trying to network in the industry. You will work with many casting directors and fellow actors intimately. The major benefit of this job is being able to audition automatically for any spots you are right for. It can also help a novice auditioner learn the ropes and reduce the intimidation that goes along with the auditioning process. One bit of advice: You may have to keep reminding casting directors that you are an actor as well. They may tend to think of you as the camera operator and overlook your larger aspirations!

The pay for an entry-level position is typically $100–$150 a day. If you direct the session or work for a particular casting director for a while, you can make as much as $200 a day, and most camera operators work 3–4 days a week. The hours are usually 10 A.M. to 6 P.M. with a one- to two-hour lunch break.

Getting this type of job can be tricky; a lot can depend on whom you know in the business. Sound familiar? If you are an actor, don't be afraid to approach the casting director, the person running the studio, or the camera operator at a commercial audition to express interest in the job. In addition, many theatrical bookstores, such as Samuel French Theater & Film Bookstore, have a number of casting director guides with contact numbers. *The Working Actors Guide* by Mani Flattery, found at most theatrical bookstores, has a chart of casting directors involved in commercial casting. Another invaluable source is *The Casting Director Directory*. Some casting directors are listed in the yellow pages under "Theatrical Agencies." You might even call reputable talent agents in your area and ask them for referrals, or contact your local chapter of Screen Actors Guild (SAG), or the American Federation of Television and Radio Artists (AFTRA), or even your city's film commission for a complete list of directors.

Good Luck

BENEFITS: good wages, learn about the process, able to network, be seen for auditions.

PITFALLS: casting directors think of you only as the camera operator, competitive position.

SOURCES: networking, contact casting directors and camera operators, yellow pages under "Theatrical Agencies;" *The Working Actors Guide* by Mani Flattery; Samuel French Bookstore in Los Angeles, (800) 8ACT–NOW for phone orders; *The Casting Director Directory;* Screen Actors Guild (SAG); or the American Federation of Television and Radio Artists (AFTRA); your city's film commission.

NEEDS: ability to work a video camera, enjoy working with actors.

Choir Work

"Hark, the herald angels sing . . ."

Did you know that it's possible to get paid for singing beautiful hymns and prayers, and feel close to God? In most major cities, temples and churches hire singers and musicians for their choirs. Even if you have no formal voice training, most organists and choir directors will listen to new singers if they have proficient sight-reading skills, as they are always on the lookout for new talent.

Church choir members typically earn anywhere from $50 to $100 a service. This fee often includes a two-hour rehearsal on Thursday evening and another rehearsal right before the service Sunday morning. Temples usually pay $50 a service. Salary may vary depending on specific skills.

Music schools such as Juilliard and Manhattan School of Music post choir opportunities on their student service bulletin boards. Most self-respecting organists and choir directors belong to the American Guild of Organists (AGO), headquartered in New York, with local chapters all across the country and a chapter in Canada called the Royal Canadian College of Organists (RCCO). Membership includes a subscription to its magazine, which lists employment opportunities.

New York Opera Newsletter costs about $50 a year and lists auditions for opera singers as well as choral gigs. It is a terrific resource for a singer considering making the move to the Big Apple.

Another way to procure employment is to look up churches in your phone book and send a résumé to the music directors. Voice teachers and their students are another useful resource.

Good Luck

BENEFITS: networking, performing, spiritual work, possibility of solos.

PITFALLS: chorus work if you want to be a soloist.

SOURCES: American Guild of Organists, headquarters in New York, (212) 870–2310, in Canada call the Royal Canadian College of Organists, (416) 929–6400; *New York Opera Newsletter,* P.O. Box 278, Maplewood, NJ 07040; contacting musical directors at churches and temples.

NEEDS: musical abilities; sight-reading skills.

> *"I've worked for countless temple and church choirs since graduating from Manhattan School of Music. For a singer it's been a valuable sight-reading and solo opportunity experience. And it's a good way to make extra money on the weekends."*
>
> ARTHUR GIGLIO, singer/voice teacher, New York

Cruise Ship Entertainer

The Love Boat was (and still remains) your favorite show.

If you can sing, dance, play an instrument, make people laugh, or do magic tricks, entertaining on a cruise ship can be a great way to make money, perform, and vacation, all at the same time.

Cruise ships hire dancers and singers for musical revues, various performers for individual acts, musicians for bands and solo work, and pianists for cocktail lounges. The act hired is specific to the cruise ship. Individual acts can be hired for two days or six months depending on the contract and the company. You can be booked directly by the cruise line or through an agent.

To be booked directly, you will usually need to send a videotape, showcasing your talents, to the entertainment operations department of the specific cruise line you want to work for. Nationwide auditions for musical revue performers and other talent are held once or twice a year. They are advertised in the trade papers (*Backstage* and *Dramalogue*), or you can call the cruise line to find out when auditions will be held.

The advantage of working with a booking agent (10–20 percent commission) is the agent's insider knowledge of specific cruise lines and ability to know where your act will fit best. One well-known agent, Larry Harmon of Fort Lauderdale, Florida, has been in the business for over 20 years. If interested in representing you, he will take a 30-minute video of your show and edit it down to a great six- to ten-minute demo tape for free.

Dancers and singers for revues are typically paid $250–$500 a week plus room and board. Principal performers in revues can make up to $1,200 a week. Contracts for revues are usually three to six months (a great way to save some money).

An individual show (comedian, singer, magician) will run about 10–30 minutes, and pay starts at about $1,000 a week plus room and board. Your work will probably consist of two shows performed two nights a week, so you're only on stage about two hours each week!

Good Luck

BENEFITS: get to perform, paid vacations, traveling, social environment, great wages.

PITFALLS: a six-month contract can take you away from friends, family, and your career.

SOURCES: cruise lines or booking agents. A few booking agents are Bramson Entertainment, 1440 Broadway, New York, NY 10018, (212) 354–9575; Don Casino Productions, 2750 N. 29th Avenue, Suite 309A, Hollywood, FL 33020, (954) 920–0137; and Morag Productions, P.O. Box 80–1736, Adventura, FL 33280, (305) 937–1492. A few popular cruise ships to contact directly are Royal Caribbean Cruises Ltd., Entertainment Department, 1050 Caribbean Way, Miami, FL 33132–2096, (305) 539–6000; Princess Cruises, Entertainment Department, Box C, 10100 Santa Monica Boulevard, Los Angeles, CA 90067, (310) 553–1770; Royal Olympic Cruises, Entertainment Department, 1 Rockefeller Plaza, Suite 315, New York, NY 10020, (212) 397–6400; Carnival Cruise Lines, 3655 N.W. 87th Avenue, Miami, FL, (305) 599–2600; American Hawaii Cruises, 604 Fort Street, Honolulu, HI 96813; Crystal Cruise Line, Entertainment Department, 2121 Avenue of the Stars, Los Angeles, CA 90067, (310) 785–9300.

NEEDS: talent, a musical act, enjoy cruises and traveling.

> *"I worked as a bandleader and piano player on seven different ships. The biggest perk was the travel. I've been all over the world for free—normally you'd have to be a Rockefeller to travel the way I have. Working on a cruise ship is a great way to gain experience—when Rosie O'Donnell called me up to be the bandleader on her show, I was ready. Working on cruise ships had given me the day-to-day experience I couldn't have gotten anywhere else."*
>
> JOHN MCDANIEL, bandleader/musical director/pianist, New York

Extra Work

You'll never forget your lines (you won't have any).

"There are no small parts"—or so the saying goes. Imagine the movie *The Ten Commandments* without the 20,000 extras—pretty boring! Extras, or "background performers," as they are now referred to in this era of politically correct lingo, are used to give atmosphere to a set and life to scenes when the principal actors are the focus.

For the novice actor, extra work is a terrific way to learn the many facets of the movie and TV industry. You get to see what goes on behind the camera as well as how fellow (albeit more experienced) thespians work. In certain situations, extras are given a line of dialogue, upgraded in pay scale, and asked to join the union.

To become eligible for extra work, go to a casting office that deals with background performers and drop off a photo. Many agencies have particular days for this, so call ahead for information. Some services charge a nominal fee for non-union members. A word of warning: Be wary of agencies that charge more than a $30 fee or insist on expensive photos. It is also helpful and more profitable (you get a wardrobe stipend) if you provide your own wardrobe for the roles you play (uniforms, upscale clothing, costumes).

Wages vary depending on your city. In Los Angeles, non-union extras make about $45 for eight hours, and SAG union extras make $65. In New York, rates start at $99. This hourly rate goes up with overtime.

For a list of reputable casting offices, check *The Ross Reports,* found at theatrical bookstores and major newsstands. Look in your yellow pages under "Casting Services" or call reputable agents and casting directors asking for referral numbers. The production services department of SAG has listings of casting directors. Cullen Chambers's comprehensive guide, *Back to One: How to Make Good Money as a Hollywood Extra* provides more information than you probably need, but it's a classic and can be found at most theatrical bookstores.

Good Luck

BENEFITS: work on a professional TV or movie set, possibility of being upgraded, contacts.

PITFALLS: long hours.

SOURCES: contact casting offices that deal with background performers. Production services department of SAG, (213) 549–6811. *Back to One: How to Make Good Money as a Hollywood Extra* by Cullen Chambers, (213) 969–4897. In Los Angeles, call Central Casting (SAG union only), (818) 562–2700; Cenex (for non-union), (818) 562–2825; Idell James Casting, (310) 394–3919. In New York, try Wilfley

Grant Casting, (212) 685–3537, and Sylvia Fay Casting, (212) 889–2626. In Hollywood, Florida, try Famous Faces, (954) 922–0700, and in Chicago, call Holzer & Ridge, (312) 922–9860.

NEEDS: professional attitude.

Industry Showcase Organizer

Following in the footsteps of David Merrick.

Organizing industry showcases for actors can be an excellent way to earn money with your creative, organizational, and networking abilities.

Showcases have become increasingly popular as a way for hopeful actors to display their talents to important industry members. Agency representatives may sign up actors they like, and casting directors or producers may call in actors to audition for specific projects. These rewards do happen often, hence the popularity of showcases and the willingness of actors to pay to participate.

Performing in a showcase is similar to being in a play, albeit an extremely short play. The showcase generally takes place in a recognized theater space, with about eight or ten scenes (usually five to ten minutes each) being performed by about 20 actors. This enables actors to show their best comedic or dramatic prepared material while "talent scouts" watch.

Your job as the showcase organizer is to recruit actors, rent theater space, organize a dinner buffet, create the showcase fliers and programs, and advertise the showcase for industry attendance. You can gather actors through friends, fliers, acting classes and workshops, advertisements in the trades, or theater companies. First-rate, centrally located theaters will draw the highest industry response.

The first thing to do is book your space. Performing arts bookstores usually have information on theaters, or you can simply check the yellow pages under "Theaters." To draw agents, managers, casting people, and producers, you can place advertisements in local papers or deliver individual packets to your targeted market.

Your profit will depend on the overhead costs. Most showcases charge $200–$350 per actor for two to four nights of performing in the arranged showcase. An actress I went to college with puts on showcases every two months. She charges $350 per actor, and each then performs a scene four nights (two nights a week, two consecutive weeks). She makes at least a few thousand dollars profit per showcase, and she often acts in them as well.

Good Luck

BENEFITS: networking, you can *perform* in them, too!

PITFALLS: gathering actors for each showcase, risk of being thought of as a producer who runs showcases, rather than an actor.

SOURCES: the trades; networking; yellow pages.

NEEDS: business mind, organizational skills, networking ability.

IDEA: This same concept can be applied to musicians and singers looking for representation.

Industry Workshop and Seminar Organizer

Act as an agent without being called one.

Organizing industry workshops and seminars for actors is becoming increasingly popular as a way to make money while staying connected to show business. Setting up an industry workshop entails renting a studio and having about 10 to 20 actors pay $20–$40 to meet and do cold readings for a casting director, agent, or producer. It may seem unfair that actors should have to pay to meet a casting director, but this type of service often leads to work or signing with an agent. Seminars feature a panel of experts, sometimes over a two-day period, and participants pay a higher fee (usually a few hundred dollars). The profit margin will depend on your overhead (space rental fee, price of flier reproduction and distribution, and cost of moderator or panel). Good business sense, organization, and promotional skills are necessary for success.

To get started, visit a few similar workshops or seminars, usually advertised in the trades (*Backstage* and *Dramalogue*) and talk to others to learn what works well and what doesn't. A good idea might be to ask your actor friends what kind of workshop they would be interested in attending. You may want to work with a partner so that your personal time will be flexible.

It is possible to start with very little overhead. You can rent a studio at a modest price (check the trade papers, yellow pages under "Theaters," or *The Working Actors Guide* by Mani Flattery for a listing) or rent a hotel room and gather actors through personal contacts and by placing advertisements in industry trade papers, at theaters, and on union boards. A casting director, agent, or manager hired to lead a particular industry workshop will need to be paid for his or her time (the going rate starts at about $100), unless you can call in a favor or do some kind of work-related exchange.

Good Luck

BENEFITS: industry contacts, you can perform in them as well.

PITFALLS: tough to gather actors and industry personnel.

SOURCES: the trades (*Backstage* and *Dramalogue*), networking, yellow pages under "Theaters," *The Working Actors Guide* by Mani Flattery.

NEEDS: business mind, enjoy working with actors, organizational skills.

IDEA: This same workshop or seminar idea can be used for musicians, singers, and writers. Or how about gathering experts for a financial seminar? Or for new parents? A wide range of possibilities can be explored.

Karaoke Performer

The chance to be Diana Ross, Frank Sinatra, and Elvis all in one night.

Welcome to the Japanese version of the sing-along. Originally imported from Japan, karaoke has become quite the rage in the States. A karaoke machine enables anyone to sing a favorite musical number by deleting the lead vocals and playing only the background and accompaniment. Lyrics are supplied on lead sheets or a video screen.

As a karaoke performer, your job is to inspire others to break out of their shells and burst into song. You don't need to be an excellent singer to work a karaoke party. Often if you are too good, you may intimidate other wanna-be singers. The quality of singing and level of experience required of a karaoke artist will vary from gig to gig, but the objective is always to make people relax and have a good time. The parties are almost always at night, although the hours vary depending on the club. Shifts usually run from 8 P.M. to midnight or 10 P.M. to 2 A.M.

To get a job with an existing company, check the trade papers (*Dramalogue* and *Backstage*) for karaoke artists. Often the jobs will be listed under the guise of a "singer wanted" advertisement. You can also go to any nightclub that has karaoke and look through its karaoke magazine to find ads with phone numbers and possible employment opportunities. Call and ask if they are hiring singers.

If you have an entrepreneurial spirit and some spare cash, you can buy or rent karaoke equipment and start your own business. You will need to advertise your service in clubs, bars, and restaurants. Or you can work private functions. Go to places that do karaoke, check them out, and ask questions.

Even if you love the idea of being your own boss, it may be a good idea to work for an existing karaoke company first to learn the ropes. Check the yellow pages under "Entertainers." When you work as an employee the pay ranges from $10 to $15 an hour. If it is your own business and you supply the equipment, charge what market value will bear.

Good Luck

BENEFITS: learn and perform songs, good hourly wage, fun, meet people.

PITFALLS: unsteady income.

SOURCES: check trade papers, call karaoke companies, yellow pages under "Entertainers."

NEEDS: singing ability, outgoing personality.

"For the past four years, one of my part-time jobs has been performing karaoke at parties. Often I hook up with a DJ and we do a DJ/karaoke combination. I rent the equipment very inexpensively from a man I met and I hire myself out. I have performed at private parties, real estate grand openings, birthday parties, and retirement parties. Even though I'm a singer, I don't go into full performance, as people are reluctant to sing at the beginning and I don't want to intimidate anyone. It is so rewarding when you finally get everyone up there singing and having a great time."

TIM GAVINSKY, singer/karaoke performer/cruise ship entertainer/singing telegrams, Fort Lauderdale, Florida

Location Manager

Blinded and dropped off in a virgin forest, you'd find your way home.

A location manager is responsible for finding places for photographers or film companies to shoot outside the studio arena, such as a home or commercial space. Your job is to make arrangements to use the space involved, facilitate the "intrusion," and see that everything goes according to plan.

Besides finding locations, you will be involved in securing permits from the city, the state, or the police department—whatever is necessary. Your job will be to negotiate fees with property owners or individual cities and towns and to handle insurance matters. The police and local film board may need to be involved to make sure all rules and regulations are followed.

To work in this field, you should be familiar with the area you're representing, including interiors. Photographers and directors may be looking for anything from a mansion to a 1940s barbershop.

To find employment, build a portfolio of pictures of places you know and can get permission to shoot in. Do your research and then go around to photographers and film companies in the area with your portfolio. Most major cities and all states have a film board to call for information on film companies. You can also call the governor's office to track down numbers. Ask for the person who handles film permits and go from there.

It is always a good idea to apprentice when starting out, but you can make excellent money as a freelancer. Salary varies depending on the city and work involved, so call local competitors for rates. Expect to earn a few hundred dollars a day.

Good Luck

BENEFITS: creativity, good pay, flexible scheduling depending on when the shoot is.

PITFALLS: long hours.

SOURCES: film companies, photographers, directors, and your city or state's film board.

NEEDS: problem-solving ability, inventiveness, people skills, patience.

> *"Because film projects have a start and finish, there is always a point at the end of a project when I can take time to pursue my other aspirations, particularly my music. And you'd be amazed at all the exciting locations I've visited!"*
>
> MICHAEL PARKS, musician/location manager/scout, Los Angeles

Magician

Most kids had posters of rock stars . . . you had posters of Houdini and David Copperfield.

On my tenth birthday, my parents hired "Amazing Marvin," a magician who thrilled me and my friends with his ability to reach into his oversized pants and pull out a rabbit! To this day I can't imagine where he actually kept it (nor do I want to know).

Performing magic tricks is a specialized skill requiring practice, acting, storytelling abilities, and coordination. If you possess these skills and have an outgoing nature, you will be well-suited for this job.

To learn magic tricks, you can purchase a beginner's instructional video for $30–$80 at a magician supply store (check the yellow pages under "Magician Supplies"). Joining the Society of American Magicians entitles you to many benefits and will enable you to learn the secrets of other magicians. It costs about $40 a year to be a member, and even though the magicians are sworn to secrecy, they are eager and willing to swap tricks with fellow members. This is a great way to get the inside scoop on all sorts of showstoppers. Similarly, the International Brotherhood (women too!) of Magicians has chapters all over the world. Headquarters is P.O. Box 192090, St. Louis, MO 63119.

There are many places to perform magic for money. Family-style restaurants often hire magicians to entertain at tables while patrons wait for their food. Card and coin tricks and balloon animals are most appropriate for this type of atmosphere. Some restaurants, however, hold more extensive evening shows and hire their magicians out for private parties. Often entertainment companies (listed in the yellow pages under "Entertainment" or "Party Planning") hire magicians as well for corporate affairs, private parties, trade shows, sales meetings, seminars, and industrials. Another idea is to do a mass mailing of fliers directly to companies that are always in need of entertainment for private parties and conventions, such as IBM or Whirlpool. Or advertise in community newsletters, local magazines, and parent newspapers (just think of all those kids' parties). Contact cruise lines (see "Cruise Ship Entertainer," this chapter) and hotels.

Typically a restaurant will pay you $50–$100 for two hours' work, or they'll ask you to work for tips only. The going rate for one hour of close-up magic (private parties) is $250. A full-scale show can pay in the thousands. The cost of buying magician props and supplies varies from a few dollars for simple tricks to thousands for full-blown illusions and spectacle. You may want to offer to work private parties and functions for free or a minimum salary while perfecting your skills and building your reputation.

Good Luck

BENEFITS: get to hone your comedy and improv skills, short hours, fun, can make good money.

PITFALLS: expensive props and tricks, takes a lot of time and effort to learn, need to market your skills, unsteady income.

SOURCES: magic stores, in New York, Tannen's Magic, (212) 929–4500. Yellow pages under "Entertainers." The Magic Agency Inc., (212) 288–9133, and Wizard Productions, (800) 400–3836. International Brotherhood of Magicians, P.O. Box 192090, St. Louis, MO 63119. Private parties, hotels, cruise lines.

NEEDS: outgoing, hand dexterity, eye-hand coordination, patience.

Party Enhancer

Your class-clown shenanigans finally pay off.

You don't have to be Robin Williams or Rosie O'Donnell to be the life of the party—or, in this case, a professional party enhancer. Take your abundant talents, your creative ideas, dialects you've spent years perfecting, and the characters you create in front of your bathroom mirror, and make money performing at parties! Corporate events, banquets, film openings, birthday parties, charity events, and private functions are a few of the many events that hire party planning companies to supply ready-made entertainment.

Recently my husband's friend, who owns a catering and event company, called me to assist him with hiring entertainers. He was handling the premiere of a major motion picture, and needed actors and comedians to impersonate the lead characters in the film during the reception. It was then that it dawned on me how popular party enhancers are. An actor I know in Los Angeles earns an excellent living (he just bought a house) impersonating Columbo at corporate parties. He has put together a polished and hysterically funny presentation and hires himself out, often bypassing an agency's cut. An actress told me that her survival job is impersonating Marilyn Monroe at events and parties. What's more, she raved about the job.

Pay varies, depending on whether you work with an agency or hire yourself out. The typical range when working through an agency is $50–$200 an hour. For employment opportunities, look in the yellow pages under "Party Planning Services" or in the classified section of local magazines. Make up a catchy promotional flier and a business card. For continuous employment enroll with a number of agencies. After you have developed your characters, consider doing singing telegrams (see "Singing Telegrams," this chapter), if you can carry a tune.

Good Luck

BENEFITS: creative, fun, good hourly wage, great food.

PITFALLS: work may be unsteady.

SOURCES: yellow pages under "Party Planning Services," classified section of local magazines, self-initiated advertising. In Los Angeles try Mulligan Management, (213) 660–4142, and A Plus Entertainment, (213) 466–0295 or (818) 901–0559. In Fort Lauderdale, Florida, try Fun Time Promotions, (954) 566–3109. Deco Productions, in Miami, does conventions and high-end entertainment; call (305) 558–0800. In New York, New Jersey, and Connecticut, try Enchanted Parties, (800) 272–7843.

NEEDS: bravery, improvisational skills, well-developed sense of humor.

"I'm a comedian and an actress, and I sing. I took these talents and created three characters: Dr. Woo (who gets the most work!) is a Chinese doctor who really wants to be a party animal; Helga, the blond storm trooper (complete with German accent, helmet, and uniform); and Red Hot Chili Pepper (need

I say more?). I put together a creative promotional flier, registered with local agencies, and spread the word. I now work on a constant basis and am having a ball doing it. You don't even have to be that funny 'cause people are usually tanked!"

DIANE ADAMS, actress/party enhancer/trade shows/singing telegrams/commercial extra work, Fort Lauderdale, Florida

Personal Assistant

Be part of the lifestyles of the rich and famous without the costly overhead!

Running personal errands, making travel arrangements, returning phone calls, organizing dinner parties, shopping, car-pooling the kids, and taking a pet to the vet are just a few of the responsibilities of a personal assistant. Many people in high-power positions—from celebrities to business executives—hire people to aid them in a variety of ways. Personal assistants need to be extremely organized, responsible, and decisive. You will be dealing with high-profile, powerful people and doing everything that they don't have time to do.

Being a celebrity personal assistant can be great for anyone starting out in the entertainment industry. A friend told me that one year of being a celebrity assistant gave her more industry knowledge, contacts, and business savvy than five years of kicking around Los Angeles. She loved the travel and the invites to benefit screenings, not to mention the exposure to the celebrity world. When traveling around town as a personal assistant, you can even work on your own career, doing your errands (such as auditions!) while doing your employer's. Be forewarned that there is a ton of responsibility involved, both physically and emotionally. Sometimes you are actually on call 24 hours a day.

Salary varies considerably depending on experience, negotiations, and the generosity of your employer. Personal assistants make anywhere from $400 to $1,500 a week. In some cases, assistants live on the property of their employer, so room and board are paid for as well. A job as a personal assistant can be elusive, especially when it's for a celebrity. Jonathan Holiff, the president of the Association of Celebrity Personal Assistants (ACPA), estimates that there are 5,000 personal assistants in Hollywood. Most celebrities and powerful people seek referrals, so if you know anyone who has personal relations with celebrities, let them know that you are interested in the job. Also, hand out your résumé to the personnel department of studios (performing arts bookstores have directories that list specific studios and contact numbers) and indicate that you are seeking a personal assistant position. You can also contact employment agencies listed in the yellow pages and look for ads in the trade papers (*Variety* and *Hollywood Reporter*), as well as in the classifieds of your local paper. Another possibility is to work at a talent agency or PR firm, or on a movie set, and spread the word that you are interested in becoming a personal assistant.

The aforementioned Association of Celebrity Personal Assistants is a nonprofit membership-based organization that can help you tremendously in your job search. The membership fee of $100 a year includes a job bank for experienced personal assistants between positions. With over 350 members, the organization will assist you in networking with other celebrity assistants and gathering valuable information. ACPA members even teach a course on becoming a personal assistant at the Learning Annex.

NOTE: In Los Angeles, the Job Factory, an employment service, helps job seekers find flexible employment and receives many personal assistant positions. It charges $60 for membership, but if you bring in your copy of *Survival Jobs*, you will receive a 25 percent discount! Membership includes a free résumé service and guaranteed work.

Good Luck

BENEFITS: travel, invitations to benefits and screenings, exposure to the celebrity world, chance to make contacts.

PITFALLS: a lot of responsibility, physically and emotionally draining, often hellish hours, catering to the whims of the rich and famous.

SOURCES: contacts, advertisements, Association of Celebrity Personal Assistants, (213) 651–3300 in Los Angeles and (212) 803–5444 in New York. Studios or people in contact with celebrities: talent agents, managers, entertainment lawyers, accountants. The Learning Annex—call (310) 478–6677 in Los Angeles and ask for course number 587, or call (212) 371–0280 for course number 465 in New York. The Job Factory, (310) 475–9521.

NEEDS: well-organized, well-groomed, responsible, flexible, good interpersonal skills.

"Working as a personal assistant to a celebrity has been extremely advantageous for me as an actress. I spend most days out running errands, which allows me to stop for auditions while I'm at it. I like the fact that I'm not confined to an office and can easily adjust my schedule."

LISA TODD, actress/personal assistant, Los Angeles

Pianist for Sketch Comedy and Improv Groups

Free entertainment!

If you play piano by ear, have a wide range of songs in your repertoire, are a quick thinker, and enjoy working with actors, then somewhere a sketch comedy group wants you! In most major cities there are sketch comedy and improv shows almost every night from about 7 P.M. to 10:30 P.M. Working as a pianist is a flexible gig in that you can turn down shows anytime you are unable to attend, as long as you give enough advance notice. The group will tell you exactly what to play or what genre of music they want to hear during the acts and blackouts, and at other times. The job is a lot of fun and a great way to meet people. Best of all, you get to see theater for free. And drinks are usually included (as long as you can keep playing).

A show generally runs for one to two hours and the pay averages $50 per show. Some musicians agree to split the house (the cover charge minus costs) with the cast instead of receiving specific wages.

For employment opportunities, contact improv or sketch comedy groups in your area and request that your name be put on a list for available piano players. You'll find that the larger market is in sketch comedy simply because there are more of those groups around. Advertise your skills by posting signs at theaters and contacting groups through ads you see in the trades (*Dramalogue* and *Backstage*). Consider contacting cocktail lounges (look in the yellow pages under "Cocktail Lounges") for piano bar work as well. And, as always, the best way to get work is by word-of-mouth.

Good Luck

BENEFITS: creative environment, meet people, use your musical ability.

PITFALLS: challenging to find a stable, well-paying group to work with.

SOURCES: word-of-mouth, advertise in the trades, post signs at theaters, see sketch comedy and schmooze, call improv groups. A few popular groups in Los Angeles are the Groundlings, (213) 934–4747; Theater Sports, (213) 469–9689; and ACME Comedy Theater, (213) 525–0233. In New York, try Chicago City Limits, (212) 888–5233, and Gotham City Improv, (212) 714–1477. Call Second City in Chicago at (312) 337–3992; in Detroit, (313) 965–2222; and in Toronto, (416) 863–1162. In Seattle, call Unexpected Productions, (206) 587–2414.

NEEDS: enjoy working with actors, play piano well by ear, wide repertoire.

Production Assistant

Tell all your friends you're in "the biz."

Production assistant is a loose term that can be applied to many different positions. Generally, PAs are hired to do the lower-level work on a film production, either in the office or on the set. The job lasts for the length of the project and can be anywhere from a few days' work on a commercial to six months on certain films. PAs are sometimes hired for longer periods of time to work with video game companies on projects that can last up to two years. In general, PAs assist directors, producers, editors, costume designers, and production companies in general.

This is a great job for anyone looking to make contacts within the entertainment industry—many now-prominent entertainment figures started out as production assistants. Many people use this job as a stepping stone to more lucrative phases of production; contacts are made and skills developed. And if you stick it out and prove yourself worthy, promotion will generally follow, with increased pay.

The job often entails high pressure and a lot of grunt work because of tight production schedules. Generally you are expected to have a car with insurance to run errands vital to the flow of production. Wages vary, typically ranging from $300 to $500 a week. Prepare to work long hours and be available for last-minute requests.

Such jobs may be found in most major cities. *The Pacific Coast Studio Directory* (the yellow pages of studios in Los Angeles), *The Illinois Production Guide,* and the *The New York Production Guide (N.Y.P.G.)* are books that can assist you in finding studios and production companies. *The Hollywood Interactive Directory* lists interactive companies throughout the country and in Canada. These books as well as others can can be found at most performing arts bookstores or by mail order from Samuel French Theater & Film Bookstore in Los Angeles. If you're interested in working for a video game company, go on line and check out http://www.ugo.net/yellowpages or http://www.gamepen.com.

Good Luck

BENEFITS: involved in all phases of production, able to network with entertainment executives, good starting point for industry career.

PITFALLS: high pressure, abundant grunt work, long hours,

SOURCES: studio and production guide directories, the Internet—http://www.vsearch.com, http://www.ugo.net/yellowpage/, and http://www.gamepen.com. *The Pacific Coast Studio Directory, The Illinois Production Guide, The New York Production Guide (N.Y.P.G.), The Hollywood Interactive Directory,* (310) 315–4815 for mail order). Samuel French Bookstore in Los Angeles, (800) 8ACT–NOW.

NEEDS: enthusiasm, reliable, good organizational skills, usually a car and insurance.

Script Reader

Find the next It's a Wonderful Life.

If you like to read, have a talent for writing, own a computer or typewriter, and prefer to supplement your income in the leisure of your own home, script reading may be just right for you. Film studios, producers, and literary agents are constantly hiring people to read scripts and then write evaluations, called "coverage." This job is especially good for screenwriters who want to sharpen their own critical sensibilities.

Flexibility is the most significant advantage of a script reading position. You are also able to make contacts and keep current on what's going on in the industry. With some experience, you can even work your way up into a development position. Many major film executives started out as script readers.

There are a number of ways to learn how to become a freelance script reader, especially in major entertainment cities like Los Angeles or New York, where jobs are plentiful. You can take a class in story analysis at adult-ed and extension schools, such as UCLA Extension, (310) 825–9971, or the Learning Annex, which is now expanding to most major cities. To gain experience and build your résumé, try interning at a reputable theater or film company in your area that accepts and reviews unsolicited materials.

Once you have gotten a feel for the basics, contact anyone and everyone you know in the industry. Supplement your personal contacts with *The Hollywood Creative Directory, The Illinois Production Guide,* or *The New York Production Guide* (N.Y.P.G.). These books are available in most theatrical bookstores and list every production company in town. Call small production companies directly, as they will probably be easier to break into and may not require much prior experience. You can offer to do a trial coverage to show off your abilities, and then you'll have a sample to pass around.

Script readers usually earn $40–$60 per script. Reading and covering a script generally takes four hours.

Good Luck

BENEFITS: work at home, make industry contacts, sharpen critical sensibilities, improve writing skills.

PITFALLS: tedious work, an overwhelming wealth of poorly written scripts.

SOURCES: take a class, call production companies, showbiz contacts, *The Hollywood Creative Directory; The Illinois Production Guide,* (312) 814–3600); or *The New York Production Guide* (*N.Y.P.G.*). UCLA Extension, (310) 825–9971, or the Learning Annex: Los Angeles, (310) 478–6677; San Francisco, (415) 788–5500; San Diego, (619) 544–9700; New York, (212) 570–6500; Toronto, (416) 964–0011.

NEEDS: enjoy reading, write well, sample coverage of a script.

Singing Telegrams

The shortest shift in this book.

For all you future "Broadway Babies" (and former ones as well), delivering singing telegrams can be a fun way to make money. The only prerequisites are a decent singing voice and minimal dance ability. And, most importantly, you'd better not embarrass easily. Some companies prefer writers, since they think up innovative and quirky telegrams. Anything goes as long as you can carry a tune.

Most telegram deliverers wear tuxedoes, or are disguised as gorillas, nerds, bag ladies, and French troubadours. The companies usually supply costumes (or pay you extra if you supply your own), except for the tuxedo, which you are expected to have. Women will need the female version of the messenger tuxedo: fishnet stockings, black heels, a short black skirt or shorts, and a jacket.

The work is flexible, but unsteady, so sign up with a few different companies if you want to stay busy. Business booms around Valentine's Day and other holidays, so stay in town and be available to work at these times. Pay is approximately $35–$50 per telegram. Some companies will pay extra for traveling time. The routine takes approximately two to 15 minutes.

To find a job, simply contact singing telegram companies in your area.

Companies are listed in the yellow pages under "Entertainers" as well as in local magazines in the advertisement section. Some may prefer that you have your own costume, but most will help you out with initial material.

Good Luck

BENEFITS: extremely short shift, good wages, fun, creative, get to perform.

PITFALLS: unsteady employment, minor travel involved.

SOURCES: yellow pages under "Entertainers." Singing Telegrams Nationwide, (800) 545–3354. In the Los Angeles area contact Zebra Entertainment, (818) 906–3809; and Entertainment Express, (818) 376–6506. In New York, a few good ones are Preppy Grams, (800) 936–SING; Life of the Party, (800) 966–7456; and AAA Entertainment, (800) 43PARTY.

NEEDS: upbeat personality, singing and dancing abilities.

> *"I apply my writing talents and create a fun short medley based on information I gather about the event. I rewrite the lyrics to songs and use a tune that the requested party likes, for example, the Beatles or Cole Porter. I love when I get to do really interesting comedic telegrams sometimes with dialects and costumes. This is one job that doesn't even seem like work."*
>
> DONOVAN GLOVER, writer (coauthor of *Stripmall Bohemia,* currently being turned into a film)/singing telegrams/children's entertainment, Los Angeles

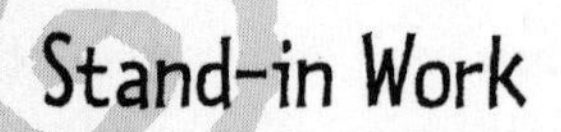

Stand-in Work

Hurry up and wait.

Production companies often hire actors to stand in for celebrities during grueling rehearsals at award shows, for contestants at trial game shows, and for lead actors on television programs. At award shows, for example, you might stand in for the host, the presenter, or the award winner throughout the three- to four-day rehearsal period. On game shows, you will play the game with the host so the production company can troubleshoot any complications that may arise. TV shows always hire at least one male and one female stand-in to fill in for any lead actors who can't make rehearsals. They will be stand-ins for all the featured roles at the beginning of each work week. TV show stand-ins need to observe and remember all the blocking of the series regulars so they can jump right in when needed.

To be hired as a stand-in, you need to have a positive attitude and improvisational skills, and be able to read a TelePrompTer for award ceremonies. Stand-in work enables you to work in the industry, earn a good hourly wage, make connections, learn a lot, and, perhaps, get to see many inspiring performances. If you are a stand-in for a TV show and are well liked, you may parlay the job into a guest-starring role on the show. A game show gig usually takes place over a week for about four hours, and a television gig typically runs five to nine hours a day.

Television jobs pay on the AFTRA scale (the minimum the union requires), about $20–$21 an hour. If you work for a particular show for an extended period of time, you can request a raise and become eligible for medical coverage. For information on current film rates, contact the Screen Actors Guild in your area.

To get a stand-in job, use any and all connections you may have. Contact production companies of shows you are interested in. You can find books that list all current production companies at performing arts bookstores, or call Samuel French Theater & Film Bookstore in Los Angeles for mail order.

When calling production companies, ask for the person who casts stand-ins and send in your picture and résumé with a cover letter mentioning any related experience. Better yet, find out when the person casting stand-ins will be available so that you can drop off your picture and résumé personally. Be forewarned: "Stand-in" is a misnomer—there is a lot of *sitting* involved while you are *standing* in. And if you are an experienced actor, this can be frustrating.

Good Luck

BENEFITS: good hourly wage, work in the industry, connections, meet celebrities, watch performances, medical coverage.

PITFALLS: a lot of sitting around.

SOURCES: contact production companies, performing arts bookstores for books listing current production companies, Samuel French Theater & Film Bookstore at (800) 8ACT–NOW for mail order.

NEEDS: positive attitude, improvisational skills, ability to read a TelePrompTer.

"I'm five-ten, and a number of years ago I worked as the stand-in for tall actresses on film sets: Sigourney Weaver, Anjelica Huston, Nicole Kidman, and Christine Lahti were just a few of the women I stood in for. The money was good and almost always above my day rate because of meal penalties and overtime. The main reason I would do it was to make my health insurance. I now realize how valuable it was to spend so many hours on a professional set. I learned the many technical aspects involved in filming and how important continuity is, and I got to go to some interesting places when we were on location."

KATHERINE NEWELL, actress/stand-in/party enhancer, Hollywood, Florida, and New York

---

Street Performer

You'll be allowed to toss knives in public.

If you have any kind of performing ability, you can hit the streets and make quick cash. From musicians and dancers to sketch artists and comedians, people making money off their talents can be found on the curb or in the subways. Wherever there are large crowds of people, you can profit. All you need is a canister or hat to hold the tips—preferably a very large one (think positive!).

There are all kinds of success stories about street performers being "discovered." Tracy Chapman was "discovered" singing in a subway station, and I know of a musician who got a record contract from performing on the Santa Monica Promenade for a number of years. A friend found his wedding entertainment by recruiting a group he saw performing at a street fair. A few years back during the holiday season, I even coerced my husband, who plays guitar, to come with me to Central Park to sing songs. I thought it would be a fun way to spend an afternoon. Some 30 minutes later, we were surprised to find out that we had made $25.

Anywhere there is heavy pedestrian traffic, such as tourist spots and recreational areas of your city, is a great place to entertain. In California, crowds congregate to see street performers at Venice Beach and the Third Street Promenade in Santa Monica. In New York, performers can be seen on subway platforms, in Central Park, at food and art fairs, at weekend flea markets, and at Broadway theaters during intermission. If you are playing an instrument, you will need to find a good acoustic area or bring along a small amplifier and microphone. Technically, in most cities, street performers are required to have a license (a vendor's permit, sometimes referred to as a peddler's license). Call your city or county clerk's office for information.

Your income will vary widely, depending on your act, the location, the weather, and how many people gather round. It is possible to earn $50–$100 for a few hours of performing. You can also earn extra money if you sell tapes of your music. During the holiday seasons, people are usually in the giving spirit and enjoy being entertained, so take your act outside and reap the benefits!

Good Luck

BENEFITS: cash, work outdoors, self-employed.

PITFALLS: unsteady income, variable weather conditions, distracting city noise.

SOURCES: popular outdoor spots, local city or county clerk's office for licensing information.

NEEDS: chutzpah, an amp and microphone for musicians and vocalists, a street vendor's license.

Theme Park Performer

Get to know Goofy personally.

Believe it or not, somewhere in the world, Groucho Marx, Charlie Chaplin, and Laurel & Hardy are still performing! In fact, theme parks often hire performers to impersonate a variety of famous comedians and TV personalities, perform in rock and roll shows, sing in musical theater, and risk life and death in stunt shows. This is a great job for actors and singers or anyone who enjoys being center stage. Millions of people visit theme parks every year, so an audience is guaranteed. You get to network with other performers, display your talents, and hone your performance skills. Typically, the job requires improvisational or musical theater skills, but stunt shows may need acrobats, gymnasts, dancers, and stunt people. Even comedians, announcers, magicians, and star impersonators can find work here.

Hours vary depending on your job and the theme park you are working for. Shifts are usually six to eight hours. A principal performer does multiple shows in a day, with each show lasting 20–30 minutes. Extra hours and shifts are available during Christmas, the summer, and spring break. Shifts are flexible, as you can usually find a substitute to cover for you.

To attract high-caliber performers, Universal Studios allows its employees to take time off for auditions and interviews as long as all shifts are covered. To make this possible, it hires full-time positions as well as "on call" positions to cover the regulars when needed. It also supports your career aspirations by allowing industry people to attend your performances for free. Many performers have gotten jobs or agents through their work at Universal. If you are a full-time employee, health benefits are available.

At Universal, you are paid per show (stint pay), and there are three to four shows in a day. Pay ranges from $22 to $55 a show, depending on experience and what the entertainment department determines. Most shows run 20 minutes, but you're contracted for the full day. If you are a full-time employee (three to four days a week), you are eligible for health benefits.

At Disneyland, usually three regular principals are hired for each job, along with a few subs. Disneyland principal performers must join the union, the American Guild of Variety Artists (AGVA) and are paid $141 per day plus benefits. Chorus members make $123 a day plus benefits. Performers are hired to work in the parades, wear character heads, and entertain people in line, but their salaries are much less, starting around $6 an hour. However, these jobs can be a good way to get in with the company, and regular pay increases are common.

Be aware that the work can be extremely demanding (demanding is a nice word for exhausting). Some shows are held outdoors, and wearing a full-body costume in summer is not always comfortable.

To get these jobs, you will need to audition. Advertisements are listed in the trade papers (*Backstage, Dramalogue, Hollywood Reporter,* and *Variety*) in the spring and fall. Occasionally people are hired in between, but these are often in-house calls when people in the shows put the word out to their friends. For information on current auditions for Disneyland or any major theme park, contact the entertainment department.

Good Luck

BENEFITS: use your talents to perform, make industry contacts.

PITFALLS: uncomfortable costumes, low hourly wage in some positions.

SOURCES: trade papers for audition information. For Universal Studios, call the entertainment department at (818) 622–3851. For Walt Disney World auditions in Florida, (407) 397–3220, and for Disneyland, (818) 558–2220. For Knotts Berry Farm auditions, call (714) 220–5386 or (714) 995–6688. A & R Wald Productions hires talent for Six Flags Magic Mountain, (805) 255–4859.

NEEDS: training in musical theater, stunt or impersonator skills.

Universal Studios Hollywood Tour Guide

Michael Ovitz started out this way.

This is a great job for articulate people who love to talk and have an interest in film industry trivia. The job entails giving guests an overview of Universal's film history in an entertaining and interesting manner, while traveling through the back lots. Shifts usually run for about eight hours, with a variety of available starting times, beginning at 7 A.M., although more guides are needed during midday. Weekend and holiday work is available. Advantages include being outdoors, seeing free screenings of Universal movies, and getting to watch shows being taped. When giving a tour, however, *you* are the star of the show, which is great for a performer's self-esteem.

The amusement park union is the International Alliance of Theatrical Stage Employees, otherwise known as Amusement Area Employee Union (AAEU), which has a $30 initiation fee. The starting hourly wage is $6, but pay raises are given regularly according to how long you have been on the job.

Open calls are held throughout the year, with seasonal positions available. You must be at least 18 years of age and must pass a prescreening interview and audition, which includes reading material from the studio guide manual. You need a working knowledge of TV and film, and a performance or speaking background is preferred. For more information, call Universal Studios or watch for ads in the trades (*Hollywood Reporter, Variety, Dramalogue,* and *Backstage*). Ads are usually placed at the beginning of each season announcing when interviews are available.

Good Luck

BENEFITS: work outdoors, free screenings at Universal, watch taping of shows, can be the star of your tour.

PITFALLS: low starting salary, difficult tourists, hot weather during the summer.

SOURCES: Universal Studios Hollywood human resources at (818) 622–6883, watch for ads in the trades (*Hollywood Reporter, Variety, Dramalogue,* and *Backstage*).

NEEDS: articulate, outgoing, love to talk and be around people, knowledge of film industry trivia.

> *"Being a tour guide for Universal Studios was the best job I ever had; I got paid to talk about movies all day. I'm a big-time movie fanatic and I saw about 250 movies a year. When my tram got stuck or my tour was waiting in line to see* Battlestar Galactica, *I'd entertain with movie talk."*
>
> CHARLES MCQUARY, actor/writer/tour guide/apartment manager/trade show presenter, Seattle and Los Angeles

---

Varied Musical Work

At your bar mitzvah you sang "If I Was a Rich Man" to your bewildered relatives.

My husband and I are a perfect example of how simple it can be to use your various musical talents to make some extra money. A number of years ago we decided that it would be fun to volunteer our talents by performing at a local Jewish senior center. We both sing and play guitar. Our first gig was rough around the edges, but soon we were taking requests and expanding our repertoire to include show tunes as well as Hebrew and Yiddish songs. Word spread, and soon we were in hot demand, earning $150–$200 for a 30- to 60-minute singing gig. We still enjoy volunteering, but it sure is nice to be paid. Besides performing at many senior centers, retirement homes, and temples, we have sung at nonprofit organizations such as ORT, the City of Hope, veterans associations, different sisterhoods, and private parties. If you love to perform, this can be a fantastic way to bring music to appreciative people and to earn good money for a short amount of time.

If you are a singer who plays guitar or piano, you can often hire yourself out as a solo performer and keep all your earnings. If not, you'll need to split the profits with a hired musician. You may also prefer to join forces with other band members and play at weddings, bar and bat mitzvahs, anniversaries, and birthday parties. Look in the trade papers to find other like-minded musicians, or enroll with one of the entertainment management firms listed in the yellow pages under "Musician." If you have sight-singing abilities or are extremely proficient with your instrument, studio work might be available. Courses to further your musical training are offered at local community and university adult-ed programs.

Salary will vary depending on your experience and the city you live in. Ask around to find out the going rates.

There are a number of ways to procure work; call the entertainment directors at various facilities to see what they pay, or start volunteering at places that don't pay and keep your business card on hand. Senior centers and retirement homes hire entertainment once a week or once a month, and many nonprofit organizations hire entertainment for their functions. To get a listing of senior centers, contact the department of aging by calling information in your area, or look in the city government listings in your phone book. Also look in the yellow pages under "Retirement Homes."

Good Luck

BENEFITS: get to perform, share your music with people, good money.

PITFALLS: work can be sporadic.

SOURCES: senior centers and retirement homes, trade papers, yellow pages under "Musician," department of aging, yellow pages under "Retirement Homes."

NEEDS: musical abilities, instruments.

Warm-up for Live TV Tapings

So that's how they get those TV audiences to laugh!

The audience at a live TV taping has a crucial role in the success of a show. They must be kept entertained and laughing so their high spirits carry over to the actors on the show. This is why warm-up jobs exist.

A warm-up is hired to keep the studio audience entertained and upbeat before and during the show's taping. This is a great side job for a comedian or anyone who has master-of-ceremony type skills. Improvisational skills are essential, as you will need to fill the time with humor, games, and prizes, and explanations of different aspects of the show.

The job is fun, the money is excellent, and it's a perfect chance to try out new material. While the hours are not demanding (a minimum of one day a week), the job itself is. You are often the scapegoat for anything that goes wrong. If an audience doesn't laugh enough, it's because of *you,* and if they laugh too much and get out of control, it's because of *you* as well.

To enhance your repertoire, visit different tapings and watch the hired warm-up to learn what works and what doesn't. Don't be afraid to ask questions of the people who hold this position. It is a good idea to make a sample warm-up tape; producers will request one to assess your abilities. Know that this is a coveted industry position, and that securing a job can be extremely tough.

To get a job as a warm-up, you'll need to network. When starting out, alert anyone you know on a series—actors, writers, casting people, or producers—that you are looking for work as a warm-up. When the main warm-up is sick, be willing to do the job at half the price. Another way to be given a chance is to say, "If you like me, pay me; and if not, don't."

If you don't have any current contacts, start making them. Contact producers who are in charge of warm-ups and introduce yourself. Listings of current TV shows are available in the *TV Guide* or *The Ross Reports.* For a list of television production companies, look in *The Hollywood Creative Directory* or *The New York Production Guide (N.Y.P.G.).* These are sold at performing arts bookstores, or you can call Samuel French Theater & Film Bookstore to order by mail.

How much you earn will depend on whether the sitcom you warm up for is shot on videotape or film. A half-hour videotaped sitcom generally tapes two shows a day, and you can expect to make $500 per show. A sitcom shot on film, however, takes about two to three hours and pays $700–$1,000 for the gig. You will generally need to show up several hours before the taping begins to see the run-through.

Good Luck

BENEFITS: great wages, fun, able to make contacts, practice new material.

PITFALLS: coveted position, 95 percent of people hired are established comics, scapegoat for problems with the audience.

SOURCES: network, contacts, call producers in charge of hiring warm-ups. *TV Guide* is sold at local newsstands, or look in *The Ross Reports,* published by the Film Group, (212) 536–5170. *The Hollywood Creative Directory* and *The New York Production Guide (N.Y.P.G.)* are sold at performing arts bookstores, or call Samuel French Theater & Film Bookstore at (800) 8ACT–NOW to order by mail.

NEEDS: comedic and MC ability, improvisational skills.

4

Do the Locomotion

Jobs for People Who Want to Keep Active

Aerobics Instructor

You can say the word buttocks with a straight face.

Working as an aerobics instructor enables you to maintain an incredible physique while earning some extra money. It is good for your ego since you are a role model for others—you become the leader, the fitness "guru." The shifts are short, the hours are flexible, and the perks generally include free club membership. Best of all, it will keep you motivated to work out when all you really want to do is stay under the covers and eat Häagen-Dazs.

Many clubs prefer that you be certified, and there are a number of ways and places to do this. The American College of Sports Medicine (ACSM) offers a national aerobics instructor certification exam that costs $150. Membership provides a career service bulletin. The American Council of Exercise (ACE) also offers an aerobics instructor exam for $175. Once you are certified, it will give you a list of gyms and health clubs in your area to help you find employment opportunities. Other certifying organizations include Aerobics and Fitness Association of America (AFAA), National Academy of Sports Medicine (NASM), National Sports Performance Association (NSPA), and National Strength and Conditioning Association (NSCA).

Many fitness centers will accept proof of completion from a local aerobics fitness program instead of these national certificates. Call continuing education programs and community colleges in your area. UCLA extension in Los Angeles offers a reputable program, as does Marymount Manhattan College Continuing Education in New York. Many clubs that don't require aerobic certification look to hire studio dancers who know how to create fun, challenging routines, and are experts on the benefits of stretching.

Once you have your instructor certificate, the International Association of Fitness Professionals, known as IDEA (the company used to be called the International Dance and Exercise Association), is a 23,000-member organization that provides continuing education, resources, and representation to fitness professionals. You do not have to be certified to become a member, and the group will help you stay certified through independent study courses.

Aerobics instructors usually earn between $10 and $60 per class. Some clubs will pay you on commission, so you'll need to fill up your class to make good money.

To apply for a job, contact the aerobics manager at the fitness center that interests you. Then fill out an application and perform your routine. Every major city has many health clubs. Check your local yellow pages under "Health Clubs" for a listing, or get a list through your membership in a certifying organization. Many health clubs have a number of locations, so when calling the numbers provided ask for the one in your area.

Good Luck

BENEFITS: stay in great shape, fun, free membership, flexible shifts.

PITFALLS: physically demanding if you have many classes.

SOURCES: classifieds and yellow pages under "Health Clubs," American College of Sports Medicine, (317) 637–9200; certification resource center in Indiana, (800) 486–5643; American Council of Exercise, (800) 825–3636; Aerobics and Fitness Association of America (AFAA), (800) 446–2322; National Academy of Sports Medicine (NASM), (800) 656–2739; National Sports Performance Association (NSPA), (301) 428–2879; National Strength and Conditioning Association (NSCA), (719) 632–6722. UCLA extension, (310) 825–9971; Marymount Manhattan College Continuing Education, (212) 517–0564. International Association of Fitness Professionals, (800) 999–4332, ext. 7; outside the United States or Canada, (619) 535–8979, ext. 7.

NEEDS: background in fitness or dance, experience, certification.

"Being an aerobics instructor and a personal trainer allows me to educate and motivate people to improve their health and wellness. It is extremely rewarding to be able to positively influence physical changes, which almost always lead to positive mental changes as well. I make good money, and having control over my schedule allows me more time for creative pursuits."

PATSY ZIMMERMAN, adjunct professor at Florida Atlantic University/aerobics instructor/personal trainer, Boca Raton, Florida

"One of my favorite survival jobs was teaching aerobics to adults and kids at the YWCA for about two years. I especially enjoyed teaching the preteens and helping them form a positive body image. It's a great job and it's never a drag to go to work. A free membership is a big plus, as well."

JONI EVANS, actress/dancer/aerobics instructor/waitress/dance teacher, Fort Wayne, Indiana

Camp Staff

Pine trees, blue skies, and panty raids.

Who doesn't enjoy sitting around a crackling campfire and toasting marshmallows? Fortunately for us, camps aren't just for kids anymore. There are senior-citizen camps as well as family, sports, religious, computer, drama, music, tennis, and weight-loss camps, to name a few. All of them need to fill staff positions. Most camps operate in the summer months, but there are also a number of winter camps.

Many college students and teachers find working in a camp extremely complementary to their work schedule. If you have any kind of special skills—lifeguarding, arts and crafts, dance, different sports, you might even be able to run one of the specific departments. Summer camp sessions generally run for eight to ten weeks, with a few additional weeks of preparation involved. There are sleep-over camps and day camps. One day off a week at a sleep-away camp plus a number of evenings off is common.

Working at a camp provides a wonderful social atmosphere. Working with children and being outdoors, often in rustic environments with a lake and trees, are other pluses. Cons might include having to sleep in a cabin with children if you are an overnight camp counselor.

Wages vary. Expect to earn a few hundred dollars a week plus room and board at sleep-away camps. Day camps usually pay a bit higher. Tips from parents on visiting day (at sleep-over camps) can add to your earning potential, especially for counselors.

Specialists, program directors, nurses, chefs, and other key staff members have their own sleeping quarters and typically earn higher wages.

To get a job at a camp, contact the camp office, which is usually open year-round, or look in the yellow pages under "Camps." Parent magazines are also a good resource, as is the back section of your local paper. Many churches and synagogues have camp programs, and the Jewish Federation, numerous Christian organizations, and the YMCA or YM-YWHA also have many popular summer programs. Your local chamber of commerce will have listings as well.

Good Luck

BENEFITS: being outdoors, working with kids, social atmosphere.

PITFALLS: can be noisy if you're a counselor and sleep in a cabin with kids, and the pay isn't terrific for the hours.

SOURCES: yellow pages under "Camps," parent magazines, federations, churches and synagogues, YMCA or YM-YWHA, local chamber of commerce.

NEEDS: energy and patience, special skill if you want to teach something specific, enjoy working with kids or the target groups.

> *"I started working as a counselor when I graduated high school. I've worked in both day camps and sleep-away camps. As a college student, it was a terrific job: low stress, fun, and a generally rewarding experience."*
>
> JEFFREY LEVY, SUNY-Albany college student/camp counselor

> *"Through an outreach program of the Lookingglass Theater Company we teach acting at schools and camps (sometimes doing a play or a one-day workshop). I just recently finished teaching a three-week drama program at a camp at the Old Town School of Folk Music to three- to ten-year olds. I have had many survival jobs in between work as an actor—from catering to handy work—and teaching drama is definitely the most enjoyable for me."*
>
> ANDREW WHITE, actor and founding member of the Looking Glass Theater Company/teacher, Chicago

Construction Work

Danger: big muscles and hardhats ahead!

When you were a kid, did your Tinkertoy projects turn into works of art? I remember how my friend Malcolm transformed our treehouse into the envy of all the neighbors. Today he runs his own construction company. Go figure!

Construction work varies depending on your level and experience and abilities. There are basically three levels of work. Day laborers, who do all the grunt work, including mixing cement, installing insulation, and unloading materials and equipment, earn $5–$8 an hour, often with lunch included. Helpers, the next level up, are expected to have an array of tools, including a full nail belt and basic power tools. They are paid approximately $12.50–$20 an hour. And finally, journeymen are expected to have table-level power tools; they earn about $25 an hour. It is wise to have health insurance if you're a journeyman since construction jobs can be hazardous.

This is a male-dominated field (apparently they've never met my Aunt Wilfred). Above all, you need to be strong and in good shape since the work is physically demanding. The job is flexible in that you can choose to work only on short-term projects. The hours are typically 7 A.M. to 4 P.M.

If you're just starting out, you'll need to work as a laborer to gain experience or work as an apprentice. These positions can be found through word-of-mouth or by simply showing up on construction sites ready to work. One way of finding construction sites is to go to city hall to find out where work permits have been pulled.

For specific construction jobs, check the classifieds under "Construction" or "Contractor," or contact companies directly by looking in the yellow pages under "Construction" or under specific contractor headings depending on your skills.

Good Luck

BENEFITS: builds muscles and stamina, both outdoor and indoor work available.

PITFALLS: strenuous physical labor, long hours.

SOURCES: classifieds and the yellow pages under "Construction" or "Contractor," word-of-mouth, city hall for construction sites.

NEEDS: some experience, strength, physically fit, tools.

"I've been working construction on and off for about 30 years. It is hard work and yet incredibly satisfying to build things."

GLENN SCHIFFMAN, writer/construction work/spiritual counselor, Burbank, California

Furniture and Carpet Cleaner

Free facials while you steam.

As much as you may not be wild about housekeeping, cleaning carpets and furniture can be a lucrative business. Apartment building owners may have carpets cleaned each time a tenant moves out, and in major cities this happens quite often. Cleaners are also hired for general upkeep and maintenance by apartment renters and homeowners, as well as by restaurants, offices, and corporations.

There are plenty of existing cleaning companies, but this is definitely a profession in which small upstarts thrive. To work for an established business, a responsible, friendly demeanor is needed. Some will want experienced cleaners and some will train you. If you want to start your own business, you will need to purchase an extraction machine. This will handle most of your cleaning needs: carpet shampooing, floor stripping, and most laundering of fabrics. Extra hand tools can be purchased for upholstery, stairs, and stains. It is always a good idea to have the phone number of an established professional cleaning store handy in case you run into problems and need assistance.

There are about six or seven different models of extraction machines to choose from that range in price from $650 to $1,500 (used machines and rentals are also available). Special chemicals must be purchased, which range in price from $3.98 to $20 and cover 20 to 30 jobs. The labels will tell you how each one is used, or someone in the store can explain which products are good for which jobs. McCalla, one of the largest retail janitorial supply stores in Los Angeles, has been around since 1938, and its employees are extremely helpful and knowledgeable. Many other large-scale stores can be found in the yellow pages under "Janitorial Supplies" or "Carpet, Rug, and Upholstery Cleaning Equipment."

The going rate is approximately 10–15 cents per square foot ($25–$40 for a 250-square-foot room) and $39–$79 for a seven-foot sofa. If you work for an existing company, you may work on commission. Your profit margin will depend on your costs, time, and labor. If you're starting out on your own, call other companies in your area for competitive rates. You will need to be insured and bonded. Call insurance agents listed in the yellow pages for rates. A city license or business certificate is also required. Contact your county clerk for information.

The best advertisement is word-of-mouth. To get your business off the ground, you can post signs at various neighborhood locations, make contacts with apartment managers, take out ads in local newspapers or community papers, and offer special discounted rates to first-time customers and friends, who will refer you to others jobs.

Some apartment associations (check under "Apartment Manager," chapter 1) have publications you may advertise in. For example, *Apartment Age* is published monthly by the Apartment Association of Greater Los Angeles for the Los Angeles County Apartment Industry. You can also let management companies and real estate agents know about your service, as well as people who remodel homes.

Good Luck

BENEFITS: flexible, relatively low initial costs to start your own business.

PITFALLS: unsteady income, work on commission, need to acquire customers.

SOURCES: yellow pages, janitorial supply stores, McCalla, (818) 786–2125. Apartment magazines, advertising. *Apartment Age*'s phone number for the editorial and advertising office is (213) 384–4131. City clerk in Los Angeles, (213) 368–7000; County clerk in New York, (212) 374–8314.

NEEDS: necessary supplies and equipment, experience.

IDEA: The same concept can be used for a number of different ventures. Invest in a piece of equipment—snowplow, lawnmower, floor sander, etc.—and offer your services.

Gourmet Food Delivery

Your fridge will never be empty again.

Any urban area will offer a number of gourmet food delivery services, which specialize in delivering prepared foods, often in carts, to office buildings during lunchtime. These services hire independent contractors, supplying you with packaged foods at an extremely discounted rate, which you then sell for profit. As you are responsible for transporting the items you sell, you will need a large cooler for perishables and a car to get from place to place. Companies generally look to hire people who are energetic and friendly, with good marketing abilities, who are likely to generate regular sales.

After a short training period, most delivery services will let you choose between a five-day existing route, substitute work, and route sharing with another person two to three days a week. The hours are approximately 7 A.M. to 2 P.M., making this job an ideal opportunity for parents who need to be available to pick up their kids after school. You are usually off on national holidays and the week between Christmas and New Year's. Potential earnings range from $50 to $150 per day.

In many cities, catering companies and gourmet food shops also deliver lunches. For a complete listing, look in the yellow pages under "Caterers" or "Gourmet Shops." Visit established office buildings in your area and ask who supplies lunch by cart and call the number. In Los Angeles, try L.A. Daily. In New York, two upscale delis that deliver lunches are Balducci's and Beauty and the Feast. If you have an entrepreneurial spirit and enjoy concocting creative lunch fare, you can even start your own similar service. Present your flier and menu at businesses around town.

Good Luck

BENEFITS: independent contractor, shifts end by early afternoon.

PITFALLS: early morning start, money varies with route.

SOURCES: L.A. Daily, (310) 559–0875 (ask for Chet). Yellow pages under "Catering" or "Gourmet Shops." Visit established office buildings in your area. In New York, Balducci's, (212) 673–2600; Beauty and the Feast, (212) 691–6135.

NEEDS: neat appearance, a reliable car with room for a cooler.

Handyman

Do you watch Home Improvement religiously?

When I was in college, I had a friend who could fix anything—from toilets to toasters, he was a whiz. He eventually used his talents to help cover the rising cost of his tuition. If you are good with tools and familiar with a variety of appliances, consider being a handyman.

There is no end to the number of different jobs you can hire yourself out for. In the past year, I have seen advertisements posted around town and even slipped under my door for painting, moving, hauling, carpentry, yard clean-up, electrical work, plumbing, and assemblage work.

If you are skilled in any of these types of services, you can easily start a business of your own, or team up with a partner to increase scheduling flexibility. There are plenty of free places to advertise, including bulletin boards at different organizations, laundromats, grocery stores, cafés, community papers, and temple or church newsletters. Introduce yourself to building management companies and apártment owners—they always like to be acquainted with someone they can call in a pinch.

The hourly rate for a handyman is usually $10–$20, depending on the level of skill required. Or you may charge on a per-project basis, calculating your prices by hours spent, tools needed, skills required, and equipment purchased. You may also want to consider an apartment management job (see chapter 1) so that you can make good use of your skills *and* live rent free.

Good Luck

BENEFITS: self-employed, good wage.

PITFALLS: unsteady work.

SOURCES: advertise on bulletin boards around town, in newsletters or community papers, contact building management companies and apartment owners.

NEEDS: jack of all trades, various tools.

"As a kid, most of the time I spent with my dad was when he was doing handy stuff. I'd hold the tools for him, and in the process, I learned a lot about plumbing, electrical work, and other odd jobs. When I got older, I was always building and fixing stuff, and people would suggest that I do it for money. Being a handyman has been extremely lucrative, paying $25 an hour. Unfortunately the work comes in waves, mostly through word-of-mouth, family, and friends. It's nice to be able to fix things for people, and to eliminate some of the stress in their lives."

CHARLTON WILSON, musician/handyman/mover, San Francisco and Los Angeles

Housecleaning

Do you already have a Dustbuster attached to your arm?

This job entails exactly what it sounds like: mopping, scrubbing, vacuuming, and dusting specified rooms in other people's homes. It is best suited to those who enjoy working alone or with a partner, and who don't mind physical labor. Even if you are the type who lets the dust bunnies collect under your bed, don't rule out housekeeping as a possibility. Many people who cannot stand cleaning their own homes actually enjoy cleaning other people's—maybe because they are being paid for it.

Each job requires three to five hours, depending on the size of the residence. You work out the schedule with the owner, which leaves room for plenty of flexibility. The going rate for housecleaning is $10–$12 an hour, or you can charge a set price (which may motivate you to work faster). A competitive set rate for cleaning a one-bedroom apartment is $40; a two-bedroom generally brings in $45–$50. Houses are usually $60 and up, depending on the number of rooms and the size. If you bring your own vacuum and cleaning supplies, you can often charge more.

If you choose to work for a service, your wages will be lower, but the service will find the work and set up your appointments, as many as four per day. The drawback is that the service gets about 50 percent of the job's cost. It is far more lucrative to have your own business and clientele, but you will need to do some basic marketing. You can advertise your services on bulletin boards, in salons, and in specific newspapers; hand out fliers and cards to everyone you know; and offer a first-time discount to people who are well-connected and likely to refer you to their friends and associates. It can be helpful to sign on with an existing business first, and then head out on your own after you have established a résumé.

If you prefer to work for an existing service, check the newspapers and the yellow pages under "Housecleaning" or "Janitorial Service." We Clean America is a big name in the greater Los Angeles area. In New York, try Townhouse Specialty Cleaning Company or Maid Power.

Good Luck

BENEFITS: flexible schedule, good wages.

PITFALLS: cleaning other people's messes.

SOURCES: call an existing service or advertise your own. Yellow pages under "Housecleaning" or "Janitorial Service." In Los Angeles, try We Clean America, (310) 839–2280. In New York, try Townhouse Specialty Cleaning Company, (212) 869–3465, or Maid Power, (914) 665–1000.

NEEDS: responsible, honest, an ability to clean well, cleaning supplies.

Mover

The chance to flex those muscles in front of the neighbors.

The average person moves approximately ten times in his or her life. The job of a mover is to go to peoples' homes, carry their belongings out to a truck, drive to the new destination, and unload their things into their new home. Packers are sometimes hired beforehand to box up the person's belongings. Be forewarned that this job is physically demanding—be prepared by bringing a weight belt and gloves. You'll get a great workout, so you can cancel that gym membership!

Movers usually work days or early evenings, with varying shifts. A typical job takes approximately four hours. Most movers are on call, which means greater flexibility but unsteady work and salary. Income depends on the company you work for and your level of experience. Generally, a mover makes anywhere from $6 to $15 an hour plus tips. A packer, who has experience in wrapping and protecting items, can make closer to $30 an hour.

For specific moving companies in your area, check the yellow pages under "Movers" or the classifieds under "Movers/Drivers." A few nationwide companies are Allied Van Lines, Bekins, Starving Students, North American Van Lines, and Moishe's Moving Company.

Good Luck

BENEFITS: flexible shifts, great physical exercise.

PITFALLS: physically demanding, unsteady work.

SOURCES: classifieds and yellow pages under "Movers." A few nationwide companies are Allied Van Lines, Bekins, Starving Students, North American Van Lines, and Moishe's Moving Company. For employment opportunities, contact the branch nearest you.

NEEDS: excellent physical condition.

Outdoor Wilderness and Teamwork Instructor

As an infant, you were raised by a loving pack of wolves.

Computer gridlock, congestion, smog, boom boxes—leave it all behind and become an outdoor wilderness and teamwork instructor. Adventure, majestic scenery, and fun await you in this physically demanding but highly rewarding job. In the field of experiential education, few jobs come close to matching this one in emotional and physical growth. Teachers, parents, students, or anyone with a block of time will find working as an outdoor wilderness instructor to be an extremely complementary part-time job. A number of schools handle this training; the most well-known is Outward Bound.

Outward Bound has over 40 schools throughout the world, and five in the United States. Clients include students, families, camps, and leadership programs, as well as corporations such as Kaiser Permanente, Deloitte & Touche, Rockport, AT&T, and US West.

Wilderness programs are year-round, and activities include mountain climbing, whitewater rafting, canoe paddling, backpacking, rope courses, and problem-solving initiatives. Programs can run anywhere from five to 80 days. Most instructors are hired for two or three courses at a time. The majority of work is in the summer, and some bases provide housing for the instructors.

The five schools in the United States work independently of one another. Outdoor experience and good leadership skills are needed to get a paid position. When you are hired, you will complete an initial training session. The school in Maine also hires interns through a program called STEP, which is based in Yulee, Florida. Working as an intern can lead to future paid positions within the Outward Bound schools; you will usually start out as a paid assistant before becoming a full-fledged instructor.

Outward Bound pays $30–$50 a day for an assistant and $50–$80 a day for an instructor. Room and board is often covered. For further information, contact the national office of Outward Bound or any of the individual schools. Other organizations in many cities have similar programs on a smaller scale. Check your yellow pages under "Youth Organizations." One independent program, Outward Bound Adventures, based in California, is a multiethnic organization that works with inner-city youth—middle school, high school, and upper elementary youths in behaviorally and academically challenging programs. Leaders who are college graduates are typically paid around $20 an hour, while counselors earn $15 an hour.

Good Luck

BENEFITS: dynamic training period at the start of the program, get to be outdoors in some exquisite wilderness, adventures, fun.

PITFALLS: the pay, can be stressful when working with kids.

SOURCES: yellow pages under "Youth Organizations." Outward Bound's national office is (888) 882–6863, or visit the Web site at http://www.outwardbound.org/obschools.html. At present, the five schools in the United States are:

1. North Carolina Outward Bound, (800) 841–0186.
2. Hurricane Island Outward Bound in Maine, (800) 341–1744.
3. Pacific Crest Outward Bound in Portland, Oregon, (800) 547–3312.
4. Voyager Outward Bound in Minnesota, (800) 328–2943.
5. Denver, Colorado, Outward Bound, (800) 477–2627.

Outward Bound Adventures (different from Outward Bound), at (213) 681–4068.

NEEDS: enjoy the outdoors, like kids, patience, handle stress well, ability to motivate others, good physical condition.

Painting Houses

You don't have to be Rembrandt.

There is always a demand for housepainters. Painting is the least expensive way to drastically improve the look of a home. Anytime someone moves out of an apartment, the management will have it painted for the new tenant, and homeowners trying to sell their houses will often have them painted to attract potential buyers.

Some of the responsibilities of painting homes or apartments include preparing the surfaces by scraping or sanding, covering the furnishings with a drop cloth to protect them, and then applying several coats of paint. If you have limited experience, go to the local paint store and gather all the printed material available to educate yourself on different methods and types of paint. You can then hire yourself out as an apprentice to learn the ropes. It is important to have an eye for color and detail. As with most things, you will become more proficient as you gain experience. The more experience you have, the more money you can make, and eventually you will be able to afford to buy your own tools and start your own business.

Going into business for yourself means advertising your services. Post fliers everywhere, especially around paint and hardware stores. Another good place to advertise is in local papers, or at community or religious organizations. As always, word-of-mouth is the cheapest and best form of advertisement.

You will also need to register your business. Call your local city clerk's office, tax and permit division, or county clerk's office. Many customers will ask to see your license. For information on licensing contact the state contractors board. I also suggest you get bonded and obtain some kind of liability insurance. Look in your yellow pages under "Insurance" and call for competitive rates.

There is an initial investment in supplies if you go solo. The job requires canvas drop cloths, buckets, brushes, rollers, an extension pole to reach ceilings, ladders, spackle, spackle knives, and . . . *paint*. It is a good idea to establish yourself with a paint supplier so that you will be able to get discounts and return your unused product.

The wage that you can expect as a housepainter depends on what is specifically negotiated with each client before you begin the job. Keep in mind you will need to include the cost of labor and all materials in your price. One simple room at 150 square feet should take you about three to four hours to paint. I was told by experienced painters that if you use middle-grade materials, the net profit will be approximately $100–$150. A 1,500-square-foot house interior, including ceilings, moldings, and doors, will take about three eight-hour days, and your net profit could be over $1,200. Get everything in writing and be sure both parties sign the contract. When you work for someone else, the pay is typically $6–$15 an hour, depending on your experience and how detailed the job is.

Good Luck

BENEFITS: abundance of jobs, good wages if self-employed.

PITFALLS: repetitious work, physically demanding.

SOURCES: advertising, work as an apprentice, referrals. State contractors board at (800) 321–2752.

NEEDS: painting experience, trustworthy, dependable. If it is your own business: materials, insurance, a business license, registration, and advertisements.

> *"I love painting houses because it allows me to be my own boss and set my own schedule. It helps me stay physically fit, and when the weather permits, I get to work outside."*
>
> DAVID NIMMS, writer/housepainter, Des Moines

Personal Trainer

Drop down and give yourself ten!

Personal trainers are not the drill sergeants of yesterday. They are highly trained, motivated individuals who assist people in becoming fit and healthy. Many dancers, martial artists, experienced weight-lifters, and health-conscious individuals become trainers. Besides the obvious benefit of staying in shape yourself, each personal training session lasts only an hour, making it extremely easy to create your own schedule.

There are generally two ways to earn money as a personal trainer: Work for a health club or work privately with your own clientele. The advantage of working in a health club is the stability of hours and clients. The club handles all advertising and equipment costs, free club and spa benefits are included, and you are often allowed to bring in your private clients when you are off the clock.

Most health clubs require you to be certified. The American College of Sports Medicine (ACSM) offers an exam for $220 that certifies you as a health and fitness instructor. The American Council of Exercise (ACE) also offers a personal trainer exam for $145. Both organizations offer a course of study and a list of recommended readings when they send you the applications for the exams. Other certifying organizations include Aerobics and Fitness Association of America (AFAA), National Academy of Sports Medicine (NASM), National Sports Performance Association (NSPA), and National Strength and Conditioning Association (NCSA). Many university extension programs offer certification in fitness training as well. In Los Angeles, UCLA extension offers such a program, as does New York's Marymount Manhattan College Continuing Education.

Once you are certified and working as a trainer, the International Association of Fitness Professionals is a useful organization that provides continuing education, resources, and representation to fitness professionals.

When working at a health club, expect to earn $10–$25 an hour. If you work as a private trainer, you will have greater flexibility and earn more money, but you will need to market your skills to gain a regular clientele. Most personal trainers who travel to their clients' homes or gyms charge $40–$60 an hour.

If you choose to work independently, good places to advertise for clients might be in a community newsletter, or at health and weight-loss establishments. Try giving complimentary or half-price sessions to first-time clients. Let established chiropractors and other health professionals know about your service, and consider a complimentary session in exchange for future referrals. Word-of-mouth is always the best source.

For employment opportunities in health clubs, check the yellow pages under "Health Clubs." One of the largest national health chains, Bally Total Fitness, hires employees based on an interview and their knowledge of equipment rather than certification. The pay is known to be on the low end, but it can be a good starting point.

Good Luck

BENEFITS: good pay, forces you to stay in top shape, flexible schedule.

PITFALLS: if you go independent, you'll need to build clientele.

SOURCES: yellow pages under "Health Clubs," classifieds. Bally Total Fitness, (800) 275–1795; American College of Sports Medicine (ACSM), (317) 637–9200; American Council of Exercise (ACE), (800) 825–3636; Aerobics and Fitness Association of America (AFAA), (800) 446–2322; National Academy of Sports Medicine (NASM), (800) 656–2739; National Sports Performance Association (NSPA), (301) 428–2879; National Strength and Conditioning Association (NCSA), (719) 632–6722. UCLA extension, (310) 825–9971; Marymount Manhattan College Continuing Education, (212) 517–0564. International Association of Fitness Professionals, (800) 999–4332, ext. 7.

NEEDS: extensive knowledge of specific exercises and equipment, certification.

"Usually by 10 or 11 A.M. I'm finished with my three clients and I've made $150. Not bad for a few hours of work. It gives me plenty of time for rehearsals or auditions and keeps me on my toes with my own physique, since no one wants a fat personal trainer!"

FRANKIE COMO, actor/personal trainer/apartment manager, Los Angeles

---

Private Mail Carrier

Never worry about becoming a disgruntled postal service employee.

We all know that insurance companies earn the big bucks—so why *wouldn't* they have their own private mail carrier?

Particularly in the insurance industry, there is a tremendous amount of paperwork that needs to be handled carefully and expeditiously. It can't be faxed, and after a while, FedEx becomes cost prohibitive. A former insurance salesperson was the brains behind Insurance Courier Services (ICS), a company currently servicing the western states and transporting those top-secret insurance documents.

As a private mail carrier, you do everything that a regular mail carrier does. You are supplied with a vehicle, uniform, route, and addresses. There are different shifts available depending on whether you are a mail carrier, a sorter, or a driver exchanging mail. Typically, a carrier works eight hours, five days a week. Hours can be shorter if you finish your route early. Sorters have somewhat more flexibility, with graveyard shifts and weekend work available.

At ICS, pay starts at approximately $8 an hour, with full medical, dental, and health benefits kicking in after 90 days.

To apply for a job, contact ICS, headquartered in Seattle. For numbers of other private mail carriers, look in the yellow pages under "Mail Carrier" or "Mail Receiving Services." Consider starting your own business by calling your local city or county clerk's office and asking about employment opportunities in your area.

Good Luck

BENEFITS: unsupervised, no-brainer work.

PITFALLS: tedious, long hours.

SOURCES: Call ICS in Portland, Oregon, (800) 929–0615; Idaho, (800) 303-2622; Utah, (800) 531–4322; and California, (800) 935–7773. Yellow pages under "Mail Carrier" or "Mail Receiving Services." Local city or county clerk's office.

NEEDS: responsible, good physical condition.

"This was a perfect job for me since it got me out of the house and required no intellectual effort, I could let my mind wander with creative ideas for my writing."

RICHARD KAHN (fictitious name), writer/private mail carrier, Burbank, California

Remodeling Homes

You added a new deck to your house . . . over the weekend.

Are you a do-it-yourself, fixer-upper kind of person? Does the idea of installing cabinets, tiling, creating moldings, or doing repair work seem as easy to you as boiling water? Then why not earn money with these skills?

There is a tremendous market for home remodeling, composed of people who need to fix up their homes before they sell them or want to improve the house they live in. People often live 25 years in a home without spending much money on it, and when the time comes to sell, they find they need to do serious work to meet the current building codes, or they decide to beautify the place so they can ask for a higher selling price. This is where you come in. People are eager to fix up their home as cheaply and as quickly as possible.

To get a sense of the business, learn the ropes, and build a résumé, I suggest working for a housing contractor. Look in the yellow pages under "Contractor—General." When starting your own business, call your city or county clerk's office for licensing information and insurance companies for public liability and damage insurance as well as bonding. You can contract other professionals if you are too busy or don't want to do certain projects. To find reputable workers, ask for recommendations at hardware stores, paint stores, and building supply companies, found in the yellow pages under "Building Materials." If you have the cash, or connect with a partner who does, you may even consider buying homes that have been repossessed from banks, remodeling them, and selling them for a very nice profit. This can be quite lucrative in areas where real estate is appreciating.

Your earning will vary greatly. Typically you should give a quote on the whole job, taking into account material costs as well as your hourly rate. Unfortunately, you'll find that often people want to cut corners monetarily but want the work to look expensive. As you learn more about the market, you'll be able to determine your own competitive price. When working for a housing contractor, expect to make about $12–$25 an hour, depending on experience.

To find work remodeling houses, advertise in local newspapers (a *Pennysaver* type paper) with promotional coupons. Often home and building centers provide bulletin boards for contractor business cards. You can also advertise at your local hardware store and in your community church or temple newsletter or bulletin board. You'll need a business card and information about past work readily available to hand to potential clients. As always, word-of-mouth is best.

Good Luck

BENEFITS: own boss, flexibility, good wages

PITFALLS: people often want to hire cheap labor, but they want the work to look expensive.

SOURCES: advertising in local papers, home and business centers, church and synagogue bulletin boards, hardware stores.

NEEDS: remodeling skills, tools, knowing reliable workers to hire out.

> *"When the company I worked for was bought out, the new owners brought in their own people and I found myself in my 40s without a job. While searching for work, I began to remodel my own home. The word spread, and soon I was remodeling other people's homes on a part-time basis while doing part-time tax returns."*
>
> MICHAEL GUNSBERG, part-time house remodeler/tax accountant, Cleveland

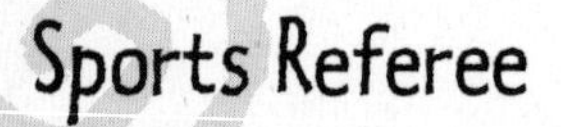

Sports Referee

You have a fashion fetish for black and white.

You always wanted to be on the varsity team as a kid. Or perhaps you *were* on the team and now want to rekindle those nostalgic feelings. If you are athletic, love sports in general or one sport in particular, being a referee or umpire may be a terrific part-time job for you.

Most sporting events need referees. They include basketball, football, swimming, diving, gymnastics, ice hockey, field hockey, baseball, softball, and track and field. The easiest way to become a referee is to start out at the high school level and work your way up. The National Federation of State High School Associates is located in Kansas City, Missouri, and for $4 plus shipping and handling it will send you a handbook that lists all the associations across the country, with contact information.

Each state has a high school association that sets its own requirements for youth league, freshmen, JV, and varsity. You'll need to take a rules class, then pass an examination. If officiating at the college level is your preference, you'll probably need to work at the high school level for a few years before applying to the college conference in your area.

To be an umpire at adult games, contact the city hall in your area and ask for the adult sports department/municipal sports program. There are adult and senior leagues in most cities. To become a ref or umpire at the adult level you'll also need to pass a test. City hall can refer you to the requisite classes provided by the community in which you live. There is usually minimal or no cost involved.

Salary varies from state to state depending on your experience and the games you ref. When working for the high school association, you can generally expect to earn $150–$375 a game. Working for the city, umping adult games, pays about $20 cash for an hour game. Not to worry, there are often three games a night!

You may also work at sports camps. Check out specific sports papers such as *USA Today Baseball Weekly* for sport camp and workshop opportunities.

SPECIAL NOTE: Ladies, don't be shy. This is no longer a men's only club! This could be the perfect job for all you "soccer moms." This way you get to keep an eye on your children and then penalize them when they break the rules. Sweet justice.

Good Luck

BENEFITS: easy way to stay fit, working with children, being around a sport you enjoy, exciting pace.

PITFALLS: irate parents and fans, people not agreeing with the officials call, can be seasonal.

SOURCES: National Federation of State High School Associates, (816) 464–5400, city hall, sports papers, *USA Today Baseball Weekly.*

NEEDS: enjoy the sport, familiar with rules and regulations, able to make quick decisions, like kids, pass the examination.

"I love softball, and being an umpire is another way to be involved with the game. I prefer working with adults so I don't have to deal with parents. I have fun, am outdoors, and meet a lot of people. The extra money is enough to cover my child support payments."

DON "TINY" TAYLOR, umpire/bouncer, Culver City, California

Tennis Umpire

Free U.S. Open tickets!

A tennis umpire is the person responsible for making sure the game is played by the rules. This job involves calling the shots, roving on as many as five to ten courts to handle disputes, and calling the score. You move up in the ranks as you gain experience. When first starting out, you will umpire junior, senior, and teen tennis tournaments. As you gain knowledge, experience, and proficiency, you can graduate to umpiring major tournaments such as Virginia Slims, the L.A. Open, and the U.S. Open.

Wages vary depending on the tournament and the number of hours worked. A 6–love, 6–1 match can get you off-court in as little as 45 minutes. Other days you may be on the court for as long as ten hours (with breaks in between, of course). You can earn anywhere from $60 to $130 a day. Hours are flexible, since you can choose the jobs that fit your own schedule. The work is primarily on weekends and sometimes in the evenings.

The USTA (United States Tennis Association) main headquarters is in White Plains, New York, and you can call for a referral number in your region. Basically, the associations all work in a similar manner. They hold a basic training umpire school a few times per year. The course is one full day and costs $15–$20. This fee covers the cost of parking, breakfast, lunch, and a copy of *Friends at Court,* which is the USTA official handbook. In the morning you'll go over the rules of tennis. In the afternoon there will be an on-court session with tennis players approximating a match and a no-fail exam given at the end of the day (my kind of exam). In other words, if you fail with the handbook closed, you can open it up, fill in the answers quoting the book, self-correct, and pass.

Good Luck

BENEFITS: fun, meet people, learn about tennis.

PITFALLS: people yelling, "Kill the ump."

SOURCES: United States Tennis Association, (914) 696–7000. Call the Southern California Tennis Association, (310) 208–3838; Northern California Association, (510) 748–7373; Mid-Atlantic Office, (703) 560–9480; New England Section, (617) 964–2030; Pacific Northwest Section, (503) 520–1877; Western Tennis Association, (317) 577–5130; and Florida Section, (954) 968–3434.

NEEDS: a love of tennis, responsible, fair, knowledge of rules, pass an examination.

Wallpapering

If the Three Stooges could do it . . .

Look up on the wall! It's a bird. It's a plane. No, it's wallpaper. Hanging wallpaper may be a skill you already have from decorating your own apartment or seeing your folks do it. If you don't already know how to hang wallpaper, you can learn this valuable skill by practicing on your own walls (it's always a good time to redecorate) or becoming an apprentice to a more experienced paperhanger. By learning the tricks of the trade—for example, metallic paper once creased is creased for good and grass cloth doesn't require a match—you can be well on your way to earning a decent hourly wage.

Paperhangers size up the room they are hanging and prepare the surface so the wallpaper will stick better. To gather tools, such as sponges, drop cloths, a ladder, and buckets, go to a supply stores. Paperhangers often work closely with interior decorators, found in the yellow pages under "Interior Decorators and Designers." To apprentice, look up "Paperhangers" in the yellow pages.

Being in good physical condition and having manual dexterity will come in handy. This job requires standing for long periods of time. It is also important to be comfortable on a ladder and have the ability to work patiently by yourself for a number of hours—possibly all day—in one room.

Pay will vary. It's customary to charge per roll of paper used. It usually takes about 20 minutes to hang a roll. Cost may also depend on the room—a bathroom will typically cost more, as there are a number of fixtures to remove, and shorter walls. A job usually pays about $300–$600 for a few days' work. Call wallpaper hangers in your area for competitive rates.

If you are not working with an established company, word-of-mouth is the best way to get work. Advertise or leave business cards in neighborhood stores, and try contacting local decorators for referrals. The International Brotherhood of Painters and Allied Trades or the International Apprenticeship Office can connect you with local unions, give professional training, and certify workers. For non-union apprentice programs, go through contracting companies listed in the yellow pages under "Wall Covering Contractors," "Interior Decorators and Designers," and "Paperhangers."

Good Luck

BENEFITS: if independent, you can control your own time and be your own boss, creative, immediate results, good wages.

PITFALLS: physically challenging, tedious.

SOURCES: word-of-mouth, advertising, local decorators. International Brotherhood of Painters and Allied Trades, (800) 437–7347; International Apprenticeship Office, (800) 276–7289. Yellow pages under "Wall Covering Contractors," "Interior Decorators and Designers," and "Paperhangers."

NEEDS: tools and ladder, experience.

> *"I learned wallpapering from my mother, who was always redecorating. I took a skill I already had, turned it into a service, and used it to make extra money."*
>
> LEONA ORCHARD, single mom/actress/paperhanger, Wheeling, Illinois

Working in a Health Club

Your workplace is the singles' club of the nineties.

For Americans, the need to work out is stronger than ever. Even my grandmother bench-presses 50 pounds (not really!). Today, just about everyone belongs to a health club. And why wouldn't they want to? Health clubs are *the* place to tone up, lose weight, de-stress, get a massage, make friends, or even meet a future spouse. Working at a health club is a great way to take advantage of all these perks—*and* make money!

Health clubs offer various employment opportunities. Receptionists answer phones, sales people sell memberships, floor management makes sure the club is running well on a daily basis, lifeguards work at the club's pool, and counter people work at the health bar. If you're a hardcore fitness buff, you may want to try your hand at being a personal trainer or aerobics instructor (see sections in this chapter). For those less physically inclined, there are plenty of other options. If you have good verbal skills and an outgoing personality, you are a natural to work in a health club atmosphere.

Working in a health club supports your efforts to stay in top shape. Facilities are at your disposal, and all those great bodies walking around will keep you on your toes. No more Twinkies! Since health clubs are open early in the morning until late in the evening, and on weekends, a variety of shifts are available.

Starting wages for counter jobs and receptionists range from $6 to $9 an hour and include free club membership. Sales people also receive commissions for enrolling new members.

For employment opportunities, check the yellow pages under "Health Clubs." Many clubs have a number of locations, so when calling the numbers provided, ask for the one in your area. One of the largest national chains is Bally Total Fitness, which has fitness centers all over the country.

Good Luck

BENEFITS: use of club and spa, incentive to keep in shape, energetic atmosphere, meet people.

PITFALLS: low starting wage.

SOURCES: yellow pages under "Health Clubs." Bally Total Fitness, (800) 275–1795.

NEEDS: communication skills, friendly, outgoing personality, *energy!*

> *"Working in a health club provides a great atmosphere—real familylike. I enjoy watching individuals achieve their goals, and a free membership is a definite plus!"*
>
> BRAD SCHRANEK, student/sales rep and personal trainer at Bally Total Fitness and Severna Park Racquetball & Nautilus, Towson, Maryland

5

Don't Be Shy

Winning Personality Jobs

Artist's Model

Are your bathing suits way too restrictive?

If you are uninhibited, comfortable with posing, enjoy silence, and are able to remain still for about 20 minutes, modeling for artists may be a good part-time job for you. Models are employed by drawing classes and professional artists to pose nude or partially nude. Many art schools have a model hiring department, and instructors have specific model books. You will often need to send in a résumé including any previous modeling work, your measurements, and a few photos, nude or clothed.

A typical session involves posing in a single position anywhere from 20 minutes to three hours, with short breaks. The reward, besides monetary, is seeing yourself in a drawing or sculpture. And it feels good to know you have helped fellow artists in their work. The pay is around $10–$20 an hour.

For employment opportunities contact art schools or the art departments of colleges and universities in your area. In Los Angeles, call Otis Design, FIDM (Fashion Institute of Design and Merchandise), and Cal Arts Institute. In New York, contact Parsons School of Design, Fashion Institute of Technology (FIT), and Institute of Design and Construction. In Chicago, contact the Media Center of the School of the Art Institute. To gain work independently, you can post notices on bulletin boards at schools with solid art departments or at independent drawing schools.

Good Luck

BENEFITS: help artists, see yourself in paintings, work whenever you're available.

PITFALLS: stiffness of joints, can be boring if you're not the silent contemplative type, no pockets for tips!

SOURCES: contact art and photography schools. Otis Design, (310) 665–6800; FIDM (Fashion Institute of Design and Merchandise), (213) 624–1200; Cal Arts Institute, (805) 496–6906; Parsons School of Design, (212) 229–8900; Fashion Institute of Technology (FIT), (212) 217–7999; Institute of Design and Construction, (718) 855–3661; the Media Center of the School of the Art Institute, (312) 899–5081 (ask for Renee Ness).

NEEDS: comfortable with nudity and posing, ability to remain still, good bladder control!

Audience Recruiting, Booking, and Coordinating

Do you love to boss around large groups of people?

Turn on the TV and you will hear audiences laughing, asking questions, or, if it's an infomercial, trying a product. Talk shows, infomercials, pilots, and sitcoms hire part-time freelance people who are good at promotion and sales to manage such audiences. There are a variety of positions available, including audience recruiters, audience bookers, and audience coordinators. Being outgoing, organized, and personable are the sought-after qualities for these positions. An actor I know has been involved in all these capacities at one time or another. He has made excellent money and found the work fun, flexible, and a great way to meet people. For an actor, these jobs can also be a good way to make important industry contacts.

Audience Recruiters

Audience recruiters are responsible for going out into the streets, malls, theaters, concerts, and parties, and anywhere else that people congregate, to hand out passes or tickets for a particular show. The tickets are coded, and you are paid by how many people show up. Pay ranges from $5 to $10 a head, although the price can be higher if it's a project that the audience will actually be involved in. The law of averages states that about 10 percent of all the people you approach will show up. It goes without saying that the percentage is higher if the show features a spectacular guest.

Audience Bookers

Audience bookers are in charge of booking groups (college clubs, social groups) over the telephone to come to shows. Groups are essential to a show's success. Wages vary depending on the studio, but the booker usually makes $50–$100 per show. Full-time workers in this area can make a salary of $400 and up a week.

Audience Coordinators

Audience coordinators are responsible for placing audience members in seats. This may not seem important, but balance in terms of ethnicity, age, and sex reflects a show's values. Once again, income will vary. Full-time workers can make anywhere from $400 to $1,200 a week, while freelance workers can earn $50–$100 per show.

As usual, having contacts is the best way to get one of these positions. Another way is looking in *TV Guide* to see what's being taped in your area and calling those specific studios. Ask for the audience relations department, and stress any promotional experience you have. Performing arts bookstores are still another source; they have updated information on shows currently being taped and the studios that produce them. One informative book is called *The Ross Reports,* published by the Film Group.

Good Luck

BENEFITS: fun, meet people, make industry contacts.

PITFALLS: freelance jobs equal unsteady money, shows are sometimes canceled.

SOURCES: contacts, audience relations department of studios, *TV Guide.* For *The Ross Reports,* published by the Film Group, call (212) 536–5170 for information, or fax your order to (212) 536–5294.

NEEDS: chutzpah, previous promotional experience.

City Tour Guide

You're sick of doing it for freeloading out-of-town guests.

A tour guide gives a factual and comprehensive history and bits of trivia about various city sites while riding on a tourist bus or private coach. Tours can range from three hours to a full day. Depending on your city, trips can include local beaches, zoos, famous sites, and the ever-popular celebrity homes.

This job is especially good for a person who knows his or her city extremely well, remembers funny stories and facts, has many hobbies and diverse interests, is familiar with a variety of local restaurants, and speaks more than one language. To be hired as a guide, you must enjoy talking and have good interpersonal skills. A good tour is really a type of performance, so the ability to improvise is also helpful.

Part-time, full-time, or freelance work is available, as well as weekend work, depending on the company. There are many advantages to this job: meeting people from around the world, seeing different locations, performing for audiences, and, if you choose to develop your own tour business, being your own boss. Depending on your city and experience, salary will range from $6 to $20 an hour, plus tips, which are usually shared with the driver.

A number of travel departments at community colleges offer tour guide courses and help you find employment upon completion. For example, West L.A. College's travel department offers a tour escorting and planning program. The program meets once a week for 18 weeks.

In certain cities, such as New York, a tour guide license is required. A license can be purchased for about $50 from the department of consumer affairs, after you have passed an exam determining your knowledge of the city. A tour guide publication specific to your city is an excellent resource to help you study. Michelin Travel Publications publishes tour guide and travel books for most major cities.

For employment opportunities, look in the local yellow pages under "Tours—Operators and Promoters." Allied Tours has offices in New York, Los Angeles, and Hawaii. About America Tours offers tours in New York, Washington, D.C., Boston, and Niagara Falls. There are numerous smaller companies as well. If you wish to start your own freelance business, check out the book *Start and Run a Profitable Tour Guiding Business* by B. Braidwood, S. Boyce, and R. Cropp.

Good Luck

BENEFITS: meet a variety of people, learn about your city, get to use your foreign languages.

PITFALLS: some companies require you to work a few tours in a day.

SOURCES: yellow pages under "Tours—Operators and Promoters." Travel departments at community colleges. West L.A. College's travel department, (310) 287–4293. Tour guide license. In New York, call the Department of Consumer Affairs, (212) 487–4161. Michelin Travel Publications, (800) 423–0485; Allied Tours in New York, (212) 869–5100; Los Angeles, (310) 215–0944; and Hawaii, (808) 924–3445. About America Tours, (212) 391–7316.

NEEDS: good people skills, affinity for trivia, excellent knowledge of your city, a license in some cities.

"Travel is something that I've always been interested in and I enjoy meeting people and teaching them about my city, so I thought this would be a good way to earn extra money. I get to utilize my knack for retaining useless bits of information and trivia, and get to perform for a captive audience."

ELIZABETH PFEIFFER, actress/city tour guide, Hollywood

Custom-Made Closets

Now we can all come out of the closet.

Organizing, designing, and installing closets has been a thriving (if little-known) business for a number of years. It all started when Imelda Marcos opened a closet door and hundreds of shoes tumbled down on her . . .

A customer who calls a closet company is given an appointment for a free consultation. Then you, as the sales person and designer, go to the home, find out what the customer's goals are, take measurements, figure out a workable design, and give a price quote. You then drop off your assessment plans, and a company installer will put the closet together and handle the rest of the deal.

This job is perfect for someone who has a flair for design and interior decorating. Keep in mind, though, that the emphasis here is on sales. You need to convince your customers of the merit of your design, and urge them to go forward with the actual installation. Working for a closet company can be both flexible and lucrative. You tell the company what your schedule is and it sets up appointments accordingly. A consultation usually takes 30 to 60 minutes, and, of course, travel time is involved.

Most closet companies hire sales people to work on a commission basis, with corporate benefits after three months. Your commission is 8–12 percent of the job. The jobs usually range from $300 to $10,000. If you work part-time, it's not uncommon to pull in $400 a week or more. Since it is commission based, the more time and energy you put into it, the more money you'll earn. The average company closing ratio is one in two jobs.

Initially there is one week of required training, and then sales meetings a few times a month. For more information on employment opportunities check the yellow pages under "Closets" or look in the classifieds. Closet World services all of Southern California. Closet Factory and The Closet Factory (two different companies) service a number of areas around the country, including New Jersey; Long Island; Norwalk, Connecticut; Hicksville, New York; Georgia; Tennessee; Florida; California; and Los Angeles and Orange County.

NOTE: You can also take your organizational skills (with or without the design and installation part) and work independently. A friend of mine who is an actress and mom literally organizes peoples' belongings in closets and offices on a freelance basis for $12 an hour.

Good Luck

BENEFITS: set your own schedule, good wage potential.

PITFALLS: commission means unsteady salary, people not showing up for appointments.

SOURCES: yellow pages under "Closets," classifieds. Closet World, (800) 452–5673, services all of Southern California. Closet Factory and The Closet Factory (two different companies) service a number of areas around the country: New Jersey, (800) 720–8270; Long Island City, New York, (718) 361–6310; Norwalk, Connecticut, (203) 854–9767; Hicksville, New York, (516) 932–3737; Georgia, (800) 756–1752; Tennessee, (800) 895–1333; Florida, (888) 741–3888; California, (800) 595–7080; Los Angeles and Orange County, (800) 692–5673.

NEEDS: helpful, friendly demeanor, sales experience preferred.

1–800–DENTIST

Help improve the smiles of the American population.

I'm sure many of you have seen those friendly commercials for 1–800–DENTIST, but I bet you weren't aware that they hire actors and other congenial, outgoing individuals as operators to actually handle the calls. These operators assist people in finding the appropriate dentist depending on special needs, location, insurance, and orthodontal requirements. 1–800–DENTIST is now servicing about 30 states, with the main corporate office in California. At the time of this book's publication, hiring is done only in California.

This is the way the system works: Dentists pay a fee to become members. They are screened by the company and checked for references and reputation, and they are eliminated from the list if there are any complaints. Upon company approval, the names of dentists and their office locations are programmed into the computer.

As a customer service operator, you will work loosely from a script, having basic points to cover when people call in. You will then determine what type of dentist is needed and give your caller the background and qualifications of the selected dentist.

This job requires a combination of basic phone operator skills and customer service and sales skills. Basic computer know-how and a personable, patient, and courteous manner are musts. It is a flexible job in that you can switch shifts freely or leave early if it's slow. Shifts are from five to seven hours, and most employees work 25–30 hours a week. A masseuse, hired by the company, comes in once a week and gives everyone 15-minute neck and shoulder massages (sounds like this company knows how to take care of its employees!).

Starting salary is $8 an hour. Raises of up to 75 cents an hour after each 90-day period are available based on performance, attendance, and attitude. The company gives frequent bonuses for a variety of reasons such as quotas being reached, incoming calls being turned into referrals, and maintaining a great attitude.

To apply for a job, call (201) 843–2144 and ask for the human resources or personnel department.

Good Luck

BENEFITS: flexible shifts, sitting down, bonuses, weekly massage.

PITFALLS: can be tedious.

SOURCES: call (201) 843–2144.

NEEDS: basic computer skills, a personable, courteous, and professional speaking voice.

Direct Marketing of Cosmetics

Ding-dong, Avon calling.

No doubt you have heard of Avon cosmetics or have seen that prized pink Mary Kay Cadillac cruising around, but did you know how lucrative it can be to work for one of these companies? Mary Kay Skin Care & Cosmetics is not only the number-one-selling cosmetics company, it is one of the esteemed Fortune 500 companies and one of the ten best companies for women to work for. There are 375,000 consultants nationwide. You are not restricted to a particular selling area, so you can sell the product line anywhere, at any time. Both Avon and Mary Kay allow their products to be sold through any number of channels—parties, setting up shop, or even door to door.

The job can be very flexible, since your earnings depend on your efforts. You need to market your products by networking with others, and you are paid 50 percent of everything you sell, plus bonuses. An actress I know offers free facials and makeovers to inspire people to test the products. New products come out every year, and they are advertised in magazines such as *Better Homes and Gardens* and *New Woman.* This is a great advertising tool, and you don't have to pay for it. Mary Kay and Avon offer free skin-care classes to teach consultants about the new lines.

For further information call Mary Kay and Avon. They will then refer you to a senior consultant in your area who will show you the ropes. There are other cosmetic companies to work for as well. Look in your local yellow pages under "Cosmetics—Retail."

Good Luck

BENEFITS: flexible, meet people, reorders, learn about makeup and skin care, bonuses.

PITFALLS: unsteady income, work on commission.

SOURCES: yellow pages under "Cosmetics—Retail," Mary Kay, (800) 627–9529; Avon, (800) 858–8000.

NEEDS: outgoing, upbeat personality, networking abilities.

Food Demonstrator

Try Vitameatavegamin.

Presenting a specific food product to the public and giving out free samples to increase product awareness and sales is a great job for outgoing Benihana wanna-bes. Demos occur at peak shopping hours, on the weekends, or early evenings during the week. Grocery stores, specialty food shops, and malls are the most popular areas for presenting food. Different locations and free product leftovers are the key advantages of this job. Most employees work two to three shifts a week, and shifts usually last four to six hours. Employees of all ages are hired, and many demo businesses will hire and train you over the phone, which cuts down on your travel time. Owning a car is a must since locations vary. Some companies will send you out only within ten miles of your home if you request it. Certain companies will require you to supply your own appliances (such as a blender or skillet) to demonstrate a product. Be aware that some jobs may require slightly more physical work if you need to lift cartons, crates, or heavy food items.

Pay ranges from $6 to $10 an hour, and most small, local agencies pay the lower hourly wage. To obtain a higher wage, seek employment directly from gourmet or specialty food stores. Some companies also provide mileage and drive time compensation.

For employment, contact different food demo businesses listed in the yellow pages business-to-business directory, under "Demonstration Service Merchandise." Ask for the supervisor in your area. Demo Deluxe services all of California, Idaho, Utah, Oregon, Washington, Nevada, Arizona, and New Mexico. A national company serving the entire country is Foodtemp, which pays $8–$10 an hour, and is the official agency that supplies demonstrators for the Fancy Food Industry Trade Show held two times a year on both the East and West Coasts. Yet another way to gain employment is to approach demonstrators you see working in local stores and ask them who they work for.

Good Luck

BENEFITS: flexible, weekend and evening work, leftover food.

PITFALLS: tedious work, standing

SOURCES: demo marketing companies. Demo Deluxe, (714) 974–1700; Foodtemp, (800) 231–9090. Yellow pages business-to-business directory, under "Demonstration Service Merchandise."

NEEDS: outgoing personality, well-groomed, love or knowledge of food.

"I started working part-time as a food demonstrator simply to pay the bills. Impressed with my people skills, the company I worked for recently offered me a full-time position in sales with the bonus of traveling around the country. Since one of my other passions is traveling, it was an offer I couldn't refuse. It will be nice to have a steady paycheck for a while."

MICHELLE ROBINSON, actress/food demonstrator, Los Angeles

Fragrance Model

Your natural pheromones consistently help get you dates.

Erase the memory of your mother struggling to avoid the spray of perfume as she walked through department stores dragging you behind her. Today being a fragrance model means something different. You no longer have to aggressively accost people with bottles of strong-scented perfume. In fact, fragrance companies prefer that you not be too pushy.

The objective of a fragrance model is to get the word out on a new perfume. The job entails spraying perfume on a card and asking interested shoppers if they would like to try a new fragrance. Outgoing, personable people with a good sense of style are hired for this position. Fragrance modeling is a freelance position. Shifts run for about four hours, and wages are usually $10–$15 an hour depending on experience and whether you work directly for a fragrance company or go through an agency.

Employment as a fragrance model can be secured in a variety of ways. You can go directly to fragrance counters in department stores in your area and ask for information. Call human resources at different perfume manufacturers, frequent department stores on the weekends, ask fragrance models for contact numbers, or go through a promotional agency. One agency, Promotional Services, has offices in Beverly Hills and San Diego. They hire models for trade shows and conventions (see "Trade Shows and Conventions," this chapter), as well as standard department store work.

Good Luck

BENEFITS: good hourly wage, meet people, smell nice.

PITFALLS: standing, pressure to sell, unsteady work.

SOURCES: fragrance counters at department stores, human resource department of perfume companies, fragrance models for contact numbers, promotional agencies. Promotional Services, (310) 659–3888.

NEEDS: outgoing, personable, sense of style.

Fundraising

"Show me the money!"

Universities, foundations, and many nonprofit companies and organizations hire a staff to help raise necessary funds. Universities typically employ students to work in their development office contacting alumni. This job is especially beneficial, as students get to see what others have done with their degrees. Fundraising parties and free admission to museums and other nonprofit organizations are some of the perks.

Telemarketing, data entry, and face-to-face solicitation are a few of the part-time, flexible fundraising positions. Weekend and evening hours are available. Telemarketers solicit contributions, and data entry employees input the data telemarketers receive, plus mailing lists and other pertinent information. Face-to-face solicitors set up meetings and work to get funds donated. Successful fundraising requires persuasive skills, tenacity, and a friendly, professional attitude. You learn how to ask for what you want, which is an ability that will serve you well in different arenas of life.

Pay scale varies, but it is usually a base salary plus commission based on the amount of pledges that come in. Expect an hourly wage of $7–$20. Data entry people make about $10–$18 an hour depending on the city. Part-time in-person fundraisers make about $25,000–30,000 a year.

To get a job in fundraising, go to the development office at your university or call different foundations. Look in the yellow pages under "Foundations—Educational, Philanthropic, Research, Etc." Most large cities have a foundation center (call information for the one in your city). Your library has a book called *The Foundation Directory,* which is an excellent resource tool, or use the World Wide Web to look up nonprofit organizations. Use your Web browser, for example, Netscape or Internet Explorer, choose one of the many search engines available, such as Yahoo, Infoseek, or Excite, and type in "nonprofit organizations."

Good Luck

BENEFITS: fundraising parties, learning persuasive skills, flexible hours, free admission to museums, contacts.

PITFALLS: dealing with rejection.

SOURCES: universities, nonprofit organizations, hospitals. The Foundation Center in New York, (212) 620–4230. Yellow pages under "Foundations—Educational, Philanthropic, Research, Etc." Your library has a book called *The Foundation Directory.*

NEEDS: persuasive, friendly demeanor, professional attitude.

> *"Fundraising has afforded me the opportunity to speak with alumni and see how they are using their degrees,* and *make some extra money."*
>
> NAKIA S.P. PIERRE, student/fundraiser, New York

> *"As a student at Wayne State University, I worked in the development office. I met faculty from all different departments, developed speaking and writing skills that have translated well into my current public relations job, and got to bring home all the sandwich leftovers from each night's phone-a-thon!"*
>
> LINDA URBAN, promotional director, Vromans Bookstore, Pasadena, California

Hairstylist

The next best thing to being a therapist.

You don't have to be Jose Eber to earn money cutting and styling hair. Many salons hire part-time hairstylists to work day, evening, or weekend shifts. Also, quite a number of hairstylists go to people's homes and work on a freelance basis. Job description may include shampooing, cutting, and styling the hair, as well as perming, straightening, highlighting or dyeing, or even styling wigs and hairpieces. It is extremely important to keep on top or ahead of styles and trends.

To start off, you need to be licensed through the state board of cosmetology (which costs only about $30); call information in your area for the phone number. Typically, 1,600–2,000 hours of beauty school must be completed, along with a theory and practical test. This will take anywhere from eight months to a year and a half depending on whether you attend part-time or full time. Beauty school typically costs a few thousand dollars, and the school will often handle licensing matters for you. To obtain a license, you must pass a practical and written exam. Primarily, sanitary measures are emphasized in these exams, as you will learn most of the specific techniques after school when you are employed as an assistant at a reputable salon. Beauty schools are listed in the yellow pages, and often in the classifieds. Some universities also offer training. You will need to renew your license every 1–2 years, which usually costs around $30–40.

Salary varies depending on whether you rent a station at a salon and provide most of your own clientele or work for a salon. If you rent a station, expect to pay about $50 for the day and earn $25–$50 an hour depending on how busy you are. At a salon where you are hired as an employee, you can expect to keep a commission of 60 percent plus tips; expect to earn $8–$20 an hour. The busier you are in either case, the more money you make. So a friendly demeanor is just as important as talent.

To get a job, network with other hairstylists, look in the classifieds under "Beauty Salons," and walk into salons and ask if they are hiring.

Good Luck

BENEFITS: creative freedom, self-expression, meet people, use haircuts to barter for other things.

PITFALLS: slow periods, trying to build a clientele, on your feet.

SOURCES: classifieds, yellow pages under "Beauty Salons," network with other hair-stylists, neighborhood salons.

NEEDS: knowledge of latest trends, a cosmetologist license.

> *"I worked many part-time jobs in order to find out what I wanted to do with my life! I realized after working in hair salons (once two at the same time) that my dream was to be my own boss and run my own business. After quite a process, I opened Angel Hair, featuring haircare, bath and body items, and cards and gifts. I am seeing my dream come true."*
>
> GIGI HUTCHINSON, owner of Angel Hair Salon, Los Angeles

Handing Out Movie Passes

The next best thing to being on the Publishers' Clearinghouse Sweepstakes Prize Patrol.

I'm sure at one time or another in Los Angeles or New York you have been approached by someone with a stack of fliers in hand, asking if you want to attend a free movie screening. What you probably didn't know is that these people are working for a company that does market research on films before a commercial release.

Outgoing, assertive people are hired for this job. You pick up a packet that includes approximately 50 tickets and you have 24 hours to return it. The job is flexible in that you choose your own hours, but companies generally prefer a four-day-a-week commitment. You are given a spec on the type of audience required in terms of age, sex, and ethnicity, and then you seek out people accordingly. The ease of this job will depend on the type of movie you are "selling" and who the lead actors are. One of the common disadvantages is being assigned an inconvenient area. Also, you may have certain quotas to fill in terms of audience selection. It usually takes between three and five hours to hand out all the fliers.

You are paid by how many people on the list you turn in actually show up for the screening. The company keeps track of this information, and if five people show up you earn $50. If ten people show up you earn $75. If 15 people show up you earn $100, and after that you earn $3 a person. If you see someone handing out these fliers, ask him or her for the number of the company. In California, call National Research Group (NRG), and in New York and New Jersey, call Matrix Alliance Market Research.

Good Luck

BENEFITS: flexible hours, good earning potential.

PITFALLS: unsteady salary, approaching strangers, specific quotas to be filled, bad locations.

SOURCES: ask a person who is handing out these passes for a contact number. National Research Group, (800) AJOBNOW ext. 1416; Matrix Alliance Market Research, (203) 698–3344 or (888) 777–3360.

NEEDS: a reliable car for Los Angeles, outgoing, assertive, personable.

> *"This job has supported me by giving me the flexibility and time to pursue other goals. The company promoted me, so I now travel around and go to a number of film festivals. As a screenwriter, this job keeps me in tune with what people want to see in the film industry."*
>
> GEORGE ZAVER, writer/actor/NRG employee, Los Angeles

Makeup Artist

Call me Chanel.

If you enjoy working with people on a one-to-one basis and helping them to look their best, becoming a freelance makeup artist can be a fun, challenging, and lucrative way to use your creative talents. Makeup artists are hired for all sorts of social events, such as charity functions, weddings, and fashion shows, and for films and TV shows. A talent for makeup application as well as an understanding of people's features and needs is required. It is also important to be a good communicator.

There are many ways to become a makeup artist. Image consulting and makeup classes are offered through beauty and continuing education schools, or you can look in the classifieds under "Schools/Colleges—Artist." Parsons School of Design Continuing Education in New York, offers classes in all phases of makeup training, as do Joe Blasco Makeup School and Studio Makeup in Los Angeles.

The least expensive way to get started is by working with a major cosmetic line at a department store. Clinique, Estee Lauder, Lancome, Prescriptives, Bobbi Brown, and Chanel are a few popular lines. If you stay with a line long enough, you will learn the art of makeup application. Makeup seminars are periodically offered to enhance your skills.

While I was a student at New York University, I worked with Clinique as a freelance "associate consultant" (I've recently met a number of women who are working this same job). It was a great part-time job. I earned good money, learned a lot about makeup application, and received free makeup (my friends and family loved that part!). Freelance consultants work the promotions (including makeovers) at various department stores. For information on this type of position, contact human resources at various cosmetic lines. You can expect to earn about $10–$15 an hour. Outside the department store, makeup artists can make excellent money. In major cities, the fee for an hour of makeup application in a person's home is typically $50–$125 and up. Makeup artists who work for photographers charge $50–$100 an application.

Many studios and hair salons hire freelance makeup artists. Check the yellow pages under "Makeup and Beauty Consultants," and "Beauty Salons." A few reputable ones in New York are Laura Geller Makeup Studios and the Makeup Center. In Los Angeles try Cinema Secrets and Naimes Film and T.V. Beauty Supply.

If you choose to become a makeup artist for a headshot photographer, look in the yellow pages under "Photographers" or in the trades *(Backstage, Dramalogue, Variety, Hollywood Reporter),* and in *The Working Actors Guide* by Mani Flattery, for contact numbers. You can also advertise your services in the trade papers, local papers, and community newsletters, and at salons and health clubs.

Good Luck

BENEFITS: good money, artistic, help people look and feel better, free makeup.

PITFALLS: can be a lengthy process to become skilled and earn steady money.

SOURCES: makeup schools, department stores, studios, advertise, beauty and continuing education schools, the classifieds under "Schools/Colleges—Artist." Parsons School of Design Continuing Education, (212) 229–8933; Joe Blasco Makeup School, (213) 467–4949; Studio Makeup, (213) 465–4002. Clinique's headquarters is in New York, (212) 572–3800. Send a résumé and cover letter to 767 Fifth Avenue, New York, NY 10153, Attention: Human Resources. Yellow pages under "Makeup and Beauty Consultants" and "Beauty Salons." Laura Geller Makeup Studios, (212) 570–5477; the Makeup Center, (212) 977–9494; Cinema Secrets, (818) 846–0579; and Naimes Film and T.V. Beauty Supply, (213) 877–2230. Yellow pages under "Photographers" or the trades (*Backstage, Dramalogue, Variety, Hollywood Reporter*) and *The Working Actors Guide* by Mani Flattery. Advertise your services in the trade papers, local papers, and community newsletters and at salons and health clubs.

NEEDS: talent at applying makeup, enjoy working with people on a one-to-one basis.

Modeling

You should be in pictures.

While modeling is often a career in itself, it can also be done part-time while you pursue another career in the arts. There is a misconception that you need to be "model beautiful" to work. Many advertisers these days are using real people and character types, not to mention fit models and specific-body-part models.

Modeling can include any of the following: print work for newspapers, magazines, billboards, and catalogs; runway work that involves showing the product by walking down a runway in front of an audience; and showroom work that entails wearing different samples of the product for potential buyers. The manufacturer or designer will often hire a showroom model with specific measurements (they vary with each line) to present the product to department store representatives or other buyers. Designers and clothing manufacturers also hire fit models to try on their clothes. Fit models are needed for most sizes if you have the perfect measurements. To find out if you are eligible, contact a design center or manufacturer listed in the yellow pages under "Designers—Apparel."

If you have beautiful hands and well-groomed nails (women's glove size of 6.5–7.5, ring size 4.5–5.5; men's glove size 8.5–10), or if you have a model shoe size (women's 6 with a narrow or medium width, men's size 9–10), being a hand or shoe model is extremely lucrative.

Modeling hours vary. "Go-see" appointments for print modeling are the equivalent of auditions and are scheduled mainly on weekdays. The more appointments, the more possibilities of booking jobs—just like acting. Modeling provides the opportunity to make a lot of money for relatively short hours, and you are often sent on location to shoot, which offers variety and adventure. On the downside, it is very competitive and you may have to go on many "go-sees" to book work. For hand and feet models, an agent usually submits a picture to book a job directly.

To get "go-see" appointments, you will need a good agent. Most modeling agents will accept snapshots of you for consideration and have open calls one day a week. If you call an agency and it will not set up an appointment, you can always stop by to drop off pictures or send a few in the mail. Needs change daily within agencies and timing is everything.

After you secure an agent you will need professional photos and a "zed card," which is a 5.5-by-8.5 composite. It usually has three photos on one side and one photo on the other, with measurements. To obtain a zed card, contact theatrical headshot photographers listed in the yellow pages under "Photographers," and specific trade papers (*Dramalogue* and *Backstage*). Local theatrical agencies (listed in your yellow pages) can also assist you with contact numbers of photographers.

Salary for modeling is open for negotiation. Print modeling pays about $250 an hour. Call Screen Actors Guild (SAG) and American Federation of Television and Radio Artists (AFTRA) for fee schedules for union work. The low end for fit modeling is about $60 an hour.

Modeling agencies are listed in the yellow pages. Performing arts bookstores carry updated books, such as *The Working Actors Guide* by Mani Flattery, *The Ross Reports,* and *The Illinois Production Guide,* which list agencies. SAG and AFTRA have lists of agencies as well. For information on fit modeling, contact the Fashion Institute of Design and Merchandising resource center or San Francisco Fashion Industries. Call and ask for the directory that lists manufacturers.

NOTE: Be wary of any agency that *insists* on your using a specific photographer or enrolling in expensive classes. It may be getting a kickback.

Good Luck

BENEFITS: good money for relatively short hours, meet people, variety of work.

PITFALLS: competitive, unsteady income.

SOURCES: call agencies, drop off pictures, open calls. Yellow pages under "Designers—Apparel" and "Theatrical" or "Modeling" agencies. *The Working Actors Guide* by Mani Flattery; *The Ross Reports,* 1515 Broadway, New York, NY 10036; and *The Illinois Production Guide,* (312) 814–3600; SAG; AFTRA; Fashion Institute of Design and Merchandising resource center, (213) 624–1200; San Francisco Fashion Industries, (415) 621–6100.

NEEDS: well-groomed, positive attitude, portfolio, zed card.

> *"I found out by chance that I fit the perfect size 8 measurements and became a fit model. It's such an easy job, requiring nothing but standing. And often when I model for a designer, my input on the clothing is respected. This job has been great for enhancing my wardrobe, as I get to buy the 'well-fitted' clothing I try on at an extremely reduced rate."*
>
> NANCY GOLD, actress/fit model/mime, San Francisco

Pharmaceutical Sales Rep

Sell drugs, make money, and never go to jail.

Pharmaceutical sales reps, otherwise known as detail people, visit doctor's offices with specific product samples and "detail" the doctor about the product, hoping for his or her commitment to try it and pass it along to patients.

Doctors are usually open to trying new and improved products for their patients' benefit. And as a result, the doctor and you both get to enjoy the many functions offered by pharmaceutical companies, including black-tie affairs and free educational programs. One of the drawbacks of this job is all the detailed paperwork that needs to be filled since you are dealing in pharmaceuticals.

Organization and a professional appearance are a must. As with any sales position, it is important not to take rejection personally, as sometimes doctors will give you the brush-off. Sales experience is preferred. Once hired, you will attend training programs on pharmaceuticals, which typically last a few weeks.

Base salary depends on experience. Part-time workers can expect to earn $30,000–$50,000 a year, including bonus and commissions. Many companies provide you with a car and full health benefits. A growing number of pharmaceutical companies now offer part-time positions, often called "job-sharing" or "working mothers" programs.

For employment leads, go the library and research the top pharmaceutical companies anywhere in the country. Look up addresses and send in your résumé. Another way to procure employment is by asking doctors about pharmaceutical companies and speaking with some friendly reps who visit their offices. Also, local pharmacists can tell you the names of the top-moving drugs and which companies are distributing them.

A few well-known companies to contact are Glaxo Wellcome, Merck & Co., Abbot, and Bayer.

Good Luck

BENEFITS: flexible hours, part-time programs available, good salary, pharmaceutical company functions.

PITFALLS: competitive market, a lot of paperwork to fill out.

SOURCES: doctor's offices, pharmacists, pharmaceutical companies. Glaxo Wellcome, (800) 5GLAXO5; Merck & Co., (800) 422–9675; Abbot, (800) 222–6883; Bayer, (213) 812–5507.

NEEDS: organizational skills, professional appearance and attitude, self-motivation, background in sales.

"I split a full-time territory with another woman, which enables me to spend more time at home with my family. I find Glaxo Wellcome to be a very family-oriented company to work for."

FRANCINE WONG, mom/part-time pharmaceutical sales rep, Santa Clarita, California

---

Retail

One word: discounts!

With the plethora of retail jobs available, it's no wonder many people choose this type of work, especially during holiday season, when there is a huge demand for sales people, stock people, cashiers, and managers. Stores look for employees who are neat in appearance, friendly, responsible, and knowledgeable about the items being sold.

It is an advantage to work in a store that fits your interests or career aspirations, as it enhances your knowledge, allows you to network with peers, and offers you discounted merchandise. For example, if you are a painter, an art supply store would probably be a good place to work. An actor could benefit from working in a drama bookstore or a clothing store (to get audition clothes), a mom or dad could work at a kids' clothing shop or toy store, a musician could work at a music store, and so on.

Scheduling flexibility varies with the store and its location. In most shopping malls, retail stores are open until 9 or 10 P.M., allowing for evening or weekend work. Most entry-level positions pay $6–$9 an hour plus commission. Not all stores offer commission, but most offer employee discounts on merchandise—anywhere from 10 percent to 50 percent. This is especially valuable during the holiday season. An added bonus is knowing when all the great sales are.

To locate stores in your area, check the yellow pages under field of interest. Visit shopping malls and thoroughly scout your own neighborhood, since you'll save driving time and money if you work near your home. Ask for the manager and inquire about employment opportunities. Previous retail experience is always a plus, as are good references.

Good Luck

BENEFITS: flexible shifts, merchandise discounts.

PITFALLS: without commission, pay can be on the low side.

SOURCES: yellow pages, shopping malls, neighborhood stores.

NEEDS: trustworthy, friendly, courteous, neat in appearance, marketing skills.

"My mom and dad told me that if I wanted to pursue theater in college, I had to pay for it myself. They saw education as an investment and didn't think they'd get a return with a theater degree! Needless to say, I have worked many survival jobs. When I was in college I worked at a Structure store in Kalamazoo. I received a 35 percent discount on top of grand opening sales—I worked there to get khakis for $12!

MICHAEL FIELD, actor/student/retail/restaurant work/box office, Kalamazoo, Michigan

Trade Shows and Conventions

Get paid for pretending to know what you don't.

At this very moment, not far from you, there is probably a trade show going on. Trade shows, usually held in convention centers, promote products such as computers and other electronics, food, and toys, to name a few. There are conventions held for all types of businesses and products. At McCormick Place (a major convention center in Chicago), conventions include the National Restaurant Association, the Chicago Gift Show, and National Manufacturing Week. For some of these conventions, 250 people a day need to be hired!

Models, actors, college students, semiretired folks, and outgoing, friendly individuals are hired to present or demonstrate products in their best light. Other types of positions are available, including convention registration assistants, who help register companies that are displaying their products, as well as retailers, distributors, and consumers. A large number of cashiers, security guards, and room models (people to hand out materials) are needed. Preshow work may include stuffing envelopes, assembling display booths, organizing books and gifts, telemarketing, and acting as an ambassador to the host city.

Scheduling is flexible depending on when the show is on. You can always decline work, and it won't affect future employment. A typical show can employ you for one day or two weeks, and different shifts are available, including weekend work. Some shows go from 6:30 A.M. to 10 P.M.

Wages vary greatly depending on skills, talent, experience, type of show and location, and the client. On the low end it can be $6–$8 an hour, ranging as high as $75 an hour for models, experienced actors, and meeting planners.

For employment opportunities, call the convention bureau in your city. Ask what registration companies hire part-time help for shows. Conference Management Systems presently hires for trade shows in Chicago, Washington, D.C., and Atlanta. They have been around for about ten years and will be expanding in the future. Two agencies that hire trade show models (these are not fashion models) are Promotional Services Inc., located in Beverly Hills, and American Model and Talent Network, a national service that is a division of U.S. Marketing and Promotions.

A library is also a good place to start when looking for promotional work. There you will find a magazine called *Promo* that lists trade companies in the promotion circuit. It rates the top 100 companies once a year. Trade papers such as *Dramalogue* and *Backstage* often have ads as well.

Good Luck

BENEFITS: good salary, interacting with people, fun and interesting.

PITFALLS: standing.

SOURCES: convention bureau; library, Conference Management Systems, (888) 751–7575; trade papers; business directory for corporations that do trade shows; *Promo* magazine; trade papers (*Dramalogue* and *Backstage*); Promotional Services Inc., (310) 659–3888; American Model and Talent Network, (800) 748–6374.

NEEDS: outgoing, well-groomed, articulate, dependable.

"We're always looking for high-quality, permanent, part-time professionals. It's permanent in that you stay on our roster and yet flexible for you in terms of hours and whether you choose to take the job at hand."

RANDY SKAJA, director of on-site personnel for Conference Management Systems, Chicago

---

Traffic School Teacher

You've been through it so many times anyway.

Comedians, actors, retirees, and other people with outgoing personalities are generally hired to teach traffic school to keep students entertained. For those of you who are lucky enough to have never experienced traffic school, it is where people with traffic violations go in lieu of having the violation appear on their record. Day, evening, and weekend classes are offered. Comedy traffic school is popular in California, Florida, and Dallas.

The job involves checking people in, collecting their tickets, and educating traffic violators in a fun, positive, and informative manner. A certificate is presented to each student at the completion of the day's course—which is an eight-hour day with a lunch break and a few other periods of respite. The fun part is that you are performing in front of a captive audience. If you are a comedian, this is a perfect chance to try out new material.

To be hired you will need to have an interview and possibly show your stuff in front of others. After being hired you will need to attend an orientation to learn basic driving rules (maybe you'll even know a few already!), watch a few traffic school classes, and then get a license at the local Department of Motor Vehicles (DMV), which costs about $30.

A teacher is generally paid $10–$20 an hour depending on the level of experience. The scheduling of shifts is flexible.

Many traffic schools are listed in the yellow pages under "Traffic Schools" or in the classifieds under "Part-Time Work." Improv Traffic

School is the number one traffic school in Southern California, with over 80 locations. It also services Northern California, Florida, and Texas. Another way to find schools is to call your local traffic courthouse for information.

Good Luck

BENEFITS: entertaining others.

PITFALLS: a small classroom where no one laughs at your jokes.

SOURCES: traffic schools listed in yellow pages; Improv Traffic School, (800) 888–8526, or (310) 286–6773; Classifieds, local traffic courthouse.

NEEDS: comedic or acting background, outgoing personality.

Welcome Wagon

Does the word yenta ring a bell?

In the old days, when you moved into a new neighborhood or town, the Welcome Wagon would come by with freshly baked cookies and a warm smile. Cut to the modern-day Welcome Wagon. This mostly suburban phenomenon is a wonderful idea for new town arrivals as well as businesses that are looking to attract customers.

The Welcome Wagon hires people (like you) who contract with businesses in the community and then meet with individuals and families moving into the area. Newcomers are given coupons and gifts from local businesses as well as information on community affairs, local policies, Little League, schools, religious organizations, and more.

Generally, businesses are charged a small amount for each newcomer. The more businesses involved, the more profit for the Welcome Wagon. You will be paid by the business per newcomer you meet, typically $10–$20 total for each. It is feasible to see five newcomers a day. Obviously some towns have more of a turnover than others. It is also possible to become a sales person for the company, selling the Welcome Wagon business in other towns as well.

You are selling individualized advertisement programs, so this job works best in areas with mom-and-pop stores and individually owned businesses. City hall will provide a list of newcomers if they see this as a valuable service—giving people materials on ordinances, licensing information, and voting information makes them more aware and responsible citizens.

For employment, look in the help wanted section of your paper under "Part-Time," or call city hall to see if it has welcoming services. Welcome Wagon International is based in Glen Ellyn, Illinois, and can refer you to the branch of Welcomers in your area.

Good Luck

BENEFITS: flexible, meeting people, fun.

PITFALLS: business can be slow if there is not much neighborhood turnover, small businesses are being bought out by super chains and foreign companies.

SOURCES: welcoming services listed in paper, city hall, Welcome Wagon International, (630) 469–8470.

NEEDS: enjoy meeting new people, friendly, assertive, sales ability to solicit funds from local businesses.

IDEA: If you have an entrepreneurial spirit, you can start your own welcoming service. When I moved into an apartment complex in Los Angeles a number of years ago, I received a welcoming coupon packet in the mail that local businesses had obviously paid for—what a great idea some smart entrepreneur put into action!

"I liked working for my town because I took pride in it. Raising two children as a single parent required flexibility as my top job requirement—this job gave me that."

KATHRYN JOOSTEN, actress/single parent/Welcome Wagon, Lake Forest, Illinois

6

If I Only Had a Brain

Jobs My Sixth-Grade Math Teacher, Ms. Schmeiman, Would Love

3D Animator

You don't have to wear those goofy 3D glasses.

How many times did your kid drag you to see *Toy Story?* All the images in that movie were created by computers. Today, cutting edge animation like the kind used in *Toy Story* is being done in most major cities. Many sculptors and traditional fine artists with computer proficiency who need freelance, part-time work have made the transition into this new medium.

Most people who get into 3D animation have extremely high computer skills or are 2D graphic artists already familiar with programs like

Adobe Photoshop or QuarkXpress. 3D falls into two categories: 3D for PC and Mac, and 3D for SGI. 3D for SGI is the more complex and highly valuable skill to have, and thus the pay is higher.

To see if this job would be of interest, take a class at a community college or university, which typically ranges from $75 to a few hundred dollars and up. Another option is to call one of the major providers of 3D software, such as Alias Wavefront. It offers intensive training programs all across the country. The courses generally run for four days and the fee is $1,950.

After developing some skills, ask your teacher which are the largest animation houses in your area to contact for possible jobs or internships. Search the Internet for employment opportunities: http://www.ugo.net/yellowpages is the yellow pages of video games, http://www.vsearch.com provides information on companies and jobs, and two job placement boards are http://www.monster.com and http://www.jobbankusa.com. *The Hollywood Interactive Entertainment Directory* and *The Hollywood New Media Directory* list interactive companies all across the United States as well as in Canada. Also, every major production company has an interactive division. For example, Disney has Imagineering and Sony has Imageworks. They specialize in new media and animated films. Pay varies depending on skill and experience. Freelance animators I've spoken with earn $350–$600 for a typical eight- to 10-hour day.

Good Luck

BENEFITS: cutting edge of technology, creative, work is plentiful, great pay.

PITFALLS: courses to learn 3D animation are expensive, finding a 3D package to learn on can be challenging, takes training to become proficient.

SOURCES: call your local college or community center for available courses. *The Hollywood Interactive Entertainment Directory,* for mail order call (310) 315–4815; the Internet for job placement boards. Alias Wavefront, (800) 451–3318 or http://www.aw.sgi.com.

NEEDS: highly developed computer skills, 2D graphic skills, familiar with Adobe Photoshop or QuarkXPress.

Adult-Education Teacher

No, these are not sex-education classes.

If you are an excellent communicator and can motivate other adults, consider becoming a part-time continuing education teacher. There are any number of interesting classes to teach. A few examples include computer technology, preparing for the GED (high school equivalency exam), art classes, and automotive mechanics.

The majority of jobs are available at vocational/technical schools, or with continuing education programs, at high schools and universities. There are also numerous independent adult schools where you can teach, for example, the Learning Annex (found in a number of major cities) or Discover U in Seattle. Requirements vary from state to state and school to school. Some programs require a bachelor's degree and a teaching certificate. Information is available from your state department of education and local school districts. Or simply contact continuing education programs at community colleges and universities and local adult-ed schools. If you want to teach a class that has never been offered before, send in a proposal to the program coordinator. Class schedules are flexible. Many classes meet in the evenings and on weekends.

Salary varies widely depending on where you teach, how many hours, and what you're teaching. If you have a product to sell, such as a book or handout, you can earn more money.

For information on listings in your area, contact the American Association for Adult and Continuing Education in Washington, D.C. This association has a membership department that provides a newsletter, publications, annual conferences, and other networking opportunities. Members are put on a list that goes out to educators. The membership fee starts at about $25.

Good Luck

BENEFITS: scheduling flexibility, teaching others is rewarding.

PITFALLS: work can be sporadic.

SOURCES: state education department; American Association for Adult and Continuing Education, 1200 19th Street, N.W., Suite 300, Washington, DC 20036, (202) 429–5131; local community colleges and adult-ed programs. Learning Annex: San Francisco, (415) 788–5500; San Diego, (619) 544-9700; Los Angeles, (310) 478–6677; New York, (212) 371–0280; Toronto, (416) 964–0011. Discover U is in Seattle at (206) 443–0447.

NEEDS: knowledge of subject, excellent communicator and motivator, sometimes a degree, teaching certificate.

Book Reader

Your favorite character in the old *Batman* series was the Bookworm.

You don't have to be Evelyn Wood to actually earn money reading books. If you enjoy reading and have a flair for writing, you can earn money as a freelance book reader at home. Literary agencies and production companies hire book readers to see if certain books would make good films, TV shows, or MOWs (movies of the week).

The difference between being a book reader and a script reader (chapter 3) is that book readers make more money with the reading part. This is an especially good job for a novelist to learn what works and doesn't work and for stay-at-home moms or dads who are afraid their brains are going to mush cooing with their infants. Basically, since you work at home, you create your own hours as long as you meet the deadlines.

To be a book reader, you will need to learn how to do "coverage" and have access to a typewriter or computer. Coverage is a report of approximately five double-spaced pages. The first section (two pages) is the cover sheet and a "log line" that sums up the book in one or two sentences. The next few pages includes a synopsis of the book and whether it can be successfully transformed into the film or TV medium. Next, you'll hit the three basics in further detail: plot, story line, and character, and occasionally talk about the setting. And finally, one page of character breakdown.

It is best to find someone who already does this to show you how the finished product looks. A background in English and writing is preferred, and owning a computer or typewriter is essential. Most major cities offer courses at adult-ed schools and community colleges on how to write coverage. Call agencies and production companies, explain why you are an excellent candidate for the job, and ask for a way to get in the door. There is a great need for book readers in major cities such as Los Angeles, New York, Chicago, and London. There are a number of books to assist you, including *Reading for a Living* by T. L. Katahn; *Writer's Guide to Book Editors, Publishers, and Literary Agents* by Jeff Herman; *LA 411* by D. Goldblatt; *The Illinois Production Guide,* (312) 814–3600; and *The Hollywood Creative Directory.*

Expect to earn $75–$100 for the first 250–300 pages read and 5 cents to 20 cents per page after.

Good Luck

BENEFITS: work at home, be your own boss, stimulating; enhances vocabulary, spelling, and speed of reading.

PITFALLS: reading boring books.

SOURCES: literary agencies and production companies. *Reading for a Living* by T. L. Katahn; *Writers Guide to Book Editors, Publishers, and Literary Agents* by Jeff Herman; *LA 411* by D. Goldblatt; *The Illinois Production Guide,* (312) 814–3600; and *The Hollywood Creative Directory.*

NEEDS: enjoy reading, learn how to do coverage, a typewriter or computer.

"When I had my baby I was looking for something to do at home, so I left my full-time job as a casting associate and became a book reader. I now have two kids and read in my spare time (ha! ha!) for money. I read approximately two books a week. It really stimulates me and keeps me on top of current pop culture and literary genres."

ALLISON BAUER, mom/book reader, Los Angeles

Bookstore Clerk

Calling all bookworms . . .

Books are food for the mind and soul, and bookstores are the restaurants that serve them. It is the perfect working environment for gathering information on a variety of subjects, learning about the current writers' market, and schmoozing with other literary folks, making this an ideal job for a writer or anyone who loves to read.

Most popular bookstores in major cities stay open until 11 P.M., so working hours can be flexible. Part-time work is plentiful, and even weekend-only work is possible. Unfortunately, like most retail jobs, the hourly wage is low, but you do receive discounts, and some major bookstore chains like Barnes & Noble provide health benefits if you work a minimum of 30 hours a week.

Requirements for working in a bookstore vary. Most stores simply want you to appreciate books and have a good head on your shoulders. Others prefer bookstore or retail experience or even an English degree. You can usually pick up an application from the cashier or call the stores you are interested in to see if they are hiring. Check the yellow pages under "Books" for the phone numbers and addresses of the stores in your area. Note that many bookstore chains now have cafés within their stores where part-time positions are available as well.

The hourly wage usually starts at about $6, and you are entitled to a 30 percent discount on book purchases.

Good Luck

BENEFITS: be surrounded by books, culture, information; 30 percent discount; flexible shifts.

PITFALLS: low hourly wage.

SOURCES: yellow pages under "Books."

NEEDS: love of books, common sense, retail experience preferred.

Creating Web Pages

Orbit in cyberspace for the rest of your life.

A number of years ago, a friend of mine who now owns Internet Outfitter, a Web design company in California, compared the Internet and advanced computer technology to the discovery of the internal combustion engine. "It will be as big as the invention of the car, Deb." "That big?" I said. "Yep," he said confidently.

These days it seems like Web addresses are everywhere, from magazine ads and billboards to junk mail. Using the Web for promotional purposes is as common as handing out a business card. As a programmer on the World Wide Web, you act as the cyberworld version of an advertising agency. Instead of creating an ad campaign for print or TV, you are designing eye-catching Web sites for companies on the Internet.

The process of creating Web sites includes everything from researching customers, to writing the code, to designing and maintaining the site. You take your clients' company literature and catalogs and translate them into viewable programming on the Web. It is always important to have your clients select some already-existing sites they like so that you can understand their taste before beginning.

Teach Yourself Web Publishing with HTML by Laura Lemay is a helpful way to acquaint yourself with process, as is *The Complete Idiots' Guide to Creating an HTML Web Page* by Paul McFedries. There are plenty of support groups, such as the HTML Writers Guild, which has over 40,000 members. For additional help, using a search engine, type in "beginning Web design" or "Web authoring." Recommended online learning resources are http://help.netscape.com/links.html, and http://ncdesign.kyushu-id.ac.jp. The book *Internet for Dummies, HTML* by John Levine can be helpful.

To get started, you will need an Internet service provider, or ISP, in Net lingo. There are plenty of ads for providers in newspapers, or you can ask around for recommendations. You'll need a computer with at least 16MB RAM, a 15-inch monitor, at least a 28.8 modem, plenty of available disk space, and a graphics accelerator card. If you want your own domain, speak to your ISP or contact http://www.internic.com and fill out an on-line application. Many ISPs offer free Web space with an account. You'll need a Web browser, which is software that lets you view Web pages. Two popular browsers are Netscape Navigator (http://www.netscape.com) and Microsoft's Internet Explorer (http://www.microsoft.com). To add graphics, you'll need a paint program such as Adobe Photoshop.

To find clients, start by spreading the word among friends and family, offering discounts or a few free sites in order to practice. Call up business owners or anyone who has a marketing idea and ask if they are interested in advertising on the Internet. For example, contact all the hair salons in your area and tell them why it would be beneficial to advertise on the Web. One idea is to create a site for all businesses in a certain location, similar to creating a "mall" on the Internet. Expect to earn $300–$1,000 to set up and create the Web site. When starting out it may take you longer than anticipated to complete a site. Once you start building a clientele, however, you can reuse programming. Another way to earn money is to host a site, rent to others, and charge monthly for space on your server.

If you want to work for an established company that creates Web sites, put your name and résumé on the Internet so companies searching for employees can find you. It goes without saying that the best advertisement for yourself is to create your own amazing Web site!

Plenty of courses will help you learn more about this dynamic field. For information, contact independent learning schools, adult-ed programs, and local colleges.

Good Luck

BENEFITS: work out of your home, large earning potential.

PITFALLS: initial investment for equipment, challenging to learn HTML, stuck in cyberspace for the rest of your life!

SOURCES: local colleges, adult-ed programs, independent learning programs, books. *Teach Yourself Web Publishing with HTML* by Laura Lemay, *The Complete Idiots' Guide to Creating an HTML Web Page* by Paul McFedries, *Internet for Dummies*, *HTML* by John Levine, HTML Writers Guild (http://www.hwg.org).

NEEDS: computer, modem, Internet service provider, Adobe Photoshop, Web browser, and Internet knowledge.

English-as-a-Second-Language Teacher

You've known it since you were three.

To teach English as a Second Language (ESL), it is often necessary to be fluent in a second language. The list of languages needed in the public school system is endless and includes Spanish, Japanese, Korean, and Russian. Knowledge of phonetics is also helpful. There are many opportunities to teach ESL full-time or as a substitute at bilingual elementary and secondary school, adult-education programs, private schools, and private tutoring sessions outside the classroom.

Requirements for teaching ESL differ within each district, so you'll need to contact your state education department or school district's teacher recruitment office for details. For example, to teach in the Los Angeles Unified School District, you need a B.A., credentials in ESL or a fifth year in student teaching, and a passing score on the CBEST (California Basic Educational Skills Test). In New York, you need to be state certified to teach in the public school system.

Salary varies depending on the city. The beginning salary at public schools in Los Angeles, for teaching four to five classes a day, is about $28,000–$29,000 a year plus benefits. Substitute teachers make about $100–$120 a day. If you teach for more than ten days at one school, the pay jumps to about $160 a day.

Private school requirements vary, as they are not under state regulations. If you have ESL experience or are fluent in a language, getting a job at a private institution can be less complicated than getting a position at a public school. Check the schools in your area for information on their ESL programs. Look in the yellow pages under "Language Schools" for further listings. Pay tends to be lower at private institutions, and classes at diocesan schools can be quite large.

Tutoring ESL is another option. Credentials are not as important, and you can advertise for free on college campuses by posting notices at the resource center, library, and student center, and on classroom bulletin boards. My friend is now privately tutoring three ESL students that she obtained by placing just such an ad. You can charge up to $50 an hour to teach privately.

Yet another idea is teaching ESL in adult-education classes. If you are interested in this approach, contact individual high schools and universities for specific requirements and pay.

Good Luck

BENEFITS: make a difference in people's lives, good money, health benefits, use your language skills.

PITFALLS: lengthy process to complete credentials to teach in the public school system.

SOURCES: state or city unified school districts, adult-education division in high schools, yellow pages under "Language Schools," advertisements.

NEEDS: teaching experience is helpful, training in ESL, B.A. or certificate.

"I've taught ESL for two years now, at night, after my day job in special education at an elementary school. I got a certificate from U.C. Santa Barbara, and started out with the lowest-level class. They couldn't write, spell, read, talk, or understand, so I had to bring in lots of pictures and act things out, as well as brush up on my Spanish. My heart goes out to my students who work so hard doing manual labor all day and then come out at night to sit in my classes and try to learn English."

LOIS CALLAN, single parent/teacher/ESL instructor/tutor/rents out house to tenants, Santa Barbara, California

Freelance Graphic Designer

You're the only person in your circle of friends who has heard of QuarkXPress and Adobe Illustrator.

When you go into a restaurant, have you ever noticed how the menu is designed to catch your eye and make the restaurant and its food seem even more appealing? Or the way a book cover and the styling of the type compels you to open it up and start reading? Well, a graphic designer helped make it that way. Graphic designers work on logos, menus, books, catalogs, Web pages, magazines, and a variety of other print media. Even if you can't draw with a pen or pencil, but still know what you like and have an eye for style, you can find work in this lucrative, abundant field. The computer is your main tool, so you don't have to be able to draw a perfect line.

To get started you will need some basic computer knowledge and familiarity with basic design principles. Classes are offered through community colleges and extension courses. Trade schools, like Platt College in California, which has a one-year program, will gear you for the field and offer guaranteed job placement. For design programs, contact specific design schools listed in the yellow pages (Parsons School of Design is in New York). Most community colleges offer courses as well.

As a graphic designer, you can work out of your home if you have a computer and a page-layout design program, such as QuarkXPress, Adobe Photoshop, or Adobe Illustrator. Freelance pay is approximately $20–$50 an hour depending on wether you work independently or through a temp agency.

If you are working independently, word-of-mouth is the best way to gather assignments. Be bold with your self-promotion. If you think a restaurant's menu needs a new look, offer your services for a fair price. Take out ads in writers' magazines (see "Freelance Writer," this chapter) or trade publications and community papers. If you are interested in book design, contact editors or designers at publishing houses, as they often use graphic design freelancers. For more corporate work, check out trade magazines such as *Adweek* or *Brandweek* for available work, or place your own advertisement. You'll also find that many temp agencies are interested in your skills—one nationwide company to contact is Mactemps.

Good Luck

BENEFITS: flexible, your own boss, creative, good wages.

PITFALLS: independent work can be sporadic.

SOURCES: community colleges and adult-ed programs, trade magazines, temp agencies; Mactemps, (800) 622–8367.

NEEDS: computer skills, creative, some design training.

> *"I knew that I wanted to work in art but didn't want to be a struggling artist. I went to Platt College, a one-year program in graphic design, and it was one of the best commitments I ever made. They provided all the equipment to learn on, had a financial planning program so I didn't have to pay until I finished school,* and *they helped get me my first job. Now I do most of my work out of my home since I have a child."*
>
> LISA BRACKEN, mom/freelance graphic designer, Agoura, California

Freelance Illustrator

If Picasso were alive today, would he own a computer?

If you have a background in graphic or fine arts, consider becoming a freelance illustrator. An illustrator creates, draws, and paints a picture, photographs it, and then puts it on the computer using a design program. You will need a computer and a few popular programs, which can include Adobe Photoshop, Adobe Illustrator, and Fractal Painter. If you are interested in the entertainment industry, you can find work doing storyboards or production illustrations. Creating the art for children's books and publications is another popular field.

For information on classes that will teach you popular design programs, contact local community colleges and adult-ed schools. If you're just starting out, it's a good idea to join a design company, advertising agency, or postproduction house in a junior position doing storyboard and sketch design. Several people I interviewed agreed that it was better for them to actually work at a company as an intern or apprentice instead of paying for classes. This way you learn a variety of skills and make industry contacts, and many times the company you're working for will eventually offer you a paid position.

In addition to a résumé, you need an impressive portfolio that contains your best work. Contact advertising agencies and facilities where there is ongoing production for TV, film, and commercials. The library and theatrical bookstores will have books on production companies in your area as well as on illustrating children's books. A few popular ones are *LA 411* by D. Goldblatt; *The Illinois Production Guide,* (312) 814–3600; *The Hollywood Creative Directory; The Working Actors Guide* by Mani Flattery; *How to Write & Illustrate Children's Books* by Treld Bicknell and Felicity Trotman; and *Children's Writers and Illustrators Market,* published by Writers Market. For design programs, contact specific design schools listed in the yellow pages (Parsons School of Design is in New York). Most community colleges offer courses as well.

Earnings will vary according to your level of experience and the project. As a freelancer, you can choose to charge per week, day, hour, or project. You can expect to earn anywhere from $12 to $100 an hour.

Good Luck

BENEFITS: illustrators are in demand, freelance with a number of companies, fair amount of artistic freedom, earn quite a lot of money.

PITFALLS: your illustrations may not make it to final edit.

SOURCES: advertising agencies, graphic departments of TV stations, film studios, design companies. *How to Write & Illustrate Children's Books* by Treld Bicknell and Felicity Trotman; *Children's Writers and Illustrators Market,* published by Writers Market; *LA 411* by D. Goldblatt; *The Illinois Production Guide,* (312) 814–3600; *The Hollywood Creative Directory; The Working Actors Guide* by Mani Flattery.

NEEDS: artistic and design talent, portfolio, computer, programs, and knowledge of software.

"When I first came to this country, my wife was pregnant, so in order to support my family, I started drawing caricatures on the street. A short time there-

after, by first apprenticing at a production house, I was able to combine my fine arts background with skills in lighting and mathematics to successfully work as a freelance illustrator."

BELA BORZSEK, freelance illustrator/computer animator/currently developing a real-time 3D digitizer, Los Angeles

Freelance Writer

You get to see your name in print.

Freelance writing allows writers the luxury of pursuing their interests while paying their bills. Magazines are ideal places to submit your work, as there are literally hundreds aimed at every audience imaginable. Writing a few regular articles a month can put food on the table *and* leave you time to write your magnum opus.

Nonfiction magazine editors look for short feature articles covering specialized topics. The best pieces are geared toward current events of national interest. If you're not an expert, become one through research. Fiction editors generally prefer to receive complete short story manuscripts. It is extremely important to be familiar with your target magazines before submitting your work, as editors want to know that you understand their magazine's audience and focus. Always contact the editor by phone first to make sure you understand submission requirements.

Order subscriptions to *Folio* and *Writer's Digest* to keep abreast of what's going on in the publishing world. *Writer's Digest* also publishes a wide range of books for writers, such as *Making Money Freelance Writing. The Handbook for Freelance Writing* by Michael Perry is another good resource, as is *The Literary Marketplace,* which is one of the most widely used reference books in the publishing industry. It lists every major publisher, publicity outlet, and supplier. Any large branch library will have these books and many others to assist you.

For further information and a listing of over a thousand magazines in subject categories, I highly recommend *Writer's Market: Where and How to Sell What You Write* by Kirsten Holm. You might also consider joining the National Writers Union (NWU), which provides resource materials, seminars, newsletters, and contract advisers. Before you submit your material, you will need to have it copyrighted. Go to the Writers Guild of America in your area or write to the Registrar of Copyrights at the Library of Congress, in Washington, D.C. 20559.

Pay will vary from approximately $30 to $400 per article. At certain magazines, you will paid by the word; $1 a word is a common price.

Good Luck

BENEFITS: rewarding, doing what you love, creative, freelance.

PITFALLS: unsteady income.

SOURCES: *Folio,* (800) 214–9539, *Writer's Digest,* (800) 289–0963; *Making Money Freelance Writing; The Handbook for Freelance Writing* by Michael Perry; *The Literary Marketplace; Writer's Market: Where and How to Sell What You Write* by Kirsten Holm; Writers Guild of America; Registrar of Copyrights, (202) 707–3000; National Writers Union in New York, (212) 254–0279 or access the Web site at http://www.nwu.org/nwu/.

NEEDS: writing ability, creative ideas.

IDEA: If you enjoy traveling, consider writing and selling your travel experiences. Check out *The Travel Writer's Handbook* by Louise Purwin Zobel.

> *"I have known I wanted to write since I was 15. I started out as a reporter at United Press International, then worked as an editor at* In These Times, *and now I work out of my home as a freelance writer for magazines including* Outside *and* Utne Reader. *I was recently approached by publishing houses to do a book based on an article I wrote, which is quite common. Editors peruse 'hot magazines' for book and film ideas. A few of my freelance writing friends have recently gotten film deals from magazine pieces they wrote."*
>
> MILES HARVEY, freelance writer/book reviewer, Chicago

Language Trainer

Buenos dias, bonjour, boker tov, guten morgen!

Whether it involves interpreting, translating, or teaching, language training is the perfect job for anyone with a foreign language skill. Interpreters generally translate the spoken word simultaneously on plant tours, at conferences, and at other important events. Translating is written work and can be done from home with a fax machine or a computer and modem. Teaching is done on site at companies or foreign language schools.

Individuals and businesses usually contact foreign language schools for business or travel purposes, although sometimes individuals want to learn a new language just for fun. Two well-known language schools are Inlingua and Berlitz.

Inlingua has over 300 schools worldwide, with 28 in the United States. Each individual school is a separately owned business but uses the company's teaching methods, materials, and support. The main focus is teaching business professionals. All employees need to be native speakers or must have achieved a native-level proficiency in their language. All teaching is done in the native tongue, so you do not need to be fluent in English. Prior teaching skills are not a prerequisite, since Inlingua has a specific training procedure and philosophy. Teachers work anywhere from five to 35 hours a week. If you are interested in translation or interpreter work, you don't need to live in the city of the school you work for. Materials are faxed to translators, and interpreters can be sent across the country depending on the client's need. Typically translators and interpreters are used for the legal system. Attention to detail, grammar, and syntax, and an understanding of the culture are important. Phone interviews are accepted. These jobs are freelance and can last a few days to a few months or more, depending on the client's needs.

Pay varies. Teachers typically earn $10–$18 per 45-minute class session. Translators usually earn 10 cents to 11 cents a word with a set minimum, and interpreters typically earn $15–$30 an hour, depending on experience.

For employment opportunities, look in the yellow pages under "Language Schools." The headquarters of Inlingua in the United States is in New York. For the translator and interpreter department, call (404) 240–1807, or use a Web search engine and type in Inlingua to find one of its sites. Berlitz has been around since 1878 and has over 60 schools in the United States and Canada, with headquarters in Princeton, New Jersey. Call the school in your area or visit the Web site at http://www.berlitz.com. Besides offering translation and instruction courses, Berlitz publishes language tapes.

Good Luck

BENEFITS: meet people of different nationalities, use your language skills.

PITFALLS: Depending on where you live, there may not be a strong demand for the language you speak.

SOURCES: yellow pages under "Language Schools," Inlingua, (212) 575–1715 and (800) 995–0988, translator and interpreter department at (404) 266–2661. Berlitz can be found at http://www.berlitz.com., or contact the school in your area for information.

NEEDS: foreign language skills, native fluent, education and business background preferred.

Paralegal

You can practically tell people you're a lawyer.

A paralegal is often employed directly by a law firm, but can also do freelance work as an independent contractor. The job involves completing government, bankruptcy, and simple divorce forms, and dealing with wills, trusts, and miscellaneous court documents. Essentially, you are to a lawyer what a nurse is to a doctor—invaluable. If you choose to work for a law office, duties may include gathering preliminary information on cases prior to the attorney's meeting with the client. The hours are flexible, and often you will be given a key to the firm and can complete your work when you wish. If you prefer to work independently, you will need to secure your own clients by advertising. You can place ads in newspapers and even paper fliers on cars at courthouses in your region.

I highly recommend taking a course in the basics of paralegal work to familiarize yourself with the required duties and give yourself an edge in the job market. Many private institutions and continuing education programs offer paralegal courses. It is preferable to take a course approved by the American Bar Association (ABA). The Service Center for ABA in Chicago can provide you with a list of accredited schools in your area. Tuition for a four- to eight-month program at these private institutions is approximately $4,000–$5,000, and day and evening classes are offered. In Los Angeles, UCLA and the University of West L.A. offer paralegal training, and in New York, Adelphi University and New York University's continuing education program offer accredited courses. For less expensive classes (not accredited by ABA), look in the yellow pages under "Paralegal" or "Legal," or in the classifieds under "Education/Training" or "Paralegal." Another way of becoming a paralegal is to take a less skilled job, such as a girl/guy friday, in a small law office and then keep taking on more tasks. Also note that some law firms will teach you to become a paralegal.

If you prefer the stability of working for a lawyer or a law firm, you can expect to make $10–$25 an hour, depending on your level of experience. If you are working independently, the going rate is approximately $300–$500 per task. Once the work becomes familiar, it only takes about 30 minutes to fill out the forms.

For specific jobs, check legal newspapers, such as the *Daily Journal* or *New York Law Journal,* or the classifieds under "Temp Work," "Paralegal," or "Legal." You can also contact law firms directly by looking in the yellow pages under "Attorney."

Good Luck

BENEFITS: good wages, steady employment, flexible hours, good introduction to law.

PITFALLS: tedious, detailed work.

SOURCES: legal newspapers, classifieds under "Temp Work," "Paralegal," or "Legal." American Bar Association, (312) 988–5522. Adelphi University, (212) 965–8340; New York University's continuing education program, (800) FIND NYU; UCLA, (310) 825–4321, or UCLA Extension, (310) 825–9971; University of West L.A., (310)

342–5200. Yellow pages under "Paralegal" or "Legal," or in classifieds under "Education/Training" or "Paralegal."

NEEDS: knowledge of legal forms, paralegal course.

"I became a paralegal to pay the bills and to decide whether I wanted to make the commitment to go to law school."

BETH ALEXANDER, law student/paralegal, St. Louis

Princeton Review Teacher

Your SAT scores were high enough to get you into a good college, but you still aren't making any money.

Teaching and monitoring practice tests for the Princeton Review is a terrific part-time job for anyone who has excelled and scored well on a standardized test. Many actors, writers, and students are employed by the Princeton Review on a part-time basis. The organization is responsible for the SAT, LSAT, GRE, MCAT, and GMAT, and special courses in each are conducted around the country. It is your job to teach students how to recognize what the tests are asking, and to prep them in specific areas before the exam date.

To qualify for employment by the Princeton Review, you must have very strong test scores on the exam you are interested in teaching, and excellent skills as an instructor. The ability to deliver information in a way that is entertaining and easy to understand is very important.

The pay is $15–$30 an hour depending on your teaching experience. Typically you are hired to work seven to 14 hours a week, and you can always rack up more hours by subbing for other teachers. Each class runs for about three to four hours, and weekend work is available. Upon hiring, Princeton Review provides training. Hiring takes place in early summer or late December. You will need to send a résumé and cover letter to the grad director or SAT director.

Good Luck

BENEFITS: good hourly wage, improves your communication skills.

PITFALLS: driving to different locations to teach.

SOURCES: call the Princeton Review at (800) 2–REVIEW.

NEEDS: above-average test scores, teaching skills, fun and energetic personality.

"My wife got into Vanderbilt Law School and suddenly I was plopped down in Nashville with two master's degrees in creative writing and literature and a book of short stories half-completed. Here I was, hyper-educated, and I found myself back in the old restaurant scene, bartending. On the suggestion of a friend, I sent my résumé to Princeton Review. Since my strengths on the GRE were in reading comprehension and the analytical section, I now teach the LSATs. This job provides a very strong supplementary source of income and is incredibly flexible, which gives me time to write. I enjoy teaching, and the work provides me with stretches of freedom, which is what all writers need."

ADAM ROSS, writer/screenwriter/teacher, Nashville

Private Tutor

You're a teacher and you get paid well!

If you enjoy teaching on a one-on-one basis, private tutoring may be a great part-time job for you.

To be a private tutor, you will need to be proficient in a particular subject or language, or skilled in a more general area, such as teaching children to read. You must be a good communicator who can assess and respond to specific problems, be encouraging, and help make learning fun. Among the advantages of being a tutor are flexible hours, intellectual and emotional stimulation, and good wages. It is a challenging job that enables you to be a mentor while helping another person gain skills and confidence. It can also be extremely demanding—working with children who have poor concentration calls for patience and dedication.

Most clients and tutoring agencies will prefer that you have a bachelor's degree, but it is not always necessary. If you live in California, it is a good idea to take the California Basic Educational Skills Test (CBEST) so that you can put it on your résumé. Call the department of education in your state regarding similar requirements. If you decide you need a little educational backup, a bookstore or library will have plenty of information to enhance your knowledge of the subject you are interested in teaching.

Tutoring usually pays $20–$50 an hour depending on your experience and whether you choose to go through an agency.

Getting tutoring jobs can be quite easy. Most schools have bulletin boards or job boards, and college and local newspapers often list employment opportunities. Substitute teaching can be a great segue into tutoring, as your principal and staff will be able to give you references. You may also want to place an ad in your community, church, or temple newsletter. If you decide to go through an established company, the yellow pages under "Tutoring" lists services that you can call for employment.

Good Luck

BENEFITS: good hourly wage, intellectually and emotionally stimulating.

PITFALLS: working with a "challenging" (politically correct for "irritating") child.

SOURCES: yellow pages under "Tutoring" for agency listings, college newspapers, place an ad in your community, church, or temple newsletter.

NEEDS: proficiency in a subject or a technique.

"I tutor math part-time in my home. I got started by placing signs at a local community college, and when I went to put up a sign at Portland State, I found out that the math department had a list of tutors to refer, and they agreed to add my name to it. My work is rewarding in that I am able to help my students with difficulties in math as well as develop relationships with them (and their families) that extend beyond their weekly schoolwork.

My schedule is flexible and, as a parent, I am able to stay at home with my daughter."

TINA KOLPAKOWSKI, mom/math tutor, Portland, Oregon

Proofreader

Winning all those spelling bees can finally pay off.

A freelance proofreader checks manuscripts and documents for spelling, grammar, and punctuation mistakes. Many writers and English teachers proofread as a side job. Publishing houses and law firms are two major sources of employment—law firms employ proofreaders to check briefs, wills, trusts, arguments for court, and brochures for legal seminars; publishers hire proofreaders to check manuscripts before they are sent off to the printer.

To get started, you will need to take a course in editing or proofreading. Most community colleges or adult-ed programs offer classes. Your local bookstore or library will have a number of useful books, such as Peggy Smith's popular *Mark My Words: Instruction and Practice in Proofreading*. Before you are hired, you will have to take a basic English grammar test and demonstrate your knowledge of proofreading symbols. Publishing houses will usually require you to own a copy of the style manual they use. *The Chicago Manual of Style,* published by the University of Chicago Press, is generally regarded as the definitive writing reference work.

Salary usually ranges from $12 to $15 an hour. It can be on the lower end if you go through a temp agency. Hours vary according to the projects you work on and the deadlines you are given.

To seek proofreading employment, call well-established, large law firms or send your résumé to editors at publishing companies. For law firms, look in the yellow pages under "Legal Services" and in the classifieds under "Proofreading," "Editing," or "Legal." The trade magazine *Publishers Weekly* lists publishing houses and has a classified section, as do many writer magazines. Corporate newsletters and trade journals (American Bar Association, American Medical Association, etc.) are yet other sources to contact. The book *Writer's Market: Where and How to Sell What You Write,* by Kirsten Holm is an invaluable resource as well.

Another alternative is to freelance through temp agencies. For a listing, check the yellow pages under "Employment Agencies." I often tell people who are seeking temp work to go directly to the source—call law firms or publishing houses in your area and ask which temp agencies they use. United Temps is a California-based employment agency serving over 100 cities nationwide, and the Affiliates Temp is an international company with over 170 offices in the United States and Canada. Its headquarters is in Menlo Park, California.

Good Luck

BENEFITS: good salary, flexible hours.

PITFALLS: tedious work.

SOURCES: temp agencies; major law firms, trade journals, publishing houses; classifieds under "Proofreading," "Editing," or "Legal." *Publishers Weekly; Writer's Market; Mark My Words: Instruction and Practice in Proofreading* by Peggy Smith; United Temps, (714) 572–4200; Core Staff, (713) 961–3633; the Affiliates Temp, (415) 234–6000.

NEEDS: proficient English language and proofreading skills, ability to work on a deadline.

Reviewer

Free entertainment!

A reviewer, otherwise known as a critic, examines a subject of interest (films, books, restaurants, plays, music, dance, or art) and reports on it for different publications. Many writers are also freelance reviewers or food critics—reviewing provides a steady writing gig while you are working on the great American novel or screenplay. You are an essential part of an industry you enjoy and are paid to share your thoughts about it. If you are a film or performing arts critic, you'll be invited to attend premieres and openings of shows with a guest (your popularity will immediately increase), and if you're a food critic, you will frequent the best restaurants in town.

Qualifications include a strong awareness of current events and in-depth knowledge of the industry you choose to write about. The ability to articulate your views on paper is essential. To gain experience as a reviewer, I suggest you contact community newsletters and local papers that hire almost anybody at an extremely low salary. This way, you can develop a solid collection of clips that are representative of your best writing. Also, study popular reviewers to see how their pieces are structured.

Once you have several reviews in your portfolio and a few gigs on your résumé, find magazines and newspapers that you are interested in writing for and send a copy of your material (a "tear sheet") for the editors to review. In your submission, explain your particular expertise on the subject matter. After you have given editors a chance to look over your submission, follow up with phone calls to get feedback.

This job is flexible, as you usually have a week to turn in the article after attending the function to be reviewed.

Pay varies depending on the publication and your experience. The going rate is anywhere from $20 to $400 an article. Certain publications pay by word; $1 a word is the standard. *Writer's Market: Where and How to Sell What You Write,* by Kirsten Holm, updated yearly and sold in most bookstores, provides a price chart for freelance projects.

Good Luck

BENEFITS: flexible, free entertainment or food for you and a guest, use of your communication and writing skills.

PITFALLS: tedious projects and bad meals.

SOURCES: *Writer's Market: Where and How to Sell What You Write* by Kirsten Holm, (800) 289–0963; magazines and newspapers of interest.

NEEDS: strong writing ability, practical knowledge or expertise in a specific field.

"As a book reviewer for Salon *(an online publication), I write about books, the media, and American pop culture in general. Online publications have expanded what's possible in terms of cultural criticism—I've written critiques on particular authors' works and then gotten into debates with them online—very stimulating!"*

DAVID FUTRELLE, writer/essayist, Chicago

Seasonal Tax Accountant

Honestly—this is not as bad as it sounds.

Becoming a licensed accountant and working out of your home during tax return months will allow you the luxury of making a lot of money in a short period of time.

H&R Block, a worldwide tax preparation company with about 10,000 offices, offers an 11- to 13-week course in tax accounting that costs approximately $250–$350. It offers basic, intermediate, and advanced courses. Each state has different tax laws and policies, and you will need to be knowledgeable about those governing your state. In many cities, after you complete the course you will need to pass a licensing exam. For more information, call the H&R Block in your area or check other listings in the yellow pages under "Tax Preparation Services."

It is customary to charge between $100 and $250 to complete a basic tax return. This process usually takes about 2–3 hours and can be done at your convenience within certain time restrictions. Your busiest time will be from the end of March through April 15. A good way to make sure you're not bombarded in early April is to offer discount incentives to people who file their papers before the mad tax season rush.

When going into business for yourself, you will need to build a clientele. The money is not steady, but you will make much more per hour than if you work for someone else. To build your private client base, offer free financial advice and planning seminars, at which time you can distribute your business cards. If you choose to work for an established firm, check the classifieds under "Accounting." Many temp agencies hire accountants. Prostaff, with headquarters in Chicago and Minneapolis, is a national employment agency that hires accountants.

Good Luck

BENEFITS: flexible, great hourly wage, work at home.

PITFALLS: need to market your skills, wages vary.

SOURCES: yellow pages under "Tax Preparation Services," H&R Block, (800) TAX–7733. Classifieds under "Accounting," referrals, give seminars, advertise, register with employment agencies. Prostaff, in Chicago, (312) 641–6851, or Minneapolis, (612) 339–2220.

NEEDS: a tax preparer certificate or license.

IDEA: To assist in preparing performing artists' taxes without any huge time or money commitment, you can volunteer at the VITA program (Volunteer Income Tax Assistance) provided through the acting unions. Call the Screen Actors Guild for more information; it provides free training for members. If you specialize in tax preparation for entertainers, advertise at casting offices, at theaters, and in industry papers (*Dramalogue, Backstage, Variety,* and *Hollywood Reporter*) during tax season.

Substitute Teacher

You have a natural ability to dodge spitballs.

Being a teacher can be extremely rewarding if you enjoy working with children. Substitute teaching comes with all the rewards and offers flexibility, as you can choose when to work. A typical work day is 8 A.M. to 3 P.M. with a lunch break and a free 45- 60-minute period.

Different cities have different requirements for teachers. Call your unified school district, educational department, or a local school for specific information. To become a substitute teacher in the Los Angeles school system, there are currently three requirements: a bachelor's degree, two or three personal references, and a passing score on the CBEST exam (California Basic Education Skills Test). For questions and placement information, you can call the Los Angeles Unified School District recruitment office.

In New York, you no longer have to pass an exam to be a substitute teacher. All you need is a bachelor's degree and a nomination from a school district. (You go directly to a school of interest to get a nomination.)

Salary depends on where you live. It is approximately $120 per day in Los Angeles and $98 per day in New York, with the possibility of earning more money if you teach an extra period.

Another possibility is substituting in private schools, which you can contact individually for specific requirements. Primarily they look at your résumé and what you have to contribute. Since there are fewer children per class, the environment is often less demanding, and it is easier to create relationships with students and the people in charge. Generally you are responsible for only three to four classes a day. The pay at private schools is usually less, around $80–85 a day.

Good Luck

BENEFITS: make a difference with children, good salary, short day, choose when you want to work.

PITFALLS: day starts early, disruptive kids.

SOURCES: yellow pages for private schools. New York Unified School District, (800) TEACH NY or (718) 935–5633; Los Angeles Unified School District recruitment office, (213) 625–6565.

NEEDS: Résumé and interview for private school. B.A., local exam, references from other school districts for public schools.

> *"I have subbed for schools in both L.A. and New York. It's the greatest survival job for an actor because you get to decide on a day-to-day basis whether you want to work. When I do work, I take home about $100 for working a six-hour day, which includes a lunch, recess, and P.E., so I even have time during the day to read or write letters. And I'm home by 3 or 3:30! Often I can schedule my auditions later in the day, so I can teach, make a hundred bucks, and still go on my audition. Unfortunately, kids don't automatically respect subs and it can get rough sometimes. Then those six hours often feel like a week."*
>
> HELEN GREENBERG, actress/substitute teacher, Los Angeles

Temp Work

You'll never be the object of office gossip (until you leave).

Temp work is one of the fastest-growing industries in the nation. It allows companies to hire individuals without providing benefits—a major cost saving for corporations. Temp positions vary, from clerical duties, word processing, receptionist work, bookkeeping, and general office jobs to customer service, accounting, and light industrial and technical positions.

Temping is a great way to gain knowledge about different businesses and make contacts in your specific area of interest. The job stress is fairly low since you have less responsibility than a full-time employee. On the downside, learning each new office routine can be tedious. Most temp agencies offer free training for different computer programs and phone systems and will place you in either long- or short-term assignments. Several temp agencies place specifically within the entertainment industry. Most major studios, production companies, record producers, entertainment agencies, and management companies use temps. If you desire, many part-time temp positions can turn into full-time (and full-salaried!) work.

Wages vary depending on the agency, your experience, and your skills. A receptionist, for example, earns $7–$9 an hour, whereas computer and word processing positions typically pay $12–$20 an hour.

When applying for a job, you will be required to take quite a few tests, such as spelling, typing, math, and computer skills, depending on the desired position. Many temp agencies offer employment, and I recommend signing up with several agencies if you want steady work. Check the yellow pages under "Employment Agencies." The large chains have a number of offices, so you can choose the one most convenient for you. If you have a particular area of interest, such as working in a bank, call banks in your area to find out what temporary agencies they work with. Kelly Services and Norell are some of the most prestigious temp agencies, employing thousands of workers worldwide. Force One Entertainment is

New York–based and services the arts, entertainment, communication, and education industries, working with the most prestigious companies in the world.

Good Luck

BENEFITS: variety of work, make contacts, meet people, free training.

PITFALLS: adapting to a new environment, can feel corporate.

SOURCES: yellow pages under "Employment Agencies." Kelly Services, (248) 362–4444; Norell, (404) 240–3000; Force One Entertainment, (212) 922–9898, http://www.kokonet.com/force1.

NEEDS: the more skills you have, the more money you can make.

> *"After I proved myself and my software skills on a few long-term assignments, my temporary agency guaranteed me a base weekly salary to have me be on call for them. When they send me on a job that requires more than basic office skills, they pay me a higher wage. The situation has been good for me in that I can count on a certain income and yet still have the flexibility to take time off (unpaid) for shows and auditions."*
>
> TOM ELLIOT, actor/temp work, Seattle

Temporary Legal Assistant/Lawyer

Meet single lawyers (maybe they'll fund your creative dreams).

Perhaps you went to law school but still dream of being an actor or of writing that Pulitzer Prize–winning novel. Well, don't give up on your less-lucrative aspirations; make your degree useful (and your parents happy) by working as a legal temp. This way you will still have plenty of time to pursue other creative activities while paying the rent and bills. And if you don't have a law degree but have a legal background and experience, consider being a legal assistant or litigation secretary. Legal temp work is simply a more specialized type of temping and calls for more specific skills. This means you will be paid about double the salary of a standard temp position.

Previous experience with lawyers and the court system and computer literacy are necessities. You must be up-to-date on computer software and proficient in a variety of programs. The ability to prepare the requisite forms and a knowledge of court rules in all counties are mandatory.

When applying for legal work at a temp agency, you may be tested on typing, computer programs, knowledge of legal documents and litigation, and basic grammar and spelling.

To learn how to be a legal assistant, you can contact community colleges and private colleges in your area. Many continuing education programs provide classes. Or call your state bar association for course information.

Part-time legal temp assistants typically earn $15–$35 an hour, depending on skills and level of experience. Freelance lawyers charge $100–$300 an hour depending on location, size of firm, and specialty.

There are a number of ways to secure legal assistant work. Most states have their own law periodicals with an employment section, such as the *Daily Journal* in Los Angeles, the *New York Law Journal,* and the *Connecticut Law Tribune. Working World Magazine,* available for free in certain cities at malls and newsstands, has listings of temp agencies that serve law firms. You can also call lawyers and law firms directly and ask if they are looking for temporary help. This will enable you to make more money, since you will have cut out the employment agency. Check the classifieds under "Law" or "Legal" or the yellow pages under "Employment Agencies." Large temp agencies have a legal division. A few respected ones in Los Angeles are the Affiliates, Legal Plus, and Kent Daniels and Associates. In New York try Strategic Legal Resources and Gregory and Gregory Legal Staffing.

Good Luck

BENEFITS: good salary, learn about the law, use your law degree.

PITFALLS: demanding work.

SOURCES: state bar association, local legal periodicals, *Working World Magazine, Martindale Hubbell Legal Directory,* temp agencies. The Affiliates, (310) 557–2334;

Legal Plus, (310) 855–1651; Kent Daniels and Associates, (818) 962–3209. In New York try Strategic Legal Resources, (212) 922–0777 and Gregory and Gregory Legal Staffing, (212) 944–2888.

NEEDS: legal background, computer proficiency, professional appearance.

Trading Stocks

You know that blue chips aren't just corn tortillas from Mexico.

The economy is down, but the Dow Jones is up. Guess what? You make money. With this job you can sit in your house, at your computer or phone, and trade stocks like a Wall Street wizard. Making a part-time income from the profits of trading stocks is not only feasible, it's fun (as long as you're profiting!). Risks can be equalized with education. You are your own stockbroker so a license is not necessary.

Trading stocks involves investing your money in stocks and bonds and other investments, like commodities or options. Most people invest in mutual funds, where a brokerage firm picks the stocks. In this setup, however, you pick the stocks yourself and sign up with a discount broker to do the legwork. To hire a discount broker, look in business and financial newspapers. Discount brokers typically charge $15–$40 a transaction.

To educate yourself, go to a library or bookstore and ask for the business/investment section. Many financial newspapers give daily stock updates; *Wall Street Journal, Investors Business Daily,* and *Barrons* (which comes out every Saturday) are popular ones. CNBC, the business channel on your TV, provides a wealth of up-to-the-minute information. If you're looking for information on particular stocks or companies, contact the companies directly or visit their homepages on the Internet. A number of software programs can help you with charts, fundamentals, and technical analysis.

The time you spend on investing is up to you, once or twice a week or every day. You need to develop a trader's disposition, built on patience, trust, instinct, work, and greed. Most agree that an initial $5,000 investment is a respectable amount to begin with.

Needless to say, income fluctuates. Shoot for a reasonable 10 percent return and have goals. Only do this job if you're willing to take a risk. As the individual stock disclaimers say: "Past performance does not guarantee future results." Caveat emptor!

Good Luck

BENEFITS: a lot of money is possible, work from home, be your own boss.

PITFALLS: risk involved.

SOURCES: financial newspapers and magazines; CNBC, the business channel on your TV; software programs.

NEEDS: interest in the stock market, penchant for gambling, trader's disposition, discount broker.

"It's not only a part-time way to earn money—it's an enjoyable hobby."

CAREY EIDEL, actor/teacher/writer/stock market investor, Los Angeles

7

You Gotta Have Heart

Good Karma Jobs

Braille Transcriber

You have a bit of Anne Sullivan in you.

Today many children who are blind or visually challenged are mainstreamed into regular public schools. They use special Braille books transcribed for them, which follow the course work. If you are bored with the typical word processing job or are looking for a part-time (or full-time) way to make money from home, this could be an ideal way to assist others and earn a good paycheck.

A Braille transcriber uses a specific Braille writer or computer with software that translates Braille. To be considered for this job, you must be certified by the Library of Congress, which will provide you with a correspondence course and exam. There is *no charge* to take the course, which is paid for by your hard-earned tax dollars. Many adult-education programs offer classes to assist you with the course work. Call local high schools and junior colleges for information.

Pay varies, as certain school districts are more intelligently budgeted than others. A Braille transcriber can expect to earn $12–$25 an hour. Wage usually depends on the level of skill used. Literary transcribers deal with a straightforward format, while textbook transcribers work with columns, charts, and tables. Math transcribers are the most technically proficient, having to work with different codes and symbols.

For employment opportunities, contact your local school district, or the city, county, or state board of education. Also try looking in the yellow pages under "Blind Institutions" or "Youth Organizations" for specific organizations for the blind. For example, the Braille Institute has five centers located throughout California.

Good Luck

BENEFITS: challenging, interesting, providing a much needed service, often able to create your own work schedule.

PITFALLS: deadlines can be stressful, wages can be low due to funding problems in public education.

SOURCES: local school district; state board of education; Library of Congress, (800) 424–8567; yellow pages under "Blind Institutions" or "Youth Organizations." Braille Institute, (213) 663–1111.

NEEDS: certification from the Library of Congress, word processing skills.

Child Care

No need to act like an adult.

It goes without saying that child care requires a love of children. And I don't mean the kind of "I love kids" appreciation when you see them in a park for a few minutes. We're talking hours here. If you really love children, this can be one of the most rewarding jobs in the book. Duties may include picking a child up from school or an after-school activity, meal preparation, overseeing homework assignments, or simply staying with the child while parents are out. The joy of this job is that you are providing a needed service while being a positive influence in a child's life. When you are working at night and the children are sleeping, your time is your own to write, read, study, or watch TV.

Child care usually pays $7–$12 an hour depending on the employer, your experience, and how many children you will be caring for.

Most child care services require you to have prior experience working with children. You may also need to have a car and car insurance. Many agencies offer 24-hour-a-day care, so there is plenty of shift flexibility. The agency will assign you to specific jobs depending on your experience and shift interest.

For a listing of agencies, look in the yellow pages under "Baby-Sitters" or "Employment Agencies," or in the classifieds under "Domestic Care," "Housekeeper," or "Nanny." Agencies are almost always open to interviewing high-quality people. You will need to fill out an application, have an interview, supply references, and usually submit to a background check. Many health clubs now provide child care, as do a number of churches and temples. If they don't provide it presently, offer to organize it!

If you are good at self-promotion, you can gather your own clientele by advertising or by word-of-mouth. You can design a flier or postcard with a personal recommendation from someone you know or have worked for. Offer to baby-sit once or twice for your rabbi or pastor's children or for any storeowner or manager who has a regular newsletter in exchange for a personal recommendation. Places to advertise your services might include community or school bulletin boards, Lamaze classes, pediatricians' offices, prenatal and postnatal classes, and parent magazines. Working in a day care center or at a child care center in a health club, church, or temple can get you more independent baby-sitting jobs. You may even decide to join with one or two other people and start your own child care service or referral agency.

Good Luck

BENEFITS: work with children, flexible hours, free time when children are asleep.

PITFALLS: building a clientele if it's your own business.

SOURCES: yellow pages under "Baby-Sitters" or "Employment Agencies—Domestic Help," classifieds under "Domestic Care," advertising, college bulletin boards, health clubs, temples or churches.

NEEDS: love of children, experience, patience.

> *"I was working in a restaurant five nights a week and was completely dissatisfied with my life. About a year ago, I started baby-sitting (for $8–$10 an hour) and entertaining at children's parties. Working with children is something I feel I am gifted in and I love being around them; I laugh more than ever and am filled with joy."*
>
> PAMELA NEWKIRK-ARKIN, actress/director/child care/entertaining at children's parties/pet care, Los Angeles

Children's Entertainment

Hear children laugh while you make a fool of yourself.

Dressing up and entertaining at kids' parties can be a creative, fun way to earn money on weekends. The instant feedback and laughter from children will give you a high unlike any other.

Party services look for spontaneous, energetic men and women who enjoy working with children in a party atmosphere. You may be hired to be any number of characters: Batman, a Ninja Turtle, a Power Ranger, Barney, Elmo, or Santa Claus. Many companies will have you create your own character or clown. The hiring company will usually provide instructions on the most popular children's games and magic tricks, including the old favorite—balloon animals. This is an especially perfect job for anyone looking to improve improvisational skills.

If you possess an entrepreneurial spirit, another idea is to create your own children's entertainment company. Two actors I know formed Send in the Clowns. They bought clown costumes, made impressive business cards, advertised, and performed popular children's games and party antics. Soon they had a thriving business and hired a number of employees.

Magic tricks, games, balloons, a pump, and a few costumes are good investments if you are interested in forming your own company. Plenty of books will provide you with fun skits, games, and activities. Costume rentals are also an option for specific occasions or theme parties. Check the yellow pages under "Costumes" for a store near you. To publicize your business, donate your time at city events that are listed in the newspapers, and then hand out your business cards. Volunteering your time at a few birthday parties in exchange for referrals is also a great way to get started. Advertise in local parent magazines and community papers, and put up signs at pediatricians' offices. The classified section of local magazines, such as *New York Magazine* and *L.A. Magazine,* have listings of party services.

Before starting your own business, work for an established children's entertainment company to learn the ropes. Such companies look to hire creative, fun, upbeat, and imaginative individuals who enjoy working with children. They are listed in the yellow pages under "Entertainers" or in parent or local magazines. A few popular ones in Los Angeles are Zebra Entertainment and Kitty Antics. In San Francisco, try Unexpected Company and Whim.

Most party services and agencies will pay you $30–$75 an hour plus tips. Unfortunately, most parties employ you for only an hour, so you may need to do quite a few weekend gigs to make a decent weekly wage. When it is your own company you can charge $100+ per hour and do the gig yourself or hire out.

NOTE: Working as a face painter is another way to entertain children and earn money. You don't even need to be that artistic—you can paint really simple designs on kids' faces. A woman I know painted faces at the Microsoft picnic (12,000 attendees!), as well as for Nordstrom and the Bon Marche. She worked through an agency (look in the yellow pages or classifieds under "Entertainment" or "Talent Agency") and earned $25–$35 an hour in Minneapolis, and $15 an hour in Seattle. You can also go it alone and paint faces at fairs and festivals.

Good Luck

BENEFITS: weekend work, creative, fun, good hourly wage.

PITFALLS: being pulled over by a cop while wearing your purple dinosaur costume!

SOURCES: yellow pages under "Entertainers," starting your own business. Zebra Entertainment, (818) 906–3809; Kitty Antics, (818) 905–0281. In San Francisco, a few popular agencies are Unexpected Company, (415) 459–0141; and Whim, (415) 383–9446. Advertise in local parent magazines and community papers, put up signs at pediatricians' offices.

NEEDS: enjoy entertaining children, improvisational skills.

IDEA: If you love interacting with children, consider calling a Gymboree Play Program in your area for a teaching position. This is an international company with over 370 franchises in the United States and Canada. Gymboree is a parent/child development center with play groups for children, lasting 45 minutes, and you're hired to teach a block of classes. For information on a center in your area, call (800) 520–7529.

"I love the children's expressions—it's so rewarding to see their faces light up as I entertain them. I do European-style clowning so as not to scare them. I have a background in mime, and I make balloon animals and face paint, as well as use puppets and masks. I also have a specialty called clowning in a bag, using giant paper bags as props. It's great fun and the kids love it."

NANCY GOLD-LEVY, actress/children's entertainment, San Francisco

CPR Instructor

Dating tip #26: say you need to practice your mouth-to-mouth homework.

Teaching a course in CPR allows you to earn money while passing on knowledge that can save lives. Everyone should know CPR. When my daughter was seven months old—around the time when she started putting everything in her mouth—we hired a CPR instructor to come to the house and give a course to me, my husband, and our baby-sitter. Teachers, foster parents, M.D.'s, aerobics instructors, health care providers, security officers, police officers, sheriffs, dentists, and firefighters are some of the people required to be certified in CPR.

Some basic teaching skills are necessary, as well as certification through the American Heart Association or the Red Cross. Generally you need to take a basic life support (BLS) for health care providers course, which is eight hours and costs approximately $30–$50, and then follow up with a 14- to 16-hour course to become an instructor. You won't get your instructor card until you've been monitored teaching a course. Once you are an instructor affiliated with a training center, you will be able to give out CPR cards and your training center will process paperwork.

Salary varies depending on experience and where you teach. Hospitals and the Red Cross have different policies on payment. Private teachers typically charge about $35–$50 per client.

Each city is different in its teaching methods. To find out more about affiliated training centers in your city, call the American Heart Association. For information on the American Red Cross, contact the office in your area. When you complete all requirements and become certified, you are on the roster of the American Red Cross. It will refer clients to you and act as an authorized provider. To find work independently, establish a relationship with pediatricians who will then recommend you; advertise at birthing classes, prenatal and postnatal exercise classes, and in local community papers and newsletters.

Good Luck

BENEFITS: helping people learn to save lives.

PITFALLS: need to be recertified periodically, which involves a review session and a recertification fee.

SOURCES: American Heart Association, (800) AHA–USA1; American Red Cross in your area, or call the national headquarters at (202) 737–8300.

NEEDS: ability to instruct others, certification in CPR instruction.

"It is very rewarding, especially as a mom, knowing that I'm teaching parents how to save their child's life. I love having the flexibility to be home with my

son. He's in preschool for half a day, so after a morning CPR session, I get to pick him up, have lunch with him, and spend time with him."

CYNDI MARGOLIS, R.N., mom/PR rep for medical center/breastfeeding, infant care, and CPR instructor, Studio City, California

Doula

Heal one mother, heal the earth.

The moment when a child is born is truly a miracle. You can take part in this life-changing experience by becoming a doula and assisting women during and after childbirth.

A friend of mine compared childbirth to running a marathon in terms of endurance and pain. (I did both, and childbirth is infinitely more challenging!). A doula offers the old-fashioned community care that used to be more prevalent and that mothers deserve. Doulas are not trained midwives, though during births they provide invaluable emotional support and nonmedical pain relief. In addition to the nurturing and coaching aspect, doulas assist in preserving the memory of the birth experience for the family. Often doulas will provide a written account of the entire birth for the parents.

As a doula, you will have to be the most relaxed person in the room. If you are a birthing doula, you may have to be on call for as long as two days. Usually there is a minimum of two prenatal meetings to connect and build up trust with the mom.

A postpartum doula is hired to take care of the mother at home. This includes helping the mom rest by taking charge of other responsibilities as well as assisting with breastfeeding and the needs of other children in the family. It is important for a doula to fit comfortably in other people's homes and not take up a lot of space energetically. Having a child is often a difficult transition for families, and sensitivity to the situation as well as to what needs to be done is crucial. A postpartum doula is usually hired for anywhere from a few days to six weeks, determined by the family.

Wages vary. Experienced doulas in major cities typically earn $15–$18 an hour. Childbirth doulas work on a sliding scale, charging $100–$400 a birth.

To be trained as a doula, contact a midwifery center or doula center in your area. The American College of Nurse Midwives is in Washington, D.C., and the Midwifery Education and Accreditation Council is in Arizona. Look in local parent magazines and newspapers as well as in the yellow pages under "Birth Centers." There are also a number of doula organizations across the country. Doulas of North America, known as DONA, in Seattle, trains and certifies doulas nationwide, offering two- to three-day workshops that cost $50–$300. It takes approximately six months to two years to become certified. DONA requires you to attend its workshop and be present at three births and write an essay on what you've learned at the births. You need a good evaluation from the parents as well as an attending caretaker (doctor or midwife). The certificate costs $50, and membership in DONA costs $40.

To get work as a doula, you can advertise at maternity stores, prenatal exercise classes, and childbirth classes, as well as in child care referral books and parent newspapers. You should also network with medical professionals and doula organizations.

Good Luck

BENEFITS: participating in the miracle of birth, rewarding on a personal and spiritual level.

PITFALLS: being on call, work can be exhausting, earnings are unsteady.

SOURCES: advertise at maternity stores, in child care referral books and parent newspapers, network with medical professionals and doula organizations. For training, contact the American College of Nurse Midwives, (202) 728–9860; Midwifery Education and Accreditation Council, (520) 214–0997; and Doulas of North America, (206) 324–5440. Yellow pages under "Birth Centers."

NEEDS: energy, patience, faith in natural processes, calmness, being comfortable in other peoples' home.

"I am 27 years old and have assisted in over 20 births. It is truly an honor to participate in these families' lives as a doula, supporting someone through the miracle of birth and the daily importance of childrearing."

ADRIENNE FUSON, childbirth and postpartum doula/massage therapist, Portland, Oregon

Pet Care

Get to play with creatures named Fanny-Noodle, Wendel-Bendel, and Dixie-Doodle.

There is a good reason that 60 percent of the households in the United States have some kind of pet: Few things are as pleasurable as the companionship and unconditional love that a dog or cat provides. Pet care is a terrific job for animal lovers, since you are around pets on a steady basis. While owners are working late hours or traveling, they need a responsible person to take care of their beloved four-legged companions. This is where a dependable pet service comes in.

A pet care service can involve dog walking, pet feeding, litter box cleaning, house visits, day care, sleep-overs, boarding, and trips to the vet or groomer. The hours are flexible. Most owners give you a two-hour range, for example, an afternoon walk between 1 P.M. and 3 P.M. There is a downside to pet care, though—pooper-scooping and cleaning litter boxes can be unpleasant (especially when it's not for your own "darling" pet).

Payment varies depending on whether you operate your own business or work for an established pet care service. A typical visit is 20 to 40 minutes, and $10 to $20 per visit is the going rate. The more extras that are added (trips to the vet or groomer, caring for more than one pet, administering medicine), the more chargeable time you have. House-sitting or boarding generally runs from $35 to $55 a night per dog.

About six years ago, I decided to combine my love of animals with my entrepreneurial spirit and start my own pet care service. From day one I began earning money and found it to be a fulfilling and lucrative side business. To get started, I simply made up a catchy flier and introduced myself to dog-walking neighbors and pet owners at nearby parks. I even placed fliers on neighborhood cars. I made up a cute business card and introduced myself to nearby pet stores and vets. Soon I had a thriving enterprise and was charging $15 a walk and $40–$50 for boarding (only two doggies at a time since I lived in an apartment!) with no overhead. I found that for a small business, it was most profitable to stick to the immediate area to minimize traveling time.

To get a business license, which costs about $100–$150 a year, call your city's tax and permit division or county clerk's office. The National Association of Professional Pet Sitters is a nonprofit organization that provides group rates for liability insurance and bonding. It offers a toll-free referral line, mentor programs, conventions, and regional meetings. The cost of membership is $130 a year and there are over 1,000 members nationwide. For further information, contact the main office in Washington, D.C. To work for an established pet care service, check the yellow pages or your neighborhood pet store, or call the National Association of Professional Pet Sitters for services in your area. In California, Mike Artreburn, previously the president of Pet Sitters Association of Southern California and owner of one of the most successful pet businesses, Little Darlin's, is currently looking for pet-sitting entrepreneurs nationwide to join his network. David Brooks, a former movie and television producer, has formed Bunkies Buddies, L.A.'s largest pet care company. You can contact him for opportunities as well.

Good Luck

BENEFITS: being around animals, self-employed, flexible hours.

PITFALLS: pooper-scooping, irregular income.

SOURCES: pet stores, dog parks, newspaper ads, neighborhood markets, and pet magazines. National Association of Professional Pet Sitters, (800) 296-7387 or (202) 393–3317. Your city's tax and permit division or county clerk's office, in Los Angeles, (213) 368–7000, and in New York, (212) 374–8314. Little Darlin's, (909) 625–7562; Bunkies Buddies, (310) 657–8766.

NEEDS: responsible, love of animals, licensed and bonded if you're an independent entrepreneur.

IDEA: Start a dog-training service, a mobile pet grooming service, or a pet taxicab service. You can work for an established company first to learn the trade or read books on the subject of interest, or buy a dog-training or grooming video and practice on your friend's dog. Various pet magazines sold at your local newsstands provide helpful information.

Professional Companion

Adopt a grandparent.

With more of the population reaching elderly status, the need for adult companionship is growing. Many adults (or their children) are willing to pay for companionship for different purposes. An elderly person might hire someone to help with tasks such as shopping, preparing meals, and doctor visits, or simply to keep him or her company.

To be a companion, you must have patience and compassion, and be extremely responsible. If you genuinely care about the people you spend time with, it is both a monetarily and an emotionally rewarding position. It is a great relief for an elderly person to know that on Tuesday from 1 P.M. to 4 P.M., someone will come over with a car to visit or take him or her to an appointment.

When starting your own business, you will need to obtain a license, which costs approximately $150. Contact your state's department of human resources for elderly care. You may also choose to look into specific car insurance if you plan to transport people for medical reasons. For liability insurance and bonding information, contact a local insurance company.

A fair rate for this service is anywhere from $8 to $20 an hour, depending on your skills and your clientele. For example, if you play an instrument, know CPR, and own a car, you may be able to charge more.

Some great places to advertise are senior centers, nursing homes, beauty parlors, and local markets, and in temple, church, and community newsletters.

Good Luck

BENEFITS: emotionally rewarding, new friendships.

PITFALLS: person may become ill or die.

SOURCES: religious and community newsletters, nursing homes, senior center bulletins, beauty parlors, and local markets. Your state's department of human resources for elderly care for licensing.

NEEDS: patience, sense of responsibility, plenty of TLC to give.

"I had a high-power position in New York that was very demanding but not emotionally rewarding. I had volunteered with the elderly for many years, and when I finally got married and moved to Florida, I was able to turn my dream of starting my own elderly companionship service into a reality. Within three weeks, just by spreading the word, I had to hire 13 employees. I charged $15–$20 an hour to my clients (usually their families hired me) and paid my staff $8–$9 an hour. I was in the business for five years and still keep a scrapbook of beautiful letters from grateful family members."

AVRIL JACOBSON, past owner of Daughter Connection, Palm Beach, Florida

Psychic

You already know what this job is about.

Can you sense when an event will take place? Have you been told by others that you possess extraordinary psychic abilities? Well . . . even if you haven't, there are still opportunities for you in this interesting and ever-expanding field. As a psychic, you can try to procure work independently or work for an established hotline.

If you do not possess an innate psychic ability, you can learn tarot cards, playing cards, or the I Ching (the ancient Chinese book of changes—considered one of the oldest and most reliable tools for divination). There are scores of books on these subjects in bookstores and libraries, often in the metaphysical, occult, or New Age sections. New Age magazines often have advertisements for courses in astrology and tarot card reading. Practice doing readings on friends until you have the process memorized. If you choose to work for a hotline, you will be tested over the phone before being hired.

What's especially beneficial about working for a hotline is that you can work from anywhere (including Canada). You'll be given a number and a code to dial on your home phone, which then hooks up to the psychic company's line. It provides you with an extension, although you will need to have a line without call waiting.

This job is flexible, as you sign up for times when it is convenient to work. Expect to work a minimum of 16–20 hours a week. Wages vary depending on experience, but you can expect to earn about 40 cents a minute and 10 percent of the sales, which amounts to roughly $7–$12 an hour. Regulations presently cut off calls at 20 minutes.

There are always new companies entering this field. Commercials on your cable TV stations will provide numbers (unfortunately, you probably will have to pay for the first minute), and you can call seeking a number for employment. Three popular companies to work for are the Psychic Network, Sylvia Brown's Gifted Psychic Network, and The Psychic Department. Some companies, such as Psychic Friends Network, require a number of years of experience.

Many psychics also earn money working out of their homes and at private functions. Building a clientele usually results from word-of-mouth. Try advertising in local papers and magazines or offering your services for free at parties, or as a side attraction in restaurants. You can even put out a sign and sit in the street or in a park like a traditional gypsy fortune-teller.

Good Luck

BENEFITS: work at home, flexible hours, assisting people.

PITFALLS: sporadic work if you're on your own, unsteady income.

SOURCES: contacting hotlines, advertising. Psychic Network, (209) 438–1930; Sylvia Brown's Gifted Psychic Network, (800) 793–3950; The Psychic Department, (305) 573–4171.

NEEDS: psychic ability or knowledge of tarot cards, astrology, or I Ching.

Rebirther

You mean I have to go through it again?

Imagine a gentle process that can rejuvenate the body and heal the mind and spirit, and all you have to do is breathe. Yoga masters and martial artists have known about the power of breath to heal and transform for centuries. The process is called rebirthing. Through rebirthing, one becomes more aware of thoughts and patterns that may prevent one from living life to the fullest. Using conscious breathing and affirmations—an affirmation is a technique that immerses new thoughts into the consciousness—you release negative thought patterns affecting your behavior. The process empowers practitioners to participate in their own self-healing.

To become a rebirther, you must first go through the rebirthing process. No professional credentials are necessary, but a number of training centers and individuals who will train you are listed in New Age magazines. Dr. Eve Jones, the director of Rebirth Associates in Los Angeles, conducts training and workshops throughout the country, as do many other rebirthers. Training is $300 for an individual session or a four- to five-hour workshop. Upon completion of training, determined by you and your rebirther, you may go into business for yourself, generally through word-of-mouth. Try advertising in local health papers and magazines or putting up fliers at gyms, health food stores, and centers for alternative medicine or therapy. Rebirthers generally charge from $60 to $120 per session, with sessions lasting anywhere from 45 minutes to two hours.

A number of centers throughout the country teach rebirthing. For further information contact the Philadelphia Rebirthing Center or Rebirth Associates of Los Angeles.

Good Luck

BENEFITS: control your own hours, healing and therapeutic work, good wages.

PITFALLS: lack of public awareness, criticism and skepticism, building clientele.

SOURCES: health papers and magazines, rebirthing centers. Philadelphia Rebirthing Center, 1027 69th Avenue, Philadelphia, PA 19126, (215) 424–4444; Rebirth Associates of Los Angeles, (213) 461–5774.

NEEDS: desire to learn the process, interest in the healing arts.

"I started out as a client of a rebirther-in-training and experienced such relaxation and increased energy that 12 years later, I am still a practicing rebirther. It is a great adjunct therapy to the other healing work that I do in my private practice."

SYLVIA DE ANGELO-CASHMAN, R.N., BSN, CPNP, rebirther/polarity practitioner/holistic wellness counselor/seminar producer, Philadelphia

---

Shomar (Watcher)

Oy vey, I thought my mother said watcher, not doctor!

One day I had a discussion with my rabbi, Steven Leder, concerning this book, and he suggested including this job. Shomar is the Hebrew word for watcher. The Talmud, the body of early Jewish civil and religious law, states that one should not leave the deceased alone. A shomar is hired by the mortuary to sit and read psalms in the room with the body (in the Jewish tradition the casket is closed). To qualify for this job you need to be Jewish and able to read Hebrew. Mortuaries look for Jews who are fairly religious, and they have a tendency to hire males.

This is not a job for the faint-of-heart, or for those who tire easily. You are required to sit and read for approximately 12 hours, sometimes longer. Short naps and bathroom breaks are permitted. On a more positive note, you are doing a mitzvah (a good deed), which is a reward in itself. You can expect to earn $125 for a 12-hour period.

For a complete listing of Jewish mortuaries, look in your local yellow pages under "Funeral." Call and ask to speak with the manager. Or call hospitals in your area for a list of local Jewish mortuaries. Weinstein Family Services has associates all over the country. Berkowitz-Kumin is in Cleveland. In New York, try Riverside Memorial Chapel and Weinstein West End Funeral Chapel. A few well-known ones in the California area are Malinow and Silverman, Mount Sinai, and Groman.

Good Luck

BENEFITS: flexible, doing a good deed, practice your Hebrew.

PITFALLS: long hours with some overnighters, slightly morbid.

SOURCES: yellow pages under "Funeral." Hospitals in your area for a list of local Jewish mortuaries. Weinstein Family Services, (800) 288–5701; Berkowitz-Kumin, (216) 932–7900; Riverside Memorial Chapel, (212) 362–6600; Weinstein West End Funeral Chapel, (212) 724–0454; Mount Sinai, (800) 600–0076; Groman, (213) 748–2201.

NEEDS: Jewish, fairly religious, ability to read Hebrew.

Social Service

Help others (while you help yourself).

Working for a social service organization is a way both to contribute to society and to support yourself financially. Many social services rely on federal and state funding and therefore often look to volunteers for assistance. However, many flexible, *paying* part-time jobs are available. Income varies greatly. For a general listing, check your local yellow pages under "Social Services."

A good example of a service organization is Jay Nolan Community Service in California. This is a wonderful organization whose goal is to keep developmentally disabled people out of institutions. Often Jay Nolan will put them in their own semi-independent private living situations—a community of friends, roommates, and families who foster self-respect, self-care, and growth. Many people with disabilities can function quite well with a little supervision and guidance. That's where you can help.

The two jobs available for people who have not been trained to care for the disabled are in residential support and relief staff. Residential support means sharing a home with a disabled person. In exchange for being a "friend" and caring for your disabled roommate, you receive a free place to live and a salary of approximately $800 a month. The extent of care varies according to the individual's needs. Often it includes doing ordinary activities together, such as shopping, running errands, and going to the movies. It can also include cooking meals, administering medication, and driving the person around. A residential support position allows for plenty of free time, rent-free living, and an income in exchange for your services. Unfortunately, this job means giving up some of your privacy. It requires a gentle, patient, communicative personality. If disabilities makes you uncomfortable, this kind of work situation is not for you.

The other position, relief staff, involves "person-sitting" when the primary caregiver needs an evening or weekend off. Pay is usually $40 for a five- to six-hour evening, with $6 for each additional hour and $200 for a weekend live-in situation. This job allows you to be of assistance while retaining your privacy. It is also more flexible—you can set a specific schedule or be on call.

Social service programs differ in their needs and requirements. Contact individual programs for specifications. When you seek employment, you will be screened by a staff member and at least one of the clients for whom you are being considered. Usually a second interview is set up for paperwork to be filled out. You must also commit to taking certain training classes—provided free of charge—which include teaching strategies.

Good Luck

BENEFITS: helping others, steady salary, challenging work, room and board.

PITFALLS: loss of privacy, detailed process to be hired.

SOURCES: yellow pages under "Social Services."

NEEDS: patient, gentle, responsible, communicative, desire to help others.

"I used to be afraid of and repulsed by people with disabilities. Like all prejudices, it stemmed from fear and ignorance. The first time I met Kevin, who is brain damaged and slightly retarded with autistic tendencies, he came out with his arms open and gave me a big hug—before this job, I would not have taken the time to get to know him. The most important thing about the work

we do is to assimilate disabled people into society rather than placing them in institutions. I am proud to do this kind of work and am a better person for it."

KIM STARZYK, mom/actress/social services/literacy program coordinator/pet care business/market research, Los Angeles

Youth Mentor

Show them all the beauty they possess inside.

These days, the media inundate us with stories of abused or neglected children. The job of youth mentor is an extremely rewarding part-time position that enables those with time and energy to make a significant difference in a child's life.

Many family service agencies have mentor programs that are paid positions, and not to be confused with volunteer organizations, such as Big Brothers/Big Sisters. Often they look for people who have a background in psychology, social work, or education. The basic job description includes planning activities and participating with young clients on a one-to-one basis. Wages vary depending on experience, but you can expect to earn $7–$12 an hour. Hours depend on your employer's needs as well as your availability.

There are a number of ways to go about contacting family service agencies. Look in the yellow pages under "Family" or "Counseling" (it may refer you to another directory listing), or call the city or county human services department and get a list of nonprofit youth agencies funded in your area. You can also try calling schools and day care programs. Agencies look for people with patience, a nurturing personality, and excellent communication skills. Often a car is required.

Good Luck

BENEFITS: flexible schedule, variety of activities, an opportunity to make a difference in a child's life.

PITFALLS: highly stressful at times.

SOURCES: family service agencies, yellow pages under "Family" or "Counseling," city or county human services department, schools and day care programs.

NEEDS: work well with kids, patience, good listener; background in psychology, social work, or education preferred; often a car is required.

> *"Working as a mentor was an ideal part-time job for me. It meant spending time with a kid who needed all the support he could get, and eventually seeing that I'd made a difference. I got to choose which clients I wanted to work with, how many hours I wanted to work, and what activities we did together. I found that it was both a challenging and wonderful experience."*
>
> JOSH LEVIN, student/youth mentor, Madison, Wisconsin

Index